G

THE GEORGE GUND FOUNDATION
IMPRINT IN AFRICAN AMERICAN STUDIES

The George Gund Foundation has endowed
this imprint to advance understanding of
the history, culture, and current issues
of African Americans.

The publisher gratefully acknowledges the generous contribution to this book provided by the African American Studies Endowment Fund of the University of California Press Associates, which is supported by a major gift from the George Gund Foundation.

Black Magic

CHLOE RUSSELL

A Woman of Colour of the State of Massachusetts, commonly termed the

Old Witch or Black Interpreter.

*Who certainly possesses extraordinary means of fore-
telling remarkable events*

Black Magic

Religion and the African American
Conjuring Tradition

Yvonne P. Chireau

UNIVERSITY OF CALIFORNIA PRESS
Berkeley · Los Angeles · London

Frontispiece: Chloe Russell, an early black American entrepreneur and writer of a book on the magical arts. Chloe Rusel[l], *The Compleat Fortuneteller* (n.d.), courtesy of the Boston Athenaeum.

University of California Press
Berkeley and Los Angeles, California

University of California Press, Ltd.
London, England

First paperback printing 2006
© 2003 by the Regents of the University of California

An earlier version of Chapter 1 was published as "Conjure and Christianity in the Nineteenth Century: Religious Elements in African American Magic," in *Religion and American Culture* 7, no. 2, Summer 1997. © 1997 by the Center for the Study of Religion and American Culture. Reprinted by permission of the University of California Press.

Library of Congress Cataloging-in-Publication Data

Chireau, Yvonne Patricia, 1961–
    Black magic : religion and the African American conjuring tradition / Yvonne P. Chireau.
        p.   cm.
    Includes bibliographical references and index.
    ISBN 13: 978-0-520-24988-2 (pbk. : alk. paper)
    1. African Americans —Religion.   I. Title.

BR563.N4 C5   2003
291.3'2'08996073—dc21   2002151315

Manufactured in the United States of America

22   21
10   9   8   7   6

To my family

Contents

Acknowledgements

My thanks go to all of those who have participated in this project from its inception as a doctoral dissertation to its culmination as a book manuscript. Without the help of many friends and colleagues, it would have been impossible for me to pursue this work to completion. I am especially grateful to the following individuals for their unrelenting support and guidance: Albert Raboteau, David Wills, Randall Burkett, and students and faculty members of the Department of Religion at Princeton University. Others who read and commented upon all or part of this work include Cynthia Eller, Paul Harvey, Robert Hall, Doug Arava, John Thornton, Charles Long, Hans Baer, and members of the Department of Religion at Swarthmore College. My deepest and most heartfelt gratitude is reserved for the late William Piersen, mentor and friend, whose passionate belief in this research sustained me through the most difficult of times. Thank you, Bill, for helping to bring out the better part of me.

Five Dollars Reward.

Ran away from the fubfcriber, on the 3rd day of March, 1796, a Negro fellow named *SAMPSON*, about 50 years old, 5 feet high, and has a large fcar on one fide of his face that reaches into his eye. He is Guinea born, fpeaks bad Englifh, is a fortune teller and conjurer, paffes as a freeman, and is fuppofed to have a forged pifs; lie was feen in Fayettevile laft fall, and very probably he is ftill there or in the neighbourhood thereof. All perfons are hereby forbid harbouring or employing faid fellow at their perd. Since he has been in this country, he has lived about Muddy-creek, in Doplin county, and is well known by the name of PICKET's SAMPSON. The above reward with reafonable expences, will be paid for his delivery to me.

Jinkin Avirett.

Onflow county, May 30. coʒt

Introduction

A remarkable moment occurs in the climax of the 1992 film *Daughters of the Dust*. The setting is a sheltered key, hidden within a cluster of islands off the coasts of Georgia and South Carolina. The time is a few years past the turn of the twentieth century. The scene opens on a golden afternoon. A family is gathering to say good-bye, for on this day some of them will travel North, to better jobs, new schools, greater opportunities. Those who depart will leave behind a community they have been a part of for generations. They will also leave behind the elderly matriarch of their clan, Nana Peazant. Nana beckons her children to join in a communion ceremony, for she wants to give them "a part of herself" to take with them. She clutches a leather pouch that is tightly wound with string and attached to a Bible. It contains personal keepsakes, such as a twist of her mother's hair and her own, some dried flowers, and various roots and herbs. Nana calls it a *hand*. Like herself, it embodies the spirits of the "Old Souls," those enslaved Africans who touched down more than a century earlier on the backwater jetty known as Ibo landing. Offering the hand to her kin, Nana calls them to pay homage before embarking on their journey. She believes that their collective memory—and the power of her charm—will sustain them as

Facing page illustration: advertisement from an eighteenth-century newspaper for an escaped slave, described as "a fortuneteller and Conjurer." *Hall's Wilmington Gazette* (North Carolina), October 1798.

they enter into a new and uncertain future beyond the shores of these Sea Islands.[1]

What is extraordinary about this moment in the film is its seamless joining of religion and magic in one powerful object. As an enduring reminder of the world to which she and her people belong, Nana Peazant has created this charm for her family's protection, even as some of the most destructive forces that they face have emerged from their own conflicts. In its composition, the charm consolidates some of the most significant icons of African American spirituality: the Bible, a token of Christian redemption; a root, a supernatural emblem and touchstone to an ancient heritage; and the most precious relic that Nana owns, the bequest of a slave parent to a child—a twisted cord of her own mother's hair. Bound together and made inseparable with twine, each element of the hand illustrates the charm's singularity of spirit.

Although the scene occurs in a motion picture, the real, historical implications present in it run as currents throughout this book. *Daughters of the Dust* enumerates the fundamental interests of one family on the eve of their dispersal, their concern for survival, their hopes for future generations, and their attempts to respect the past and to preserve memory. It is also a story of the cultural and spiritual resources to which a people might turn when they are in need. I suggest that *Daughters* might be read as an allegory of the religious sojourn of blacks in America, with Nana's charm as a metaphor for a legacy that some have chosen to preserve, and others to reject. Rather than dismissing the hand as an object of superstition, I want to argue for its deeper significance, as a symbol of the survival of a kind of magical spirituality in the African American experience.

This book is about the creations that black people have woven into their quest for spiritual empowerment and meaning. It is about magic, as that term refers to the beliefs and actions by which human beings interact with an invisible reality. But it is also about religion, which may be defined as a viable system of ideas and activities by which humans mediate the sacred realm. In some African American spiritual traditions, ideas about magical and religious practice can enclose identical experiences. Christianity may presume a person's acceptance of a kind of supernaturalism, as a religion that calls upon God, Jesus, and the Holy Ghost to directly intervene, when petitioned, in the life of the believer. Individuals may utilize the rhetoric of *miracle* to characterize this kind of spiritual efficacy, or they may adopt a lexicon that is associated with magic. Or they may choose both. A fixed dichotomy between these ideas is not always apparent.

It is clear, then, that we are dealing with contested notions of belief. In contemporary scholarship, "magic" has acquired a plethora of associations, many negative, and others that appear to be virtually identical to "religion" in certain historical contexts. In the chapters that follow I examine the ways that these ideas have interacted—and separated—in African American experience, and the ways that they have been appropriated, critiqued, and recreated by both practitioners and antagonists. Although magic is generally characterized as the antithesis of religion, it seems just as often to reflect the latter, to be its mirror image. When seen from different perspectives, the divisions sometimes break down, revealing the arbitrary nature of the categories. In the words of one writer, "Stated simply, magic is . . . the religion of the other."[2]

This book is also concerned with the actual experiences that gave rise to the introduction of "magic" into that complex generally recognized as "religion" in black American experience. Since few terms have prompted more disagreement than these two, it might be useful to clarify my own use of them. Magic is a particular approach or attitude by which humans interact with unseen powers or spiritual forces. In contrast with religion, it is efficacious, with its spells, curses, incantations, and formulae. Magic is used for specific, personal ends. It operates mechanically—as opposed to prayer, which is communal, devotional, and noncoercive. "Magic," notes a famous treatise by the nineteenth-century Scottish classicist James George Frazer, "often deals with spirits," but "it constrains or coerces instead of conciliating or propitiating them as religion would do." Religion is, accordingly, a public and social activity; magic is private, manifested in solitary, focused events, and has no church or sustained collective.[3]

Yet if we return to Nana Peazant and her conjuring hand, we are confronted with a problem. Should the hand and the accompanying ceremony be interpreted as "magical" or "religious?" Or is there an intermediate category in which to place ideas of the ways that humans have engaged a reality beyond their own, a reality delineated by the presence of divine beings, forces, and other invisible entities? To address this question, this book examines a range of spiritual traditions such as Conjure, Hoodoo, and root working. Viewing these traditions through the interpretive lens of "vernacular religion," I draw a contrast between the official doctrines of institutional religions such as Protestant Christianity and the vast territory of behaviors that human beings may invest with religious meaning.[4] These behaviors, we will see, may be embedded within activities such as work, recreation, or leisure. Hence the boundaries of "religion" can be difficult to locate. Charles Long, who has most strongly advocated an original methodological approach to black religion, asserts that "the church [is] not the only context for the meaning of religion" for black people, but that "religion . . . mean[s] orientation—orientation in the ultimate sense, that is, how one comes to terms with the ultimate significance of one's place in the world." These "extrachurch orientations," Long adds, "have had great critical and creative power," often touching "deeper religious issues regarding the true situation of black communities."[5]

"Religion," then, not only pertains to the formal creeds, doctrines, and theologies of a church-based faith tradition but includes beliefs that are embedded in the ordinary experiences and the deeply held attitudes, values, and activities of members of a group or community. It may also include what David Hall has called "lived religion," or the practice and "everyday thinking and doing of lay men and women." African American religion, according to this perspective, not only embodies ecclesial formations of faith but also encompasses noninstitutionalized expressions and activities.[6]

It is my belief that permutations of the supernatural in practices such as conjuring, the African American tradition of healing and harming, have been resignified as "religion." Generally, however, observers have not viewed Conjure and religion as elements of a single complex, choosing instead to retain the "magic-religion" dichotomy when looking at African American spirituality. Perhaps one reason is that most interpreters set "Christian" and "non-Christian" traditions against each other, with little regard for the range of relationships that might exist between them. This approach, with its value-laden assumptions, has shaped academic studies on African American religion from the past to the present. While it may be useful for academic interpreters, a rigid dichotomy between Christian and non-Christian expressions in black folk traditions belies practitioners' own experiences.[7]

Instead of viewing supernaturalism as a marginal subset of African American religion, I have identified supernatural practices as they appear within and outside black spiritual traditions. These include those that might be classified as "magical," whose participants claim an allegiance to conventional spiritual authorities (e.g., Christian ministers, or members of black churches) while taking part in Hoodoo, Conjure, and root-working practices. Take for example a former slave, self-proclaimed preacher, and healer in a 1930s Texas community by the name of William Adams. Adams, as did others in his day, found in the Christian scriptures a timeless collection of potent spells, charms, curses, and esoteric lore. "There am lots of folks, and educated ones too, that says we-uns don't understand," he claimed. " 'Member the Lord, in some of His ways, can be mysterious. The Bible says so." Spiritual powers and supernatural abilities, he argued, were available to those who were divinely gifted or specially inspired by God.[8]

This book considers other cases as well, such as that of Bishop Charles Harrison Mason, the founder of what would become the largest African American Pentecostal denomination, the Church of God in Christ. Mason possessed an uncommon fascination with strangely formed natural objects—objects that were reminiscent of the "roots" or magical artifacts used by black Conjurers throughout the nineteenth and early twentieth centuries. Mason, however, described his roots as "wonders of God" and contemplated the miraculous as he delivered sermons to his Afro-Christian followers. Shifting to a very different context, we may consider the Kongolese in the sixteenth and seventeenth centuries, pious African Catholics who assigned supernatural significance to the gnarly, rootlike incarnations of their patron deities. Far from representing religious oddities, do these phenomena point to continuities that reach from Africa to America? To begin to answer this question I present a spectrum of beliefs and practices by illuminating the "magical" aspects of African American spirituality.

African American magical practices and beliefs possess an extensive historiography, as writers in the fields of black studies, religion, history, folklore, and anthropology have all examined conjuring traditions. Theophus Smith formulated a theory of black spirituality in his *Conjuring Culture: Biblical Formations of Black America* (1994), which viewed African American magic as expressing a cultural idiom, and conjuring rituals, performative signs, and symbols as articulating human intention. At the other end of the bibliographic spectrum stand older studies, such as Newbell Niles Puckett's *Folk Beliefs of the Southern Negro* (1926), which offered the author's particular insights into the social and cultural milieu from which black spiritual traditions in late-nineteenth- and early-twentieth-century America were derived. First-person narratives of Conjure traditions are best exemplified by the vast collection of supernatural charms, mystical experiences, spiritual formulae, and other raw materials collected in *Hoodoo — Conjuration — Witchcraft — Rootwork,*

collected by Harry Middleton Hyatt in the 1930s and 1940s. There is also
a voluminous secondary literature on African American supernaturalism that consists of monographs, articles, and ethnographies of black folk
tradition in the United States dating from the early 1800s. There are no
single academic studies, however, that deal directly with the relationship
between magic and religion, the congruency of these phenomena in actual spiritual experience, and the shifting, fluid meanings that they have
acquired in African American culture. The present text addresses these
concerns.

The sources I utilize are drawn, for the most part, from a mix of primary and secondary documents, autobiographical narratives, and perhaps most important, folklore accounts. Only partial answers to my questions were to be found in the standard historical documentation, which
did not usually give voice to the inarticulate majority, the black "folk."
I have emphasized wherever possible the words and experiences of
African American witnesses over those of scholarly interpreters. Relayed
by persons of varying status—including former slaves and their descendants, men and women "in the pews," staunch secularists, and nonbe-
lievers—African American sources feature vivid personal remembrances,
oral testimonies, and rich ethnographic descriptions. For a people who
have relied on the oral transmission of knowledge and culture as black
Americans have, the spoken narrative of folklore is as vital as the written documentation on which many histories of African American religion are based. As argued by the historian William Piersen, folklore can
function as "moral truth" rather than "historical truth" for those who
recount it, giving evidence of a "deeper" reality that endures in shared,
communal recollections of the past. Accordingly I have also relied on
documents such as the Federal Writers' Project Slave Narratives, compiled from interviews with former bondmen and their descendants in the
United States after the turn of the twentieth century. Other materials used
as resources for *Black Magic* include oral "texts" such as those drawn
from the black performative tradition, including folk music and the blues,
whose contents have circulated for generations as valuable repositories
of African American thought.[9]

Although this book opens with a fictional sequence situated among
the Gullah-speaking people of the Sea Islands, the book's focus is not on
that territory, nor on any single region or population where African
American supernatural traditions are found—not even New Orleans, a
demographically unique city that is more often associated with black
"magic" than any other. Rather, I argue that widespread affinities are

manifested in black folk traditions, be they practices from Christianity in its numerous sectarian forms, or spiritual traditions such as supernatural healing and divination. The conclusion that I have arrived at is this: African American "religion" is not always distinct from what others call "magic." Instead, these are complementary categories, and they have historically exhibited complementary forms in African American culture.

The chapters in this book are arranged thematically. The first chapter considers the centrality of supernatural traditions such as Conjure and Hoodoo in the African American spiritual experience, presenting images and examples from various historical contexts. The second chapter discusses the potential sources of black American supernaturalism, beginning with the spiritual life of African slaves in early America, and the traditions that, in African societies, had once encompassed all human relations and institutions. Among enslaved blacks, older cosmologies gradually merged with concepts that were extracted from newly formed Afro-Christian ideas such as a radical monotheism, dualistic notions of good and evil, and concepts of spiritual intervention. Elements of the older African worldview also intersected with a network of Anglo-American supernatural traditions. The simultaneous emergence of African-based supernaturalism (later identified as Conjure and Hoodoo) and black Americans' embrace of Christianity resulted in the reinforcement of magic and religion as convergent phenomena.

Chapters 3 and 4 examine the contours of African American folk tradition as exemplified in supernatural harming and healing practices. Supernatural harming is usually called *Voodoo,* which is also the name of an African-derived religion originating on the island of Haiti. Voodoo, as it is used in the American context, connotes an illicit form of spirituality, and many images have been used to bolster the notorious associations between it, racial blackness, and evil magic. Yet this Afro-Caribbean religion (*vodou,* in Kreyol) is quite distinct from the aggressive spiritual practices that arose in the United States, practices that were initially employed as sources of resistance by black people. The continuity of these supernatural harming traditions suggests that African-based beliefs in spiritual power as a force for self-defense persisted in African American spiritual beliefs.

If harming was an important concern in black American spirituality, so much more was healing. Chapter 4 considers African American understandings of the supernatural as both theoretical and practical ideas by which members of black communities interpreted suffering. Like the

African roots on which they drew, black American supernatural traditions promoted authorities and practitioners who bridged the physical realm and the invisible world. These spiritual professionals were competent at dealing with affliction and its prevention; they provided diagnoses and cured intractable ailments. As Theophus Smith has noted, the "curative intention" of practices such as Conjure can be seen in African American practices and beliefs that "revised and re-visioned" conditions such as violence and racial victimization. Similar to the traditional healers in African societies, African American supernatural practitioners "deciphered" evil and sickness, locating affliction within the ills occurring in society itself. Personal misfortune, therefore, could possess underlying causes such as anger, selfishness, and jealousy. A tragic accident, an unforeseen illness, a calamitous event sometimes figured as an affliction with spiritual origins.[10]

The final chapter briefly examines more recent manifestations of Conjure and Hoodoo in black and white America, beginning with the public perceptions of African American supernaturalism in the last quarter of the nineteenth century, and later in the twentieth. After the Emancipation Proclamation was issued in 1863 and following the movement of blacks during the Great Migration from the South to the northern states in the early 1900s, a variety of forms of African American magic developed within metropolitan environments. In these contexts, conjuring specialists and spiritual practitioners were prominent figures in the black urban landscape, and in some cases their roles were reconfigured in African American churches. In the cities, magic was also reproduced as a commodity, reshaped by innovative profiteers, and appropriated by commercial interests and industries. Although black American spirituality was still oriented toward human interaction with efficacious powers, other expressions of the supernatural informed black American popular culture, with the blues and literature as two important artistic products that manifested the influences of Conjure in the twentieth century.

Black Magic does not purport to be a definitive history of African American magic or religion; rather, it is a selective examination of key themes in African American religious history. It is my contribution to a conversation among students of black religion that provides a more nuanced view of "religion" and "magic," by tracing the elements of these two parallel and sometimes indistinguishable ideas. Ultimately, the effacing of these categories may lead to a richer understanding of the myriad dimensions of human spirituality. It is a reminder that as we look at African American religion, certain themes appear to be inescapable: where there are preachers, there are also Conjurers; where there are conversions, there are dreams and visions. And where there is faith, there is, and ever continues to be, magic.

THE
LONG LOST FRIEND.

A COLLECTION

OF

MYSTERIOUS & INVALUABLE

ARTS & REMEDIES,

FOR

MAN AS WELL AS ANIMALS.

WITH MANY PROOFS

Of their virtue and efficacy in healing diseases, &c., the greater part of which was never published until they appeared in print for the first time in the U. S. in the year 1820.

BY JOHN GEORGE HOHMAN.

HARRISBURG, PA.—1856.
T. F. Scheffer, Printer.

CHAPTER I

"Our Religion and Superstition Was All Mixed Up"

Conjure, Christianity, and African American Supernatural Traditions

Henry Abraham, an African American farmer, migrated from the low-country plantations of South Carolina to the pine fields of Florida early in the twentieth century. A story tells that one day he was sent to draft some laborers for work in the turpentine camps. Approaching a truck-load of potential recruits, Abraham tried to persuade them to sign on with the company he represented. Then, according to one witness, he threatened to "throw the worste [sic] spell" on them unless they went with him. In fear, the men went along, and thereafter Abraham acquired the reputation of someone who was able to "fix" whomever he wanted or to "throw a fix," that is, remove the spells of others. Knowledge of his powers spread, and Henry Abraham thus began his career as a "Hoodoo doctor" for the "sick and spell-bound." His spiritual work included creating and distributing small, powerful healing charms that he called "Christian letters" to his many patients, including some who came from as far away as Canada to see him.[1]

Figures such as Henry Abraham have held a fascinating role in black America. A supernatural practitioner who was committed to good

Facing page illustration: texts favored by black Hoodoo practitioners included magic manuals of European Christian extraction, such as this English translation of John George Hohman, *Der lange verborgene Freund* (The long lost friend; 1856). Courtesy of the Library Company of Philadelphia, Rare Books Division.

works, Abraham channeled his gifts into a ministry that endured for more than thirty years. His great success demonstrates how African Americans in the early twentieth century, like their nineteenth-century predecessors, embraced beliefs that extended well beyond the prescribed territories of the church and the Sunday school and into their everyday lives. Although it is not clear that Henry Abraham would have claimed the title, his career manifests strong parallels with those of other African American supernatural healers, the Conjurers.

Conjure is a magical tradition in which spiritual power is invoked for various purposes, such as healing, protection, and self defense. The relationship between Conjure and African American religion—in particular, Christianity—is somewhat ambiguous. Conjure is usually associated with magical practices, unlike Christianity, which is seen as a "religion," a dichotomy that suggests that they are in conflict with one another. Yet from slavery days to the present, many African Americans have readily moved between Christianity, Conjure, and other forms of supernaturalism with little concern for their purported incompatibility.[2]

It would be incorrect to assert, however, that Conjure and Christianity have always functioned in total harmony. From the beginning, Conjure was disparaged by critics as incompatible with true religious piety. Yet in most cases Conjure appears to have operated as a counterpart to religious belief and practice. The following anecdote illustrates the complex relationship that existed between the two. Shortly before the turn of the twentieth century, an amateur collector of Negro spirituals and folklore recounted a conversation she had had with an unidentified black clergyman. According to the collector, the clergyman, "one of the most scholarly and noted ministers of the colored race," admitted that even as a professed Christian he had found himself sometimes "under the influences of *voodooism*," his term for African-derived spiritual practices. He explained that as a young pastor he had grown "completely discouraged" after numerous unsuccessful attempts to attract new worshipers into his congregation, until one day an unexpected visitor happened his way. "I was in my study praying," he recalled, "when the door opened and a little Conjure man came in and said softly: 'You don't understand de people. You must get you a *hand* as a friend to draw 'em. Ef you will let me fix you a luck charm, you'll git 'em.'" The minister accepted the charm from the Conjurer and found to his surprise the very next week his church was full. "For four years," he reflected, "the aisles were crowded every Sunday." Disgusted, he eventually destroyed the charm, unable to reconcile his increased popularity with the apparent potency of the supernatural object. "I knew it was not the gospel's power, but that wretched 'luck ball.'" Perplexed, he concluded, "I . . . have never been able to draw an audience since."[3]

This intriguing account highlights a number of issues. Although the author never identifies the Negro clergyman, she presents this as a "true" event, noting only that the incident portrayed an instance of the "peculiar persistency" of magical ideas among the descendants of Africans in the United States. If we read this account as folklore, it underscores how religion and Conjure were sometimes viewed by African Americans as strange but potentially suitable bedfellows. The relationship between Conjure and Christianity, seen according to the perspective of the preacher, was inimical. Seen from another perspective, however, the story suggests that the charm was beneficial, providing a power that supplemented the minister's own spiritual gifts. For him, the Conjure hand delivered immediate results, while his own religious faith lacked the guarantee of efficacy. This story advances possibilities for understanding the intricate notions that operated for persons who might have practiced or believed in Conjure. It indicates that two perspectives might have been dominant in African American spirituality. We want to know how these distinctive ideas, Conjure and Christianity, were reconciled. What did they mean to those who embraced them? In what ways did they interact? To explore these questions let us begin in slavery, among persons who viewed their world through a supernatural lens.

Persons believed to possess special powers were present in black populations throughout the United States in the slavery period, as affirmed by both black and white witnesses. The black abolitionist William Wells Brown surmised that the role of the supernatural practitioner was institutionalized within most antebellum slave communities in the South. "Nearly every large plantation," he stated, "had at least one, who laid claim to be a fortune teller, and who was granted with more than common respect by his fellow slaves." White witnesses concurred. A prominent slaveholder in South Carolina observed that in most slave quarters there were one or more blacks who were "ambitious of being considered in the character of Conjurers" in order to gain influence among other bondpersons. Conjure practitioners, it is believed, were "the most powerful and significant individuals on the plantation." While it is impossible to say precisely how many such practitioners existed, it is certain that during slavery, and even beyond, Conjurers were highly visible figures on the cultural landscape in black America.[4]

In the nineteenth century some observers noted that Conjure and

African American Christianity seemed to have been nurtured in the same soil. One plantation owner in antebellum South Carolina recognized discernible incongruities between religion as practiced by the blacks and by whites and attributed those differences to African American predilections for the supernatural. "In all instances which I remember to have noticed with reference to such fact," he remarked, "I have found among the religious slaves of the South traces . . . of a blending of superstition and fetichism [sic], modifying their impressions of Christianity." Frederick Law Olmsted, the noted architect and travel writer, toured Virginia in the 1850s, observing that while a good portion of slaves were churchgoers, their religion was dominated by a "miserable system of superstition, the more painful that it employs some forms and words ordinarily connected with true Christianity." Almost thirty years later, the folklorist William Owens corroborated the appearance of a strange admixture of Christianity and supernaturalism, remarking that black "American-born superstitions" were "interwoven with so-called religious beliefs" and represented "a horrible debasement of some of the highest and noblest doctrines of the Christian faith." Others would note that African American practitioners of Christianity often mingled unusual practices with their traditions. As stated by one elder, an ex-slave commenting on the eclecticism of black spiritual beliefs: "Our religion and superstition was all mixed up!"[5]

Religious leaders in slave communities were entrusted with the knowledge and responsibility for maintaining spiritual traditions. These leaders included both Christian ministers and Conjurers. Occasionally, these offices were shared by a single person. William Webb was one such individual. Enslaved in Kentucky in the early 1800s, Webb recalled how he had prepared special bags of roots for other blacks to carry in order "to keep peace" between masters and slaves on local plantations. The roots, he explained, were to be used in conjunction with prayer. When asked by other bondmen about the bags, he explained, "I told them those roots were able to make them faithful when they were calling on the Supreme Being, and to keep [their] mind at work all the time." Webb, who also believed in the mystical significance of dreams and prophecy, apparently combined the roles of conjuring specialist with plantation religious functionary.[6]

William Webb was not unique. Quite a few African American spiritual authorities shifted between Christianity and the prospects that Conjure offered. In the 1840s the wife of a wealthy white landowner in Virginia, Mary Livermore, described a black preacher she had known who was "a man of many gifts." According to Livermore, "Uncle" Aaron, a minister and exhorter, was popular as a "Conjurer who could raise evil spirits, and a god-man who wore a charm, and could become invisible at any moment." Another slave, known only as Elihu, was recognized by witnesses as "an old and creditable member of the church," who was "as punctilious as a Pharisee" in his own religious observances, according to one nineteenth-century writer. Elihu, however, also placed great faith in charms, Conjure, witches, spells, and his own gifts for the "miraculous cures" of animals and humans that he performed in the South Carolina countryside. Other black preachers of note explored equally eclectic spiritual venues. John Henry Kemp, a slave in Mississippi, considered himself a loyal representative of the True Primitive Baptist Church, who preached "one faith, one Lord and one religion." Kemp was also gifted with the ability to determine the future, to read palms, and to cure sickness with the aid of "charms, roots, herbs and magical incantations and formulae" for "those who believe[ed] in him."[7]

The activities of such enslaved Conjure men and women have been well documented. In nineteenth-century North Carolina, a journalist described a plantation bondwoman whom other slaves believed to be "in communication with occult powers," as an accomplished seer and prophet: "Her utterances were accepted as oracles, and piously heeded," for it was thought that "she could see through the mists that hide the future from others." Slave Conjurers offered consolation to other bondpersons who were at risk. According to his famous autobiography, young Frederick Douglass was once assisted by a Conjure man named Sandy Jenkins, who gave him an enchanted root prior to a confrontation that Douglass had with a notorious "Negro-breaker" or slave disciplinarian, in Maryland. As recounted in another African American slave narrative, the bondman Henry Bibb went to a Conjurer on the advice of a friend, who subsequently provided him with a supernatural preparation that he believed protected him from beatings by his master. The black abolitionist and writer Henry Clay Bruce, who had been enslaved in Virginia, described a community of slaves that hired the services of a Conjurer to prevent their deportation and removal to a plantation in the Deep South. The Conjurer's powers, they believed, obstructed the slaveowners' attempts to separate them, for at the last minute the scheduled relocation was aborted. The assurance that these individuals supplied to persons who accepted the virtue of supernatural actions was often indispensable. Such defenses against the psychological and physical assaults of slavery were essential for many African Americans, who endured a system in which their humanity was devalued and their collective efforts at self-determination were constantly hindered.[8]

While Conjure possessed multiple uses, its most salient functional value for blacks had to do with practices of racial opposition. Conjuring arbitrated the day-to-day conflicts in which slaves were confronted with white slaveholder domination, which was often directed and enforced through violent means. African American testimonials describe how some slaves believed that the power of charms and amulets provided them with protection from whippings and other forms of abuse. Louis Hughes, a bondman who had lived on plantations in Mississippi and Tennessee, explained that he had carried a leather bag containing "roots, nuts, pins and some other things," which was given to him by an old man. The "voodoo bag," Hughes claimed, was believed to have the "power to prevent any one who carried it from being whipped." Stories of Conjurers who subdued whites were also prominent in the narratives of slaves and former slaves. Clara Walker, an ex-bondwoman in Arkansas, told of a black "witch doctor" who punished a slaveholder by creating "a little man out of mud" in his image, and then sticking a thorn into the back of the doll. "Sure 'nuff, his master go down with a misery in his back," she claimed. "An de witch doctor let de thorn stay . . . until he thought his master had got 'nuff punishment. When he took it out, his master got better." Perpetuated through hundreds of accounts of this sort, supernatural lore was passed on by men and women who weathered the ordeal of bondage. Conjuring narratives form some of the most compelling accounts of their experiences.[9]

The significance of Conjure as a putative deterrent against slaveholder persecution may have extended beyond its actual use by the slaves. The exploits of conjuring specialists are ubiquitous in slave histories, autobiographies, narratives, and especially, in folklore. It is likely that some folklore traditions were based on real-life situations. From this perspective, Conjure was a powerful psychological device for many African Americans. Wells Brown described an incident involving a clash of wills between a slave driver and a plantation Conjurer, Dinkie, a man "deeply immersed in voodouism, goophering and fortunetelling," who was "his own master" on the Missouri plantation where Wells Brown and the other slaves lived in the early nineteenth century. The overseer was an aggressive and sadistic man who had been hired to manage the farm and was determined to enact his authority through the physical intimidation of the slaves. The eventual confrontation that erupted between Dinkie and the overseer was inevitable, as Wells Brown tells in this portion of the autobiography:

"Follow me to the barn," said the impatient driver to the Negro. "I make it a point always to whip a nigger, the first day that I take charge of a farm,

so as to let the hands know who I am. And now, Mr. Dinkie . . . I shall give
you a flogging that you will never forget."

At this juncture, Dinkie gave a knowing look to the other slaves, who
were standing by, and said, "Ef he lays the weight ob his finger on me,
you'll see de top of dat barn come off."

As the two disappeared into the barn, the other slaves tensely gathered
and waited. Moments passed, and when Dinkie and the overseer emerged,
they silently went their separate ways. Either by shrewdness or through
some extraordinary occurrence, Dinkie had avoided the driver's lash and
remained unscathed. The other slaves were deeply impressed by this
event, while Wells Brown, for his part, remained the impassive narrator:
"how the feat had been accomplished," he reflected, "was a mystery."
The others, however, interpreted Dinkie's achievement as a supernatural sign. "Dinkie's got de power," declared one witness, "he knows things
seen and unseen, an' dat's what makes him his own massa." Incidents
such as these may have contributed to the development of popular figures in African American folklore, such as Big John, High John the Conqueror, and Bandy Joe, colorful mythic characters who were attributed
with acts of defiance and bravery in the African American community.[10]

It is clear that in many cases, supernatural beliefs served to mediate
relations between blacks and whites. Conjure also might have allowed
black people to attain a measure of control over their lives, as bondpersons. The world that the slaves inhabited was unpredictable and uncertain. Anxiety over inevitable violence, separation from loved ones, or the
unforeseeable risks of escape must have engendered persistent insecurity
for African American slaves. Blacks also endured the ever-present realities of racial subjugation and other forms of affliction such as sickness
and destitution. According to one historian of slavery, "Conjuring constituted a pragmatic and realistic method, given a situation of extremely
limited alternatives, that slaves could use to cope with their masters."
Nevertheless, slaveholders often found that the dilemma posed by
Conjure lay not in the question of direct efficacy—that is to say, whether
such practices "worked" against them—but in the ways that the slaves
utilized these beliefs to challenge their authority.[11]

Supernatural traditions were integral to slaves' strategies of resistance,
available not only to individuals like Frederick Douglass, who attempted
to avoid an overseer's lash, but, as I will show in a later section, to leaders of slave uprisings as well. Conjure traditions also gave some slaves the
determination to engage in subversive activities. Horace Overstreet, an ex-
bondman in Texas, described the confidence that some African Americans

derived from their faith in supernatural practitioners. Overstreet told how a Conjurer once gave a bondwoman he knew a special "bag of sand" in order to keep her cruel master from whipping her. "Dat same day," he noted, "she got too uppity and sass de massa, *'cause she feel safe.*"[12]

Their Conjure beliefs enabled some black bondpersons to chip away at the foundations of slaveholders' authority, sometimes through small, disabling acts. The clandestine operations of Conjurers and supernatural specialists, for example, were a scourge to slaveowners. James Henry Hammond, the prominent proslavery ideologue of South Carolina, described his great frustration with the rampant destructiveness of Conjure practitioners on his estate, who had been involved in numerous incidents of vandalism, unauthorized doctoring, and theft of his personal property. Unsuccessfully, Hammond had tried to expose those who were involved with prohibited spiritual activities, but his slaves' belief that they were supernaturally protected from his reprisals allowed them to thwart his attempts to dominate their collective wills. They had adopted a conceptual framework to which Hammond had no access.[13]

Black Americans utilized conjuring traditions not only because they saw them as a valuable resource for resistance, but because they believed that the supernatural realm offered alternative possibilities for empowerment. Aside from its subversive uses for slaves, Conjure may have been the cause of some concern for slaveowners because of their own belief in its power. Apparently many whites were acquainted with supernatural practices and beliefs, in part through their own exposure to black folk traditions. "Most of the superstition among the whites," wrote Wells Brown, "was the result of their close connection with the blacks." Wells Brown recalled that some African American caregivers would tell magical folktales and stories to young white children in nurseries, but "they learned more, as they grew older, from the slaves in the quarters, or out on the premises." White writers reflected on these traditions in their published reminiscences of their youth. Edward Pollard, a novelist and Civil War historian, stated that he was deeply affected by the "superstitions" that he had imbibed, growing up among black household servants. In many cases, children of both races were inculcated with images from a rich folklore tradition that served the twin objectives of admonition and instruction. Conjuring tales no doubt made a great impact on impressionable children. The Reconstruction legislator William Councill wrote that as a child he had been sent to live on a small plantation where he met "Aunt Phillis," a "noted Conjure woman," who took him into her care. "She exercised complete control over me—soul and body," he stated. "I believed in her. I feared and worshipped her." In such biracial contexts, the vivid depictions of spirits, invisible powers, and other, malevolent forces from black folklore may have functioned as a means of control over youngsters. The former slave Abram Sells, for example, recalled how his grandfather, an elderly man, was assigned to care for the black and white children on a Texas plantation. "Us sure have to mind him," he explained, " 'cause iffen we didn't, us sure have bad luck. He always have the pocket full of things to conjure with." The dreadful "hants" and powerful Conjurers that inhabited African American folklore may have helped reinforce social norms and invoke sanctions for both black and white children's behavior.[14]

These examples demonstrate how belief in the power of black Conjure practitioners transcended racial boundaries. This would not be strange, given that similar traditions had also circulated among segments of the Anglo American population. Diverse occult practices, witchcraft, divination, astrology, and supernatural healing held great appeal for European Americans of broadly disparate educational backgrounds, social rankings, and religious commitments from the colonial period onward. Fears of malevolent spiritual harming were still prevalent among whites in the antebellum era. In the South, adherence to such beliefs left Anglo-American plain folk open to chastisement by religious leaders and class-conscious elites. An 1855 editorial in a Charleston, South Carolina, newspaper, for example—bemoaning the abject spiritual state of the citizenry—linked the widespread belief in witchcraft to the superstitious fears of "poor and ignorant" whites. Yet Wells Brown, who had fled his native Missouri in 1834, asserted that "all classes" of white persons he had ever known were obsessed with witchcraft and other supernatural traditions. He observed that the whites were "possessed with a large share of the superstition that prevail[ed] throughout the South." Describing an African American Conjurer whose duties varied from providing cures for ailing slaves to predicting the romantic prospects of white spinsters, and a black fortune-teller on whom white businessmen called for legal advice, Wells Brown depicted a brisk trade in supernatural practices to which both whites and blacks subscribed. These beliefs were maintained, he concluded, not only by "the ignorant Negro, who brought it with him from his native land, but also by a great number of well-educated and influential whites." Interest in the supernatural apparently persisted among some Anglo-Americans in some parts of the South in the years following the Civil War. In 1867 a letter appeared in a local newspaper, written by a schoolteacher who reported that "more than half of the white people" in the area surrounding Beaufort County, North Carolina, believed in "witches and jugglery."[15]

Although accepted by some whites, conjuring traditions thrived within the slave quarters, the social and cultural hub of the black community. Conjure spoke to the practical concerns of African American bondpersons, from their personal aspirations to matters that affected everyone, such as health, wealth, and conflict. Within interpersonal relations Conjure was also utilized as a popular means of enticement in romantic matters. Dinkie, the plantation Conjurer with whom Wells Brown was acquainted, provided consultations, charms, and potions for an avid clientele of lovelorn ladies. The bondman Henry Bibb described his experiences with a talisman given to him by a Conjure man that promised to "make any girl love" him, "in spite of herself . . . no matter who she might be engaged to, nor whom she might be walking with." Although his charm ultimately failed to fulfill the desired effect, Bibb was not deterred; he simply sought another Conjurer's assistance. Another case, recorded after the turn of the twentieth century, described a former slave in Tennessee who had bought a love charm from a "coal black" Conjure man named Old Bab Russ, who, it was noted, could "talk African." In this farcical account of failed courtship, the suitor narrowly escapes the wrath of the girl's protective parents, who had discovered his amorous intentions. In these and other slavery-era accounts, the inventory of recipes and formulae utilized by African Americans for matters of seduction was virtually limitless.[16]

Supernaturalism thus was an inseparable part of the composite of cultural practices that emerged in the context of the American slave experience. Even beyond slavery, conjuring traditions showed great variety, as the following "list of uses" compiled from a folklore source in the early 1900s indicates. Conjure was an all-purpose utility, employed for "injuring or destroying enemies, getting rid of rivals or undesirables, softening hearts, winning or holding love . . . breaking up homes, calling the absent, getting jobs, dodging the law, protecting property, detecting criminals, gambling, collecting debts, disciplining servants, stopping trains and steamboats, producing fertility or barrenness in women, promoting crops, controlling weather, foretelling the future, and locating lost and stolen goods, water, and buried treasure." To believers, these supernatural traditions clearly served multiple purposes, but at the heart of conjuring practices lay a fundamental quest for power, explanation, and control.[17]

Who were the Conjurers? Colorful, diverse, and enigmatic, Conjure practitioners maintained distinctive styles and expressions of their craft. European American observers provide the first accounts of black

Conjurers, the earliest dating from the seventeenth century, and often describe practitioners of the supernatural as "cunning men" or "witches." By the nineteenth century the terms for African American Conjurers would change. "Hoodoos" and "root workers" were the most common vernacular expressions that depicted persons who were believed to be able to manipulate unseen forces or "work the spirits." "Root doctors" was a prevalent euphemism that described persons who practiced healing only, whereas "Conjure doctors" could include those who possessed the power to do harm as well as heal. "Goopher-doctors," "Two-Head doctors" or "Wise men" were region-specific titles for folk practitioners, as were "Longheads," and "Double-sighters," root workers who could be found in Florida, South Carolina, and Georgia. Throughout Louisiana and Mississippi, black Conjure specialists were variously called "Voodoos," "wangateurs" and "horses." "Trick doctors" and "Witch-doctors" dealt with the spiritual sources of misfortune. "Conjurer" eventually became the most commonly used term for African American supernatural practitioners, but it is unclear precisely when the word came into its widest use. Some nineteenth-century witnesses seemed unfamiliar with the term, as for instance Frederick Douglass, who remarked of one Conjure practitioner in his acquaintance, "he professed to believe in a system for which I have no name."[18]

The words used to describe them accentuate the uncommon qualities that were associated with Conjurers. These supernatural practitioners were often thought to possess extraordinary powers—such as the ability to control the weather, to become invisible, to fly, or to shape-shift at will. Many demonstrated a genius for receiving and interpreting communications from the realm of spiritual forces. Most of all, unusual and discernible physical traits set the Conjurers apart from other persons. A fascinating enumeration of bodily deformities particular to Conjure specialists, such as distinguishing birthmarks or abnormalities such as harelips, red eyes, or eyes of different colors, have been noted by observers during the nineteenth and twentieth centuries. The folklorist Ruth Bass recalled in the 1930s that a "distinguishing physical characteristic" set apart most of the Conjurers she had known in her childhood in Mississippi. "One was tall and dark with grave eyes," she wrote, "one was an undersized, dwarfed mulatto, almost an albino, with green eyes and a cunning little face. I remember one who had a twisted back and walked with a sickening, one-sided limp." Similarly, the African American schoolteacher Mamie Garvin Fields described an elderly practitioner she encountered while she was living in rural John's Island, South Carolina, in 1909:

The old man was very short—a runt—and his head was tied with an old red bandanna. They say his hair was never combed. And ragged! He was so ragged and dirty until [sic] you couldn't see what the body of his clothes was made of . . . he carried a real snake in his hand. . . . He whipped that snake around his head, cracking it like one of those big whips that you have for horses.[19]

Other descriptions focus on the apparel of African American Conjure practitioners. Some specialists adopted accessories that they claimed had supernatural significance. Tinted or dark glasses, for example, a symbol of second sight that "blocked a man's view" of the Conjurer's "eyes and thoughts" were a noted item among some practitioners. To enhance their status as the descendants of Africans, some Conjurers acquired exotic paraphernalia, such as Wells Brown's Dinkie, who wore a shed snake-skin about his shoulders. Others carried elaborate carved walking staffs and canes as the trademarks of their profession. Some supernatural specialists were also known to dress in styles suggesting sexual inversion. One account from the post-Emancipation period tells of "Reverend Dr. H." in Virginia, a Conjurer who "had his hair braided like a woman, and [had] rings in his ears." Gender mutability may have been a dramatic means by which Conjure practitioners exploited their reputations as eccentric individuals.[20]

Although males appear to be more prominent in nineteenth- and early-twentieth-century accounts of Conjurers, African American female practitioners apparently made their mark in significant numbers as well. Charles Colcock Jones, Jr., a white southern historian and namesake of a prominent antebellum missionary, alleged that Conjure women predominated in black communities in the coastal regions of Georgia and the Carolinas. "The fabrication of Fetiches, and their sale to those who desired to utilize the powers of the deities which they were supposed to represent, were monopolized by old women," he wrote, "who derived considerable gain from this calling." The novelist Charles Chesnutt attested to the supernatural powers of the elderly black women he met in North Carolina while researching his 1899 work, *The Conjure Woman and Other Tales*. Other black female supernatural specialists were represented in a gamut of gender stereotypes in fiction and folklore, from the sinister, decrepit hag to the dangerous, bewitching mulatta. African American Conjure women inherited a legacy of powerful spiritual roles that had been instituted by their foremothers.[21]

It was not unknown for Conjurers to undergo a period of study or training in order to master required skills. In South Carolina at the turn of the nineteenth century, General Assembly records noted that a slave who had been accused of murder had apprenticed at a "free school to learn To Conjure sixteen years." Other supernatural specialists participated in various methods of initiation. Zora Neale Hurston, the anthropologist and novelist, found herself taking part in secret rituals of initiation among Hoodoo practitioners in New Orleans in the early twentieth century. Mary Owen, a white folklorist, also detailed the ceremonies of initiation for members of a "Voodoo" cult of black Conjurers in the late nineteenth century. Nevertheless, it appears that most often the secrets of conjuring were passed on from one practitioner to another, between family members, or learned by those who were seen as especially proficient or in possession of unusual talents. " 'To be strong in de haid' . . . is the most important characteristic of a *Cunjurer,*" concluded Owen, whose observations point to the link between Conjure and other diasporic spiritual traditions such as Haitian *vodou* and Cuban *santería,* religions in which a devotee's head is believed to be governed by a particular force or divinity.[22]

Conjurers were sometimes summoned to their professions in ways that evoked the traditional Christian "call" to ministry. The career of Henry Abraham, who came to be known as the "Hoodoo doctor" of Lawtey, Florida, began with his receiving a divine revelation, as described by Hurston in the following account:

> One day as he was plowing under the parching sun, he suddenly stopped, his face bathed in perspiration. Calling his wife he said, "Honey, I jes' can't do dis yere work; I has a feelin' God's done called his chile for higher things. Ever since I been a boy I done had dis yere feelin' but I jes' didn' obey. *Quench not the spirit, saith de Lord.*" Throwing down his plow Abraham left the field, never to return to it again as a laborer.[23]

Many supernatural specialists were "born with the gift"—marked, or chosen, at the start of their lives. Anomalous births were considered significant in the conjuring tradition. Being born with a caul, the amniotic veil covering the face of the newly delivered infant, was interpreted as evidence that one was gifted with enhanced insight into the invisible realm. Another well-known belief held that the seventh child of a seventh son or daughter would enjoy an auspicious spiritual lineage. "If you are a double-sighted person and can see ghosts, if you happen to have been born on Christmas Day, or are a seventh son, you are born for magic," claimed one folklorist.[24]

These anomalies sometimes led the depiction of Conjurers as outsiders, inhabitants of the fringes, dwelling within a cultural demimonde. Speaking of a well known Conjure practitioner in antebellum Tennessee, one slave observed, "she ain't got father nor mother, an' nobody don't know whar she come from nor what she's a-goin' to." Social marginality allowed some practitioners to accumulate material wealth from their professions—or to at least achieve the illusion of having done so. In the post-Emancipation period some African American practitioners mastered the commodification of the supernatural arts, accepting monetary remuneration and even becoming self-reliant spiritual entrepreneurs in the freedperson's community. In Virginia a student at the Hampton Institute described a specialist from his hometown who he said had made a "fortune" from conjuring activities. "I heard him say out of his own mouth," insisted the student, "that he made over five hundred dollars a week, sometimes." A black senator in North Carolina, William H. Moore, was said to have left his seat in the state congress to become a Conjure doctor in 1878. Moore, in the words of a hostile white legislator, "prospered sufficiently on the ignorance of his patients to maintain a handsome horse and buggy and many other comforts" following his departure from state politics. The Virginia historian Philip Alexander Bruce, writing in 1888, noted that nomadic "Trick" doctors were perceived to be economically threatening to white landowners in the southern Virginia tobacco belt. According to Bruce, the demand for their charms was especially high among the freed black population. "It is doubtful, indeed," Bruce surmised, "whether a Negro could follow a more lucrative pursuit." In the latter decades of the nineteenth century other practitioners such as Doctor Buzzard, one of the most famous of all southern root doctors, was said to have amassed a great fortune from his conjuring activities in South Carolina. Jimmy Brisbane, a prominent Conjurer in the early twentieth century, owned a house, property, and several automobiles in his home state of South Carolina. It was commonly asserted in black folk narratives that root doctors earned more money than formally trained physicians.[25]

For black people, wealth was one of the most tangible symbols of empowerment. Attaining power—over one's destiny, over one's circumstances, over one's environment—was a particular concern for African Americans, who had suffered the debilitations of slavery, poverty, and institutionalized racism. It may be argued that conjuring traditions allowed some blacks to achieve a conceptual measure of control and power over their circumstances. Religious faith functioned in much the same way when slaves were confronted with uncertainty in their lives. The religion of Christianity, however, operated as more of a salvific or soteriological philosophy than a utilitarian system. It was, as Albert Raboteau has noted with regard to slave religion, "well suited for describing the ultimate cause of things and the ultimate end of history." In the theological schema of Christianity, salvation and morality were given priority—perhaps more so than individual security. In contrast to the way that faith issues were conceived in Christianity, Conjure beliefs applied to an individual's most pressing and immediate conditions, such as physical well-being. Spiritually pragmatic, black Americans were able to move between Conjure and Christianity because both were perceived as viable systems for accessing the supernatural world, and each met needs that the other did not.[26]

The relationship between Conjure and Christianity was fluid and constantly shifting. Supernatural practitioners often adopted symbols from Christian traditions for use in their own practices and rituals. Protective charms, for example, were endowed by specialists with spiritual potency "in the name of the Lord." Accoutrements adopted from both Catholic and Protestant traditions were enlisted by black Conjurers for supernatural protection. The slave Old Divinity, a Mississippi Conjurer who claimed to be the grandson of a witch, was buried clutching his cherished silver medal of Saint Anthony and the infant Jesus. W. D. Siegfried, a Baptist missionary who lived among the freedmen in Augusta, Georgia, after the Civil War, complained bitterly of the sale and dissemination of religious books and pictures to African Americans, who frequently adopted them as charms and protective objects. Especially notorious was the "letter from Jesus Christ" that, according to Siegfried, circulated extensively among black families. "The poor people have been deluded into the belief that the Letter is genuine," he railed, "that it was written especially for them, that those possessing it and exhibiting it in their dwellings will enjoy certain great protection and blessings enumerated in the letter." The letter, which guaranteed protection of its owners from natural disasters and theft and ensured safe childbirth deliveries for women, was apparently derived from the stock of Roman Catholic merchandisers.[27]

Lore and images from the Christian Bible also provided fertile territory from which African American specialists could acquire conjuring materials. Charms containing inscriptions of the Psalms provided wearers with luck and prosperity. According to Hurston, the Bible, with its miraculous formulae and magical legends, was viewed by many Conjurers as the "greatest Conjure book in the world," while Moses, as a powerful African miracle worker, was "honored as the greatest Conjurer." Other literary-minded Conjure practitioners swore by the knowledge they attained from popular Euro-American nineteenth-century magical manuals such as the *Albertus Magnus,* John Hohman's *"Pow-Wows,"* or the *Sixth and Seventh*

Books of Moses, the last one an esoteric treatise of occult science and philosophy that was considered by some to be the "Hoodoo Bible."[28]

The medicinal items that African American supernatural practitioners employed for treating their patients were often given religious
names and identifications. Herbs identified as angel's root, devil's
shoestring, bowels-of-Christ, and blood-of-Jesus leaves were utilized
to heal and give the carrier control and protection. "Jew David" was
a plant that was especially prized among slaves for its therapeutic properties, whereas "Adam and Eve" root brought luck. Individuals who
possessed Sampson's root or St.-John's-wort boasted of supernatural
security. The leaves of the peace plant and the king-of-the-woods, pat-
terned in the shape of a cross, were sacred and powerful if used with
a prayer to "the Father, Son and Holy Ghost."[29]

Christian accoutrements were utilized in other unusual ways by African
American Conjurers. A common procedure for divination used by slaves
involved the use of a Bible for detection of criminals. Jacob Stroyer, who
was enslaved in South Carolina in the 1840s, gave a detailed account of
a ritual involving prayer and the Bible that was used in order to find bur-
glars and thieves in the slave community. An identical system of supernatural detection was noted in a postslavery report, a practice known as
"turning the sifter," involving a "man of standing in the church" who
was able to detect a wrongdoer by balancing a sifter between two chairs.
One nineteenth-century writer assumed that the ritual was an African survival that had been adopted by black Americans: "Substitute a raw-hide
shield on two upright spears," she proposed, "and you have the rite as it
is practiced today on the Guinea Coast." The distinctive "Africanness"
of the style of many African American supernatural practitioners, we will
see, was a quality that both whites and blacks commented upon.[30]

It was not unusual for practitioners of Conjure to profess their simultaneous commitment to Christianity. A devout Baptist and former
slave, "Uncle" John Spencer, told Works Progress Administration inter-
viewers in the mid-1930s that he still believed in "tricking" or malign
spiritual practices of the sort that had been used extensively in the days
when he was a slave in Virginia. Another twentieth-century account refers
to a bondman in Georgia, Braziel Robinson, who proudly described
himself as a "member of the church" with a "seat in [Methodist]
Conference." But Robinson had been born, he said, with a caul and could
see spirits, one that "prowled around," and another that inhabited his
body. He felt no disparity between his religious beliefs and his spiritual-
istic ideas, because, as he put it, "My spirits are good spirits, and have

power over evil spirits, and unless my mind is evil [they] can keep me from harm." Robinson believed that his personal protection derived from his faith in his supernatural allies.[31]

After slavery had ended, parallel streams of Conjure and Christianity developed in every part of the United States where African American freedpersons settled, occasionally entwining and merging within the lives of practitioners. In some places Conjure made its way into the institutional church. In Missouri at the turn of the twentieth century, Mary Owen wrote of a sexton in an African Methodist church whose authority extended to his role as a powerful Conjurer. He and others in his circle of "Voodoos," who were members of the church as well, saw no contradiction between the two the positions he held. Sarcastically, Owen commented, "The old-fashioned Negro . . . conjures in the name of his African devil on Saturday, and goes to a Christian church, sings, prays and exhorts, and after 'meetin' invites the minister to a dinner of stolen poultry on Sunday." Some black supernatural specialists appear to have been quite comfortable in their dual roles. Allen Vaughn, an early-twentieth-century Conjurer "of great repute" in North Carolina, "conducted prayer meetings and sat on the mourner's bench" in the Baptist church, as was explained in a chapter of a book about his family titled "The Conjurer-Churchman." Other Conjurers supported Christian religious work in other ways. Perhaps the most famous black Conjure man of all, the Gullah "Doctor" Buzzard, was said to have financed the building of the largest church on St. Helena in the Sea Islands in the early 1900s, to aid and sustain the Christian ministry.[32]

To be sure, African American Conjurers were often devoutly religious. William Adams, an ex-slave from Texas who was interviewed at the age of ninety-one, cultivated a distinguished reputation among his peers for his esoteric interpretations of biblical lore. Adams, who was sought after for his healing knowledge, attributed his expertise to the power of God and found sanction for his beliefs in the doctrines of Christianity. He believed that "special persons" were chosen to "show de powah" of God, as was written in the Gospel of Mark. Such justifications of practice that were based on the believer's private exegesis of biblical texts were not uncommon for African American practitioners. The black conservative writer George Schuyler's elderly grandmother, "an able Bible student" who lived in New York's Hudson Valley in the early decades of the twentieth century, claimed with great conviction that persons could be "fixed" by evil Conjurers and witches, as was seen in the Bible. Schuyler recalled that his mother denounced his grandmother's beliefs

as "ignorant" and "superstitious" but, he stated, to no avail. "My grandmother," Schuyler wrote, "held stubbornly to her beliefs and cited an
impressive list of apt anecdotes in support of them." Appalled, Schuyler's
mother "chided her for believing in Christianity and occultism at one
and the same time." A similar flexibility of spiritual ideas could be found
among blacks in rural Mississippi in the 1940s, where the anthropologist Hortense Powdermaker interviewed several "Voodoo doctors" who
were also well-known "Reverends" with ministries that were supported
by members of the community. "those who are devoutly religious are
also devout believers in current folk superstitions," she wrote, "and do
not look upon Christianity and voodoo as conflicting in any way."[33]

As religious persons, many Conjurers relied on divine guidance or supernatural inspiration. A student from Virginia's first black college, the
Hampton Institute, wrote a letter in 1878 concerning a well-known practitioner who was also a deeply religious woman. "she had a special revelation from God," he remarked, "as do all the Conjure doctors I have
ever heard of." Similar statements characterize the beliefs of other
African American Conjure practitioners. When asked by a white professor where she had obtained her knowledge of divination and "tricking" (casting spells), a Conjure woman in Alabama named Seven Sisters
said, "It's a spirit in me that tells—a spirit from the Lord Jesus Christ. . . .
I tricks in the name o' the Lord." At the turn of the twentieth century
Chesnutt interviewed an aged Conjure woman whom he described as a
"dreamer of dreams and seer of visions," who was well versed in conjuring lore and explained that she was guided by Jesus and "de Spirit er
de Lawd." In his research on Conjure and folk beliefs in the late nineteenth and early twentieth centuries, the southern-born sociologist
Newbell Niles Puckett noted the virtue and conscientiousness that distinguished many of the supernatural practitioners that he came across.
Far from projecting irreverence, Puckett noted that many Conjurers believed that they should embody the qualities of piety, devotion, and holiness that were expected of a faithful Christian. Similar ideas of piety
and moral behavior were reflected in more recent accounts, as noted by
the anthropologist Norman Whitten, who found that clients and neighbors generally believed Hoodoo practitioners in North Carolina's Piedmont Village in the mid-1960s to be morally righteous, "good" persons.[34]

African American Conjure practitioners experienced the invisible world
as a reality rather than as a theological abstraction. It is in this sense that

a supernatural perspective truly interpenetrated the beliefs of many black believers, churchgoing Christians or not. In the African American religious imagination there were a host of forces that intervened directly in human life and its affairs, including spirits, ghosts, and angelic personalities that were periodically summoned to assist human beings in their endeavors. The biblical God of Jesus and Moses was also the sovereign of the unseen world whose power was witnessed in "signs and wonders" on the earth. To many, it was all a matter of correctly perceiving the nature of things. "The old folks . . . knows more about the signs that the Lord uses to reveal his laws than the folks of today," recalled a ninety-one-year-old former slave. "Some of the folks laughs . . . says it am superstition, but it am knowing how the Lord reveals His laws." For this former bondman and many other descendants of African slaves, traditions such as Conjure could demonstrate the vastness of God's power and presence in the universe.[35]

For addressing specific conditions in one's life, Conjure and Christianity offered contrasting possibilities. Although sharing images and symbolism with Christianity, Conjure could both support and challenge traditional religious ideas. Some African American specialists, for example, claimed membership in churches that tolerated their practice of acts of supernatural harming, if they were turned to positive ends. "The witch-doctor . . . is the antidote to evil," asserted one late-nineteenth-century writer, "he may keep his standing in the church, and be highly respected, if he uses his knowledge only for good." In South Carolina, kin of the early-twentieth-century black Conjurer Jim Jordan proudly affirmed their church affiliations, which reached several generations back into slavery. Jordan's biographer stated, "The Conjure doctor who sided exclusively with good spirits in the fight against evil was often a church leader." In other cases, Christian faith functioned as a weapon by which victims of affliction could defend themselves against supernatural harming specialists and their powers. This was aptly demonstrated in the remarks of a former slave in Texas, who recalled how her grandfather, a "hardshell" Baptist preacher, was sought out by church members who wanted him to "break spells" that had been placed on them with "de charms by the Conjur doctor." This particular example underscores the ways that some African Americans may have conceived of Conjure practitioners and Christian ministers as competing figures of spiritual authority.[36]

Yet not all the works of churchgoing Conjurers were benign. A source from Arkansas in the 1890s notes that a former slave was believed to have "hoodooed" unsuspecting victims out of "meanness" even while a member of a local Baptist congregation. It was said that he did so because he knew he had " 'surance er salvation anyhow." Another Arkansas Conjurer was "renowned in three counties" for his alleged role in the deaths of at least ten men and women by supernatural means. "He is a pious man and a deacon in the church," scoffed the reporter, "which used to surprise me until I knew more about the African brand of piety." Puckett uncovered a strand in southern folk beliefs that explained this seeming duplicity: "there are good and bad hoodoos," he found, "the good hoodoo often being part hoodoo and part preacher."[37]

The Christian church and its membership were also sometimes the objects of spiritual malevolence, either from Conjure practitioners or other supernatural specialists. Sarah Rice, a black woman coming of age in rural Alabama in the early twentieth century, believed that Conjure was used by a pastor's wife against a member of the local church who was a source of great resentment for her and other members of the congregation. She recalled,

> The . . . church had another member, a beautiful woman who was named Bishop. She had long, pretty black hair, and she was a pretty brown color. Just from her hips down, she was invalid. . . . They said she was such an attractive woman that every minister who went to their church fell in love with her. One minister's wife who believed in witchcraft said, "She'll never get my husband." The old wives said the minister's wife fixed her so she wouldn't be bothering any other ministers, and that's why she was paralyzed from the waist down.[38]

In 1899 the white folklorist Jeanette Robinson Murphy described a woman who was "the most prominent member in the Baptist colored church" in an unidentified northern city. According to Murphy, when another member of the congregation "got jealous of her power to holler the loudest," the woman fell sick, believed to be the victim of Conjure. When doctors failed to provide a cure, a conjuring specialist was called and, according to the writer, "for twenty-five dollars undertook the case." The woman recovered shortly thereafter.[39]

Persons were victims of Conjure harming because of the envy of others; because of their own selfishness; or, sometimes, in the words of one observer, because of jealousy over their "power in prayer at de meetin' house." Clergy were also the victims of Conjure harming. Hurston noted one case where an individual approached a specialist in New Orleans for a "job" against "a very popular preacher." Distrustful of the minister's increasing power and influence, the client explained that the problem was that he was "getting too rich and big," and it was necessary to have "something done to keep him down." The implication was clear: "They tell me he's 'bout to get to be a bishop," she warned, "I sho' would hate for that to happen." These examples give voice to the belief that ministers and other church officials were not immune to supernatural harm perpetrated by their enemies and rivals.[40]

The intersection of Conjure and Christianity also illuminates the perceived dangers that could strike at the most faithful of believers. The antebellum businessman Thaddeus Norris wrote of a young slave in New Orleans who, "although a consistent professor of the Christian religion," believed that he had been "bewitched" by "one of his co-worshippers." Terrified, the boy was taken to a city physician and later recovered from his ailment when the doctor conceded that his ailment was the result of the work of Conjurers. So common was the threat of malevolent supernaturalism in some religious circles, that when the "most prominent member in the Baptist colored church" in an unidentified northern city fell sick, she was immediately convinced that she was a victim of a "fix" caused by a jealous choir member. Neither were church ministers, deacons, and other officials immune to the Conjurer's powers. According to an account by an ex-slave in Lynchburg, a pastor who had graduated from Virginia Seminary believed that he had been poisoned by a spurned woman. Even after receiving medicine from a Conjure doctor, he took ill and died. A similar story from a former slave in nineteenth-century Georgia claimed that a Baptist preacher died from Conjure after believing that snakes had invaded his body. And in an 1874 article, the New York Times stated that it had been confirmed reports in Clarksville, Tennessee, that a black preacher had been 'hoodooed' and, going "hopelessly insane," ultimately had to leave his pulpit.[41]

These examples leave us with the problem of Conjure harming—the malign use of supernatural power by practitioners. How did blacks respond to persons who utilized Conjure for malevolent ends? There were few organized crusades to drive out those who engaged in supernatural harming practices within their own communities. Neither were there collective attempts to cleanse public spaces of evil magic, as with the witchfinding movements of Africa and the Caribbean, where purging "fetishers" using prayer became a frequent practice for establishing the supremacy of the Christian deity. In nineteenth-century West Indian slave societies, it was common for churchgoing folk to engage in collective digging expeditions of *obeah* charms. Not so in black America, where Christianity and Conjure were not so much actively resisted as they were reconciled by practitioners, sometimes in innovative ways. When warfare against Conjure did occur, it involved confrontations that were usually played out on ideological terrain. These confrontations, which will be discussed further in chapter 5, engaged the first generation of emancipated slaves and their children. Incipient tensions between the meaning of the past—shaped by the black folk traditions and the slave experience—and the evolving present—informed by distinctions of class, culture, social ranking, and economic status—had a profound impact on the ways that freedpersons perceived Conjure. Those who retained the older supernatural traditions, we will see, often found themselves in a struggle to balance their spiritual values with their practical needs.[42]

The lack of a sharp dichotomy between the sacred and the secular realms led many African Americans to view the spiritual realm as directly impinging on human experience. It is perhaps owing to such a perspective that the emphasis on supernatural mediation in black religious life both before and after Emancipation can be understood. African American spirituality put a premium on experiences of empowerment, which were potentially available to all believers. This dynamic element of black spirituality has historically taken many forms. The exuberant practices of African American communal worship, "shouting" and spirit possession, mystical visions and revelations—these aspects of black belief served to bring the individual and community into a transcendent experience that effaced the boundaries between self and spirit. Conjuring—the practice of appropriating invisible forces for efficacious intent—achieved similar results. Conjure emphasized the acquisition of supernatural power by gifted professionals, and the means by which persons could tap that power to make it "work" for them. In this respect, Conjure should be understood as a system of appropriation of spiritual energies for specific needs—hence its association with magic. It was this practical, utilitarian orientation of Conjure, and its relation to African American Christianity, that produced much of the variety, and some of the tension, in the lives of the slaves and their descendants.[43]

Of course, there were those persons who remained skeptical or disbelieving of Conjure and Conjurers, as some did of the Christian faith. Some blacks repudiated Conjure yet equivocated when reflecting on other supernatural traditions. "I never know much about de hoodoo, but de spirits, yes," explained one former slave. "God is a spirit, ain't he?" George Wood, who had been a bondman in South Carolina, insisted that he had never seen ghosts and had never heard of anyone being Conjured. "I don't believe in those things anyhow," he declared, also discreetly mentioning his wariness of the reputation that South Carolina blacks had for practicing Hoodoo. Katie McCarts, an ex-slave in Old Fort, Georgia, rejected any notion of the efficacy of charms. "Now me, I don't believe people can put something under steps or under your house that will harm you." She did, however, place much stock in signs and omens, especially portentous dreams and good luck practices, traditions with which she was "plenty 'sperienced." For others, faith in the benevolent power of Christianity was the most powerful charm to challenge the works of evil Conjurers and witches. One former bondwoman in Mississippi said that she feared the curses of supernatural practitioners until she "got religion." When Jack Atkinson, a former Georgia slave, received a "second blessing from the Lord," an allusion to the Christian experience of sanctification, he maintained that thereafter "no Conjurer [could] bother him." Another convert claimed that when God had saved him from being "Conjured by a hoodoo," in return he promised to "serve Him the balance of [his own] days."[44]

Nevertheless, there remained numbers of blacks who tenaciously held onto the supernatural beliefs of their African ancestors. These persons embodied the spiritual legacies that had been forged in the crucible of slavery, but had origins in Old World cultures. In style and in outlook, African spirituality governed much of the ways that African Americans knew and saw the world. Among future generations, supernatural practices would be strongly associated with Africans, even as most adherents and practitioners were American-born. These associations were made not only by individuals who came into firsthand contact with native African practitioners—those deemed to be most familiar with magical styles of spirituality—but others, who adhered to an axiom that stated the most widely respected Conjurers were "full-blooded Africans," a designation that affirmed the geographical and spiritual roots of conjuring practices. In the eyes of many blacks, these supernatural traditions were the bridge that connected the spiritual heritage of the ancestors with the adopted traditions of North America. We turn now to the African origins of Conjure lodged in New World magic.

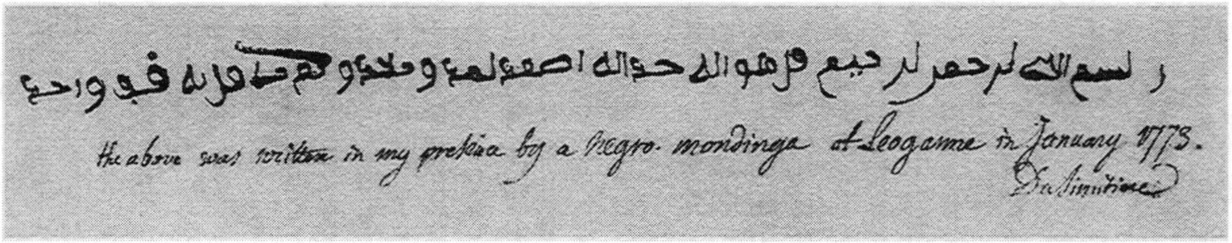
The above was written in my presence by a Negro mondinga at Leogame in January 1773.

"Africa Was a Land a' Magic Power Since de Beginnin' a History"

Old World Sources of Conjuring Traditions

New Providence, Bahamas, circa 1760. A schooner embarks for the English colony of Georgia on a fair spring morning. On board are a small crew, several black slaves, and a young Ibo freedman named Olaudah Equiano. Suddenly the wind blows high and the boat careens toward the rocky coastline. Desperately laboring against the surging waves, the sailors secure the vessel and return to port. Once safe, some of the passengers speculate that the storm was brought about by witches and wizards on board among the captured slaves. Undaunted, Equiano professes his trust that God will protect the travelers on their journey. Heartened by his faith, again the crew sets sail, arriving safely in Georgia within seven days' time.[1]

This brief episode in the life of one of the first English-speaking, African-born autobiographers sheds light on the convergence of "magical" and "religious" modes of thought in the eighteenth century. To Olaudah Equiano and his shipmates, the unexpected chaos of a violent squall possessed meanings that went beyond the apparent realities of the visible world. The elements of sea and air bore evidence of forces that were subject to both divine will and human intervention and manifested

Facing page illustration: Gris-gris with Qur'an verses, purchased by an American collector in the Caribbean, late eighteenth century. Typically such charms were carried for good luck, health, and spiritual protection. From the collection of Pierre Eugene DuSimitiere, courtesy of the Library Company of Philadelphia.

a wildly dangerous struggle for control over nature. It was an ancient conflict, one in which both Africans and Europeans had engaged for centuries and addressed in various theological debates and formulations. *Who governed the forces that could endanger and destroy life or preserve it?* For Equiano and this band of helpless travelers, fate rested either with the benevolence of the Christian God, or in the hands of a few shipboard witches, for both forces were real, and both were powerful.

Equiano's narrative draws together some of the disparate intellectual currents that were present in the modern era, such as Providentialism, or the belief in the manifestation of divine purpose, and older entrenched notions of spiritual contingency such as *maleficia,* also known as witchcraft. The account illustrates how easily and spontaneously both blacks and whites integrated these diverse perspectives into their lived experiences. As was also true for Europeans, Africans' belief systems featured an array of practices, as well as practitioners who were able to channel supernatural power for their own needs. To some extent, Equiano embraced both African and European viewpoints. A similar mixing of ideas would occur among black people in America and persist for centuries to come.

This chapter considers the African, European, and American sources of Conjure as it emerged among blacks in the United States. Its origins are attributable to a combination of factors, such as the religious orientations of Africans before their enslavement; the congruence of African and European-based supernaturalism; and the rise of Christianity among Africans and native-born blacks in America. The starting point for charting these developments thus becomes the arrival of the slaves and their gradual formation of religions and cultures in the New World, for the story of Conjure is fundamentally an account of the relationship of black American spirituality to both its African past and its American present.

The acknowledged presence of "Africanisms" in black American religion, such as the use of rhythm as a liturgical device and performance traditions like the "shout," spiritual dancing and possession, shows the organic connection between African and African American religious cultures. What is less clearly articulated, however, is the relationship between African religion and black American supernatural traditions such as Conjure. This relationship has been considered, to some extent, in studies of the material aspects of black culture in both the old and new worlds. Some scholars have argued that the manufacture of *minkisi,* the sacred "medicines" of Kongo tradition, is reconfigured in black charm-making practices in the United States. "Voodoo" dolls and figures, as seen in southeastern cities such as New Orleans and Miami, have been identified with artistic motifs originating not only in Kongo, Central Africa, but in Benin and Togo, West Africa.

But it is not only in visual creations that strong influences of African spirituality appear in black American supernatural traditions. A consideration of African cosmologies shows that a proliferation of ideas—ranging from concepts of divinity to theories concerning cause, effect, and the responsiveness of spiritual forces to human will—have informed expressions of black American religion and magic. A brief look at the religions of African people before the transatlantic passage of the slaves can illuminate the characteristics that black spirituality would later acquire in the United States.

The indigenous religions in the areas from which the slaves were taken—those of the western and central regions of sub-Saharan Africa— were extremely diverse and paralleled an equally diverse range of linguistic groups. It is arguable that most practitioners, irrespective of their national origins, adhered to characteristic traits of African religions: highly structured cosmologies, concepts of a diffused monotheism, rituals of sacred mediation, an emphasis on devotions to ancestors and the dead, and the use of spiritually efficacious objects.[2]

Throughout Africa, certain cosmological precepts appear to have been relatively congruent from people to people. Precolonial Kongolese, for example, envisioned the world as a multidimensional structure, with two mountains connected at their foundations and divided by a barrier or horizon line, symbolized by water. They believed that on death human beings would pass into the other realm, a land paralleling that of the living and inhabited by ancestors, ghosts, and spirits who were able to affect the lives of those in the earthly realm. Many representations of the Kongo universe show a cosmogram, a circle partitioned by a cross, its center bisected by a horizontal line, the symbolic division of the world of the dead from that of the living with a vertical path linking the two realms. Similarly, the Yoruba pictured the universe as a triple-tiered structure, arranged with the earth and the heavens in separate arenas "enfolding" an "islandlike world" that enjoined the three spheres. Human beings, according to this model, exist in the middle domain, between earth and sky. Both Yoruba and Kongo cosmologies, like so many other African systems, map an anthropocentric universe.[3]

Elaborate cosmologies inform the great variety of ways that human beings sought to influence the forces of the universe. Some scholars have characterized these systems of influence and interaction according to their "micro-" or "macrocosmic" focus, on immediate and local matters, or on a much larger design, universal matters. These foci correspond with the forces within a particular cosmological framework. For example, in addition to human beings, there are intermediary spiritual beings, coexisting with the supreme (yet otiose) creator deity in most African religious systems. In the spiritual realm, the micro- and macrocosmic converge with the social, political, and ideological dimensions of existence. As formulated in traditional African thought, the universe is a densely structured realm of living entities and inhabitants, some visible, others invisible.

According to most Western interpretations, African spiritual systems can be transposed into three main categories: religion, magic, and witchcraft. These categories reflect the liturgical or practical emphasis of human-otherworldly interactions as coercive or propitious practices that are communal, individual, socially beneficial, or antisocial. But typological categories can obscure the fact that indigenous African religions are not compartmentalized. Many African people of the past, as now, drew few distinctions between the substance of their beliefs and the other aspects of the world in which they participated. A spiritual reality governed human life, within belief systems that were not elaborated as philosophical or speculative knowledge but rather enfolded ways of being and living.

Africans arriving in the West during the period of the slave trade would have subscribed to a view of the universe with no divisions between sacred and profane. Theirs was a universe that reflected the pervasive power of spirit and life force. "African peoples are aware of mystical power in the universe," writes the Kenyan scholar John Mbiti. "This power is ultimately from God, but in practice it is inherent in, or comes from or through physical objects and spiritual beings." Though stemming from more recent observations of indigenous African religions, Mbiti's remarks apply to older African understandings of the supernatural or nonmaterial world. The concept of *force vitale,* an omnipresent energy, has been articulated in diverse ways in traditional African cultures—as *ashe, nommo, chi,* and *da.* The power of this life force was believed to dwell within organic and inorganic objects, in the elements of nature, and in the bodies of all animate beings. Through ritual, it was thought that human beings would be able to tap supernatural power for manifold purposes.[4]

What came to be seen as "magic" for the Africans who lived in

America appears to have actually been a fusion of ideas that derived, in part, from older indigenous African religious concepts and the New World perspectives to which they were linked. Thus, as I noted, a sharp delineation between "magic" and "religion" can be misleading, for these notions were nearly always connected in practice. "Magic" and "religion" were reflected in attitudes toward the human relationship to the unseen, or supernatural, world. As the authors of an influential study of religious movements in Zaire have written, "the constituent components of magic are the same as those of religion . . . in practice religion and magic are often blended in ritual performance." A Yoruba historian, Bolaji Idowu, further notes that "although African traditional beliefs recognize a clear distinction between what is man-made and what is of the spirit, the intermingling of religion and magic is always present in every ritual." Perhaps it is more appropriate to refer to *magico-religious* acts and beliefs in order to describe this complex fusion of ideas.[5]

The differences between magic and religion in African traditions, as viewed by most observers, hinge on two important concerns. First, magic is seen to operate automatically and mechanically, by principles of imitation or contagion, instead of through entreaty to supernatural powers. Idowu has argued that the efficacy of magic "depends upon the form rather than the spirit." Others have challenged this view, noting that the performance of magical acts in African traditions is normally not mechanical but nearly always depends on a secondary "supernatural agency" such as a deity, a spirit, or some otherworldly force. For example, the near-ubiquitous use of charms in Africa is an example of magic that is governed by a supernatural agency, for certain manufactured objects can be activated by invisible powers and persuaded or compelled to act according to a person's will.[6]

According to some observers, magical acts are also distinguished from religious activities since the private use of the supernatural by individuals typically characterizes the former. "Magic," note the authors of the Central African study, "is concerned with maximizing the attainment of specific goals of personal importance to the actor," in contrast with religion, which is communal and group-oriented. The difference between magical and religious acts, in this analysis, is also suggested by the formulation of their purposes. Magic is a self-serving enterprise that derives from personal, egotistical motivations; religion, a public activity, yields benefits for an entire community.[7]

And yet this delineation of private versus public interests did not apply in all cases. In many accounts of indigenous African religious life, spiritual forces were involved in rituals for personal needs as well as those affecting the larger group. The seventeenth-century German barber-surgeon Andreas Ulsheimer noted this when he observed that the *futisse* (fetishes) of Cape Coast Africans were often petitioned for the success of crops, for prosperity in trade, for prevention of illnesses, for the fecundity of women, and on the likelihood of war—matters of both private and public concern. Other witnesses corroborate the fusion of private and public interests within indigenous African rituals.[8] So closely were magic and religious practices entwined that their separation was impossible.

The European term "fetish" was widely used as a concept to describe one of the most salient features of African spirituality: the construction and use of sacred charms and other supernatural artifacts. Conceived as a practice, an invisible force, and a commodity, "fetish" derived from the Portuguese verb *feitico,* to fabricate, referring to the handmade quality of these material creations. Colonial observers in Africa often identified the fetish as the primary substance of African spiritual life. As Willem Bosman, a Dutch administrator at the West African port of Elmina in the late 1600s exclaimed, "they cry out, Let us make Fetiche; by which they express as much, as let us perform our Religious Worship." The avatar of the national deity of Whydah, a serpent, was called a fetish by white missionaries on the Slave Coast in the late seventeenth century. Bosman spoke of fetishes as "all things made in Honour of [their] False Gods," as did Wilhelm Müller, a German Lutheran prelate who wrote from the Gold Coast that Akan fetishes incarnated "the Devil himself, from whom . . . they seek advice, comfort and help," a being who was incarnated in the figure of a "tall, abominable, black Moor." At a future point *fetishism* would be associated with magic, but most accounts suggest its link to various forms of traditional African religion.[9]

Although contemporary writers have done away with the term "fetish," viewing it as a derogatory, anachronistic referent, the association of the word with certain material forms appears to have carried into New World characterizations of indigenous African religions. In some diaspora traditions in the United States today, for example, spiritual forces are believed to be brought into human experience in the creation of supernaturally empowered objects. Joseph Murphy, who has depicted "ceremonial spirituality" as a fundamental principle of New World religions such as *santería* and *vodou,* highlights this concept. In African-based religions, spiritual force can be isolated and enclosed in time and space. "The focus on ceremonial spirituality reveals an interdependence of humanity and spirit," Murphy notes, "this means that the spirit . . . *can be localized or 'fixed' into physical objects and human bodies."* This emphasis on spiritual power appears to be a hallmark of African ritual that was carried over from the Old World to the New.[10]

Let us now turn to the American colonies, where hundreds of thousands of black Africans arrived during the four centuries of transatlantic slave trade. We must speculate that, embedded within the consciousness of these bondpersons, African spiritual perspectives also traveled the lengthy Middle Passage to the New World, evident when enslaved women and men performed ceremonies that ritualized the arrival of unseen forces on the earth or when they took part in elaborate mortuary observances to ensure secure passage of the dead into the realm of the ancestors. In mainland British North America, these activities occurred as they did elsewhere in the New World colonies, although in varying degrees.

In slave communities from the Caribbean to Brazil, African people carried the rituals, theological principles, and liturgical practices of their ancestors into new environments. Slave religious traditions were supplemented with alternative practices and beliefs, some extracted from non-African sources. These processes differed according to the conditions of acculturation and the particular demographic arrangements that shaped slavery from region to region. For instance, in sharp contrast with other parts of the Western Hemisphere, in the British colonies of mainland North America the African religious heritage was dramatically attenuated. And yet the gods did not die. While Africans were unable to replicate their religious institutions, they usually created new, sometimes clandestine traditions that served their collective needs. Although they transformed the older religions, Africans maintained their ancient spiritual moorings while in America.[11]

Historical sources are limited in what they tell us concerning the religious experiences of African peoples in the first hundred years of settlement in mainland North America. This is not to say that religion was not an important concern for Africans, or their enslavers, at this time. Despite the standard rationalization by Europeans that blacks would be brought into a knowledge of Christianity through their bondage, inattention and indifference marked the attitude of most colonial slaveholders toward the spiritual plight of the bondmen. Converting Africans took a back seat to concerns over the economic and political implications of religion—would Christianity make slaves dangerous and difficult? or would baptizing slaves require their manumission?—until a formal missionary program was initiated by the Church of England in America during the late seventeenth century. Slaveholders' hostility, linguistic barriers, financial constraints, and the cultural intransigence of Africans themselves greatly hindered the progress of Christian missionaries who attempted to convert the enslaved in the colonial era.

Historians have agreed that the majority of Africans in the mainland colonies remained generally untouched by missionary Christianity until the early part of the eighteenth century. Only after the turn of the nineteenth century did any widespread, self-perpetuating evangelical activity take place among black slaves. Following the onset of the Great Awakenings, the first black churches were founded (late 1700s), and by the time of the Great Revival of 1801, Christianity was established within most African American communities. Significantly, descriptions of African American "magic" appear in the early 1800s as well.[12]

Until the nineteenth century, observers provide only occasional witness of supernatural spiritual traditions and magical rituals among the slaves. Philip Reading, a minister with the Anglican philanthropic society Thomas Bray's Associates in Delaware, noted that African slaves bore great "prejudices" against converting to the Christian faith, partly, he believed, because they were "strangely predisposed in favour of superstition and Idolatry." The London-based secretary of Dr. Bray's associates, John Waring, warned clergy of Africans' fervent devotion to "the idolatrous Rites and Practices of their own Country." Francis Varnod, a missionary with the Society for the Propagation of the Gospel in Foreign Parts, wrote to his superiors of the spiritual disposition of slaves in South Carolina, observing that "some of our negro-pagans have a notion of God and a Devil, and dismal apprehensions of apparitions." Other comments by white clergy in the eighteenth century provide an indeterminate picture of black spiritual life, vaguely characterizing African slave practices as "heathenish" and "pagan" with little elaboration or detail. Evidence does indicate, however, that despite severe challenges and prohibitions, African slaves in the Anglo-American colonies retained their spiritual perspectives.[13]

By the end of the 1700s, for example, some African forms of supernaturalism were already viable in black American communities. In New England, enslaved and free "Afro-Yankees" perpetuated divination, witchcraft, and healing traditions in an indigenous folk culture, according to sources from the late colonial era. In the South, supernatural beliefs found expression in dramatic harming practices that were occasionally brought to light in criminal charges against African slaves. Other important clues to the spiritual activity of black people include the plethora of charms, talismans, and ornaments that have been unearthed in archeological excavations of plantation sites. These excavations have yielded a thriving material subculture of African-derived, American-made objects. The recovery of remnants of crystals, beads, divining vessels, and a variety of unusual shells, stones, and irregular objects point to the use of supernatural artifacts that date back nearly three hundred years.[14]

A major difficulty in identifying the forms and expressions of African spiritual beliefs in early periods has to do with the task of distinguishing African-based traditions from other cultural practices. It is likely that the supernatural traditions of Africa were fortified by traditions that were adopted from Anglo-Americans. As did Africans, Europeans envisioned the universe as a territory inhabited by a hierarchy of forces and spirits. They developed rituals to allow them to interact with benevolent forces and defend themselves against the malevolent forces that existed within that universe. While some Anglo-American practitioners incorporated beliefs from Christianity, others did not. Given that there were some significant similarities in their beliefs, it is certain that accommodations, or exchanges, of the ideas of Africans and Europeans occurred during the colonial era in the realm of supernatural beliefs, as they most certainly did in later periods.[15]

There are numerous documented cases of cultural interactions between blacks and whites in various areas of life. African-European encounters had a broad impact on the development of language, work methods, and artistic forms. Africans and Europeans possessed comparable ideas concerning supernatural power, the efficacy of spiritual force, and practitioners who were able to mediate the unseen world. Within interracial contexts blacks and whites came to learn of the others' spiritual practices. Africans were impacted by popular notions of the "worlds of wonder" that so captivated whites in seventeenth- and early-eighteenth-century America, just as they were by evangelical Christianity.[16]

The correlations between African and European ideas of the supernatural world underscore the fluctuating boundaries between magic and religion that characterized the preindustrial worldviews of both groups. The unstructured and fluid nature of supernaturalism may have permitted an admixture of black and white beliefs. The spiritual traditions to which Africans were exposed in early America were by no means pure or orthodox; the religious lives of Anglo-Americans sometimes disclosed pagan, pre-Christian influences. Although formally condemned by ecclesiastical authority, even the most stalwart Christian strongholds were besieged by dissident spiritual challenges from within and without. As European Americans struggled to resituate themselves in the wake of their own transatlantic displacement, their religious institutions came under the assault of sectarian reformers, heretical dissenters, and radical insurgents. Beneath the overarching shadow of the church arose alternative spiritual inclinations that persistently attracted the attention of the lay population. These heterodox interests included supernatural spiritual experiences, many of which white European settlers revived.[17]

A great variety of sources supported the development of supernatural traditions among whites in America. Among learned elites and intellectuals, complex occult philosophies filtered through a post-Renaissance ferment of astrology, alchemy, hermeticism, and other pseudo-sciences. Unlettered commoners, including nominal Christians and uncommitted individuals, adopted practices from an older storehouse of folk tradition and oral lore. Although soundly condemned by officials of the church establishment, Anglo-Americans also dabbled in divination, sorcery, and witchcraft, unconventional practices that ebbed and flowed with the tides of colonial spiritual life.[18]

Given the sparse historical evidence—and the extent to which African religious practice was suppressed in America—the claim that European American spiritual beliefs and practices may have actually sustained African traditions might appear to be contradictory. And yet certain elements from indigenous African religions, particularly those with European cognates, are discernible in some of the earliest descriptions of black American "magic." To take one example: both Africans and Europeans in colonial America held certain common cosmological perspectives, such as that of a universe that abounded with divine activity and power. Both groups incorporated their otherworldly visions into their understanding of earthly experiences. English Protestants often read unusual events as evidence of the divine presence in everyday life, acknowledging the activity of a creator deity who operated through omens and portents within the natural order, or signs and wonders in the heavens, a philosophy known as Providentialism. "Comets, hailstorms, monster births and apparitions" and other disruptions of the ordinary were demonstrations that foretold God's will or signaled His displeasure with humankind. Africans' understandings of the universe were also inspired by visible manifestations of spiritual forces within nature. They too viewed thunder, lightning, and other elements as heralds of sacred hierophanies, the awesome presence of numerous divine beings. These conceptions of the supernatural held firm for their free black descendants in

America, who glimpsed the power of God in catastrophic earthquakes, lunar eclipses, and meteor showers.[19]

The informal nature of European-derived supernaturalism may have facilitated its integration into African and African American cosmologies. Parallels can be seen in both groups' perceptions of the invisible world. Many Anglo-American Christians, for example, believed the celestial domain to be occupied by an almighty, benevolent deity *and* a host of spirits, including angels, archangels, and other more malevolent entities, powers, and principalities. Similarly, West and Central Africans would have viewed the cosmos as a heavily populated world in which a reciprocating traffic of invisible and visible beings moved, interacted, and influenced each other. While Anglo-American Christians utilized a colorful language of "wonder" and "remarkable providences" to bear witness to the proximity of the supernatural in their lives, Africans depicted the universe in myth and beckoned the timeless inhabitants of the spiritual world with ritual. In some cases, images from European folklore wove their way into the cosmologies of Africa. The earthly reality of witches, demons, and other purveyors of misfortune underwrote the oral traditions and beliefs of both races. Stories passed on of restless souls and apparitions—such as "Raw Head and Bloody Bones," a fiendish specter appearing in African- and Anglo-American folklore traditions—demonstrate the assimilation of European and African supernatural motifs into a shared complex by whites and blacks.[20]

While the two populations' supernatural concepts may have resonated, the traditions of African and Anglo-Americans themselves obtained vastly different meanings. Africans adapted their beliefs to the specific circumstances of their status as an enslaved people and utilized their traditions toward these ends for personal or collective empowerment. Some accounts provide eloquent evidence of the efforts of slaves to preserve their culture in these traditions, as well as their lives. For example, blacks in America transformed the handmade charms, amulets, and figurines that were so necessary to African religious ritual into objects of security and resistance. In colonial York County, Virginia, the Anglican minister Morgan Godwyn would complain of slaves' attachment to spiritual charms, declaring that they often turned to these personal talismans in times of need. Fugitives and runaways in particular, he warned, "plac[ed] confidence in certain figures, and ugly Representations . . . believing these deities able to protect them in their flight and from Discovery." These "puppets," he believed, lost power to help those possessing them once they were discovered and seized. Material artifacts became customary cultural forms for Africans in America, as they had been in precolonial Africa, where ritual activities facilitated the "fixing" of unseen entities into created objects.[21]

The discursive logic that underlay the construction of supernatural objects explains the persistent use of amulets and phylacteries in African traditions and in African American practices as well. European travelers, who found protective charms to be ubiquitous among African peoples, called them *gree-gree* or *gris-gris,* a term from the Mande language that related to spiritual force. "The Religion here, if it may be called such," wrote John Atkins in the 1700s from Sierra Leone, "is their Veneration to *Gregries.*" Some of these items were worn on the body or kept conspicuously about in the open to guard against misfortune and evil. The French trader Jean Barbot described *gris-gris* charms in seventeenth-century Upper Guinea (the present-day Senegambia) that were displayed by elites "all over their body, on their head, neck, arms, waist and legs" that contained "scraps of paper written with Moorish or Arabic." In areas that had been influenced by Islam, Africans placed "unlimited faith" in the power of *gris-gris,* leather and cloth packets commissioned from Muslim priests and *marabous* that guaranteed health and protection to their wearers.[22]

Throughout Africa charms were created that were conceived as portable containers for spiritual entities. These containers were believed to possess efficacious powers. In Kongo, Central Africa, the manufacture of *minkisi* blurred the lines between magic and religion. *Minkisi* were spiritual beings who interacted with and often assisted humans in earthly endeavors. They could be found in composite, fabricated materials or manifested in unusual objects that were identified as having sacred significance by the persons who found them. These included *minkisi* that were incarnated as twisted, misshapen roots or stones or strangely deformed things. Others were synthetic creations, bags, sculpted containers, or figures containing a combination of natural and inorganic ingredients such as leaves, roots, animal parts, shells, or metal. As the loci of supernatural power, *minkisi* were believed to incorporate divine forces, and through them, humans could produce transformations within the natural world.[23]

African *minkisi* and *gris-gris* illustrate the fundamental similarities between indigenous African spiritual artifacts and those supernatural artifacts created by blacks in early America. Such objects were normally energized by the activation of their internal components in ritual. Their internal elements included "medicines," that is, various additives that gave them life, and other ingredients assembled according to their innate properties or powers. For instance, the addition of human remains, such as hair or bones, into a charm assimilated the essence of a departed being, and combinations of natural with inorganic substances tied a supernatural entity to a desired trait, such as aggression or belligerence. Charms functioned through a formulaic system of metaphoric and metonymic signs and associations. Outer materials such as clay, cloth, or ceramic demarcated the powers of the otherworldly beings that charms contained. Some charms were tightly bound with cord, to represent attachment, impenetrability, or entanglement; others were formed with hollow spaces so as to be inhabited by spirits that would be made to work for their owners with prayers and oaths. Wooden figurines such as *minkisi minkondi,* the distinctive "nail fetishes" of Kongo, were pierced with iron spikes and pegs to provoke the forces within them. These spirits were then commanded by their owners and given specific appeals or imprecations.[24]

The emphasis on materiality carried over into black American supernatural traditions. Like their enslaved forebears, Conjure practitioners in the nineteenth and twentieth centuries relied on created material objects. They used an array of charms, amulets, and talismans known among black Americans as "hands," "mojos," "gris-gris," "jacks," "tobies," "goopher bags," and "wangas" for empowerment and protection. The contents of a practitioner's "trick bag" varied enormously. One Conjurer's favorite item, described in an account in the late 1800s, included balls of tar, sulfur, and assorted lumps of color that blazed when set afire. The other popular items included red flannel bags filled with dried leaves, potent crumbling powders, or metallic dust. Bottles of pungent liquids, pins, and needles were interred by practitioners or strung on trees as a snare for invisible forces. Some material creations teemed with life, as one surprised observer discovered, according to one account, when he opened a hidden Conjurer's cache to find "a tin trunk and a great many articulate creatures." Other created artifacts transformed into animate beings, mysteriously shifting and relocating when left alone. The fabrication of "Voodoo bags," "luck balls," and other supernatural artifacts was the mainstay of successful Conjure practitioners. The ex-slave Patsy Moses of Fort Bend, Texas, described the creation of her protective charm. "A good charm bag," she explained, "am make of red flannel with frog bones and a piece of snakeskin and some horse hairs and a spoonful of ashes. Dat bag pertect you from you enemy." Moses claimed that she learned her magical knowledge "from my daddy and mammy and de old folks." She added, "most of dem things works iffen you tries dem."[25]

Over time, certain ingredients emerged as staple components in the material rhetoric of Conjure practices. The gravel and earth gathered from the surfaces of cemetery graves and stone markers, sometimes called "goopher dust," was a near-universal element in the pharmacopoeia of African American supernaturalism. A rabbit's feet or the highly sought after bone of a black cat endowed a practitioner with great power. Materials were selected both for their sympathetic associations and for aesthetic purposes: red pepper to produce heat or irritation; lodestone to draw desirable forces magnetically; bone fragments to signify the passage of powers from the otherworld; soil from gravesites to symbolize the presence of spirits in transitional places; acrid herbs to displace evil essences metaphorically. Some of the most powerful charms required exuviae from the body itself: hair, nails, skin, or waste matter such as urine or excrement. The inventory of conjuring materials has remained remarkably consistent for hundreds of years.[26]

One of the most important ingredients in the apothecary of African American supernaturalism was not handmade at all but consisted of the root matter of designated plants. In particular, the root known as High John the Conqueror, with its twisted, tuber-shaped bulb, was most valuable. Of all the charms carried by African American practitioners, these roots were especially prized for their potency and effectiveness. "Thousands of Negroes carry Johnny the Conqueror roots," wrote the Louisiana folklorist Robert Tallant, "not only in New Orleans, but all over the country." The genealogy is obscure, but the magic of roots in black America may be linked to an older African sacred lore. In Central Africa, Kongo legends relate the kinship between local divinities and anomalies within nature. A patron spirit called Funza, also known as the "creator of charms," was believed to be incarnated in all deformities, including abnormal children, oddly shaped animals and insects, stones, and contorted plant formations. Other regional spirits in Kongo were believed to appear on the earth as "unusual, bizarre or twisted natural objects," such as misshapen roots and branches. It may be that the prominence of roots in African American Conjure traditions harks back to Kongo beliefs in *minkisi,* incarnations of the powerful spirit beings that quickened an artifact. Other sources of the High John root tradition can be found in ex-slaves' narratives, where roots are described as having the power to bring love, luck, and protect the wearer if carried or chewed. The emphasis on roots as spiritually powerful objects appears to be peculiar to black American supernatural beliefs.[27]

Nevertheless, while creative African spiritual traditions were prominent, whites in the English colonies possessed strong charm-making customs as well. Although Africans may have borrowed and appropriated these traditions, the white charm beliefs often reflected their medieval Christian origins. For instance, one of the harshest critics of magic in seventeenth-century New England, the Puritan divine Increase Mather, described a charm that suggests a symmetry between European and African supernatural artifacts. Inflamed by the presence of "Enchanters" and "charmers" in the community, Mather reported that a white layman in Boston owned an object marked with religious inscriptions that he utilized for spiritually efficacious purposes. Reminiscent of the African *gris-gris*, the charm consisted of "a Sealed paper . . . wherein were drawn several confused characters, and these words written, *In Nomine Patris, Filii, et Spiritus Sancti, Preserve thy Servant, such an one*," a formula obtained from a Roman Catholic liturgy. Elsewhere in New England, descriptions of other objects with supernatural purpose were reported, such as magical "puppets," dolls, and "little images" ostensibly designed by Anglo-American practitioners of witchcraft. These too were similar in form to *minkisi* and *vodun* dolls, the miniature effigies of Dahomey, West Africa.[28]

In Africa as in America, charms, dolls, and other supernatural artifacts were endowed with personalities. Africans' charms were usually treated as living beings, tended, provided with offerings, and under some conditions consulted for advice by their owners. Similarly, African American slaves "fed" offerings of whiskey, camphor, and corn liquor to their charms in other to vitalize them. Many blacks also believed that their charms possessed the power to pursue and attack wrongdoers on behalf of their owners, retaliating for intentional harms and sometimes inflicting mortal punishment on malefactors. As we will see in the following chapter, African Americans commonly employed such "harming" techniques for resistance, attack, and protection.[29]

African American Conjurers thrived on the spiritual borderlands in early America, where various supernatural traditions were in wide circulation among whites. Correspondences between these traditions can be seen in several areas. The roles, for example, of black and white practitioners were similar. For English colonials, "spiritual professionals" included not only the official and authorized dispensers of divine grace, the clergy, but also "cunning" men and women, supernatural experts who drifted across early American villages and towns, revisiting pre-Reformation traditions of magic and miracle. Believed to be adept at treating sickness, cunning persons functioned as popular spiritual seers, diviners, and fortune-tellers in Anglo-American communities.

African American Conjurers were also sought out for their abilities to read the future. Divination was a system of sacred disclosure that had been a common religious specialty in Africa, where it was viewed as a reliable procedure for mediating the invisible realm. Other methods of divination such as augury, geomancy, and spirit mediumship were practiced by religious authorities in indigenous African societies. In his seventeenth-century description of the "Fetu Country" on the Gold Coast, Wilhelm Müller wrote of priests who "boast[ed] of their ability to foretell the future" who traveled "all over the country for the sake of gain." According to Müller, a successful diviner at Kormantin was held in such high esteem by English officials that he was constantly sought after for his soothsaying talents, loaded down with valuable gifts and "large presents." In eighteenth-century Accra the English captain John Atkins witnessed Ghanaian "Fetish-women" who became famous through their ability to "pretend Divination, [and] give answers to all Questions." To Africans, divination specialists were discerning religious authorities who were able to provide vital moral and spiritual guidance to members of their communities. Considered to be a form of revelation, divination involved the consultation of spiritual forces that held hidden information and knowledge.[30]

African divination traditions surfaced among blacks in America in a variety of forms. In eighteenth-century Georgia a runaway slave by the name of Luce peddled her spiritual gifts, "cutting cards" and telling the futures of others for payment. In New England, the famous "Old Witch or Black Interpreter" Chloe Russell advertised her divining talents "By Astrology, Physiognomy, Palmistry . . . Anatomy . . . Geometry" and the spiritual interpretation of "Moles, Cards and Dreams" in a self-published production (see frontispiece for her portrait). From the late 1700s on through the turn of the nineteenth century, African American women and men plied their talents in an active trade of fortune-telling or prediction. Like the white cunning persons, some were commissioned to locate lost goods. In the same manner that African priests and diviners received monetary compensation for their services, African American practitioners profited from their spiritual knowledge. In America, however, divining traditions were ultimately divorced from their religious context.[31]

Like the white cunning persons, black diviners sometimes served as

healers and spiritual counselors in early America. These roles were rein-
terpretations of the practices of traditional African priests. Conjurers,
for instance, revived older divinatory vocations in the practice of fortune-telling. Whereas some divining specialists were reclusive individuals who dealt solely in private transactions, others were public functionaries and itinerant adepts. In New England, supernatural specialists
accounted for almost half of all persons identified as "fortunetellers,"
according to an occupational census of professions taken beginning in
the mid-1600s.

Some supernatural professionals acquired methods that suggest affinities between African and European styles. One specialist called Long
Hercules was said to have performed miracles for citizens in eighteenth-
century Savannah, Georgia. Hercules, who was known locally as "Doctor
Hercules," was renowned for his "remarkable conjurations" of "pigs
feet" and "rattlesnakes teeth" that he was said to have removed from
the bodies of "several sick people." A contemporary of Long Hercules
was Negro Sampson, a practitioner in South Carolina who frequently
went about with "rattlesnakes in calabashes," which he would handle
freely, putting them "into his Pockets or Bosom, and sometimes their
Heads into his Mouth, without being bitten." Beliefs surrounding snakes
and rattlesnake fascination also had powerful occult overtones for whites
in the New World environment. While it is unclear whether Sampson's
proficiency extended to other spiritual matters, his expertise with poison remedies (and serpents) point to indigenous African concepts and
beliefs. In chapter 4 I explore the relationship between African American
supernaturalism and healing.[32]

Black American Conjurers sometimes flavored their performance
practices with sleight-of-hand feats and visual tricks, styles of trickster-
ism and subterfuge that had African precedents. Writing from the windward coast, a skeptical English physician, Thomas Winterbottom, remarked that deception might have aided in the successes of African
specialists and their powers to work *gris-gris*. "I have met with instances
at Sierra Leone," he stated, "of persons who might be supposed to know
better, being so far imposed upon by the grimaces and pretended magical ceremonies of one of these greegree men, as to believe that he had extracted from their sides the bottom of a quart bottle, which . . . he assured them had been conveyed there by some unfriendly witch, and had
occasioned all their illness."[33]

Certainly not all practitioners made use of such trickery, but accounts
suggest that artifice might have been a factor in more than a few public

healing rituals. For example, the treatment of illnesses by black slaves in America often featured techniques that were similar to older African healing practices, as in the distinctive practice of extracting unusual foreign objects from the body. An report from a Sea Islands newspaper described such a case, in which an African American "doctor" resorted to supernatural ritual to treat his client. The doctor, noted the writer, "profess[ed] (with the aid of a magical cow horn and certain herbs) to be able to remove the witchcraft out of [the] person bewitched."

> when the doctor pulls old lizards, etc., out of the horn . . . and asserts that he has drawn them from the sufferer, [the patient] not only firmly believe[s] this to be the case, but will describe in extravagant language the feelings experienced during the operation.

Such healing practices were perhaps known by whites as well as blacks. The above report, written at the end of the nineteenth century, demonstrates striking similarities with a graphic description of an Anglo-American healer written more than two hundred years earlier. John Hale, a Congregational clergyman in colonial Massachusetts, scorned the skillful deception of European American cunning men and women. These persons, whom he called "white witches," by "devillish means . . . pulled fish bones out of a wound, cured tooth ache, agues, warts, and stopped blood" for their patients and other afflicted persons.[34]

African American supernatural traditions represented the continuum of African spiritual practices in the New World. By the start of the nineteenth century, unique products had emerged out of the tangle of African and European cultures of the colonial era. The emergence of distinct African American practices has itself been the subject of intense scholarly discussion. While the supernatural beliefs of Anglo-Americans at the end of the seventeenth century became "folklorized"—that is to say, less visible, shifting to marginal sectors of society, underground, or out of the public sphere—among blacks, supernatural beliefs began to proliferate. African tradition clearly influenced the rise of Conjure practices. What is not clear is the context in which the new practices unfolded, a process that coincided with the exposure of African Americans to Christianity. It is probable that African-based supernatural practices and ideas drew on Christian signs and symbols, with a kinship gradually developing between these practices and black American religion.[35]

How do we account for the dramatic presence of black diviners, spiritual healers, witchcraft, and descriptions of supernatural ritual in accounts from the late 1700s to the late 1800s, when the numbers of Africans in America had been supplanted by greater numbers of American-born blacks? Perhaps documentation of black spiritual life was more widely available after the turn of the nineteenth century, or perhaps the shifting demographic configurations of slave populations at this time explains its emergence. The largest percentage of enslaved Africans entered the mainland British colonies between 1720 and 1760, with these forty years representing the highest annual rates of importation of slaves from the transatlantic trade. After 1800 most blacks living in the former colonies were American-born, making them one of the largest native populations on the mainland. Paradoxically, the rise of black American supernatural traditions, particularly in the South, coincided with a decline in the direct importation of native Africans to America.[36]

The impact of African spirituality in America was mitigated by a number of factors, but perhaps most significant was the number of native Africans in any given slave population. The transmission of indigenous African traditions to first- and second- generation American blacks would have been hindered by the isolation and dispersal of these "saltwater" Africans, and by the slaveholding authorities' harsh repression of public forms of African religiosity such as ritual sacrifice and the use of the drum. Yet even while the institutional foundations of African religious life were disrupted, a diminishing form of African spirituality was kept alive by individual slaves. Though the exposure of blacks to their ancestral traditions was in all likelihood fortified by the occasional appearance of new native Africans among the bondpersons, slave culture after the mid eighteenth century reflected its African *American* experience.[37]

The flowering of traditions such as Conjure occurred more than half a century after the peak in numbers of sustained arrivals of African slaves. This suggests that the development of African American supernatural practices was not contingent on the firsthand exposure of blacks to African cultures but rather on the adaptation of older beliefs and practices within a new cultural context and framework. The expansion of Christianity among slave populations also explains why black supernatural practices and practitioners appear more consistently in the historical record after 1800, a time when Conjurers became a regular feature in accounts of slave life. African American supernaturalism was augmented, rather than constrained, by the emergence of Christianity. The development of magical forms first became evident when African Americans began to turn to Protestantism in large numbers in the latter part of the eighteenth century. Although some blacks, both enslaved and free, had been exposed to Christianity in the colonial period, educated in missionary schools, and baptized under the auspices of white benevolent associations and churches, from about 1750 to the period following the American Revolution blacks responded proactively to the call of African American Christian preachers. By the start of the nineteenth century, African Americans were creating their own denominations, choosing their own spiritual leaders, and adopting distinctive styles of worship. The rise of African American supernatural traditions in this period corresponded with the development of Protestant Christianity among numbers of second- and third-generation black Americans.[38]

Although the African cosmologies were eroding, they still provided the philosophical basis by which new beliefs could be assimilated. Even as blacks in America embraced Christianity, they retained perspectives that harked back to older African ways. The new formations' continuities with African religious traditions included an emphasis on ritual efficacy, the appropriation of invisible powers, and ceremonial spirituality. This fusion of perspectives was achieved in a powerful synthesis of African spirituality and Afro-Christian Protestant traditions, and it surfaces in many Conjure practices.

African American supernaturalism continued to develop throughout the early nineteenth century, even as Christianity was being planted in black communities. The comments of a white physician at a slave plantation in North Carolina, written in 1829, are illuminating in this regard. On observing the collective activities of "several old Guinea Negroes," the physician Edward Warren remarked that despite being "rampant Christians" they also demonstrated a profound "faith in evil genii, charms, philters" and "habitually indulged in an infinitude of cabalistic rites and ceremonies, in which the gizzards of chickens, the livers of dogs, the heads of snakes and the tails of lizards played a mysterious but very conspicuous part." The significance of these African-derived practices does not become clear until we place them in the context of a developing African American Christian tradition. Emerging in various forms, these synthetic "Christian" practices would have been familiar to African Americans of various cultural positions, both Creoles and native Africans, slaves and free blacks. Variations in African rituals and belief, in this case maintained by an older African-born population, would endure among American blacks because they offered power to their practitioners, because they were meaningful, and because they came to meet essential needs.[39]

✤   ✤   ✤

The distinctive "Africanness" of black supernatural traditions in America, we will see, was a quality that witnesses nearly always seized upon. Conjuring practices carried the residue of the Old World and were consistently identified with Africans and African ways. For example, in many early accounts, slave Conjurers were classified simply as "outlandish" or associated with African cultures by their particular dress, accoutrements, or visible features such as filed teeth or facial scarification. Remarkably, as late as the 1890s, some black American Conjurers were conducting African-based rituals such as animal sacrifice. Even the lexicon that came to be associated with conjuring in the United States included terms like "toby," "goopher," and "mojo," which emanated from West and Central African linguistic antecedents. Above all, blacks in America viewed Africa, the spiritual site of the ancestral homeland, as having special significance. "Africa," according to one former slave resident of coastal Georgia, "was a land a' magic power since de beginnin' a' history." This claim to power, based in geographical location, became one of the distinguishing marks of black American supernatural practice.[40]

Yet other, non-African, sources shaped the development of black American supernatural traditions. Anglo-American influences, for example, may help account for the great range of titles for Conjure practitioners over time and from place to place. In New England during the 1700s, black fortune-tellers and transient diviners were called "cunning persons" by whites. In the southern colonies, Africans who used spiritual powers were known as "witches" or "sorcerers." Other reports by whites include descriptions of black ritual specialists as "Ober [obeah?] Negroes" or simply as "doctors." In the early nineteenth century, African magic practitioners were characterized in ways that recalled Euro-American depictions of Indian shamans. "The slaves, being educated in ignorance, are therefore very superstitious," relates one account, "having their poison-doctors and their *Conjurers*. Some become wizards, by chewing live coals, first gathering the saliva." The word "Conjurer," though it is of English extraction, became the most common appellation to describe African American supernatural practitioners, although it did not acquire conventional usage until the nineteenth century. Before this time, the term alluded mainly to performances by traveling magicians or the acts of suspected witches, both black and white.[41]

There is an additional cultural source that deserves mention. Some black American Conjure specialists claimed a direct connection to

American Indians, a relationship that would be most fully drawn in late-nineteenth- and twentieth-century ex-slaves' testimonies. Some black American specialists declared that their skills came from knowledge of Indian shamans and supernatural practitioners. Harriet Collins, who practiced folk medicine in Texas, acknowledged that African and native American beliefs provided the foundations for her own healing practices. "My mammy learned me lots of doctorin', she claimed, "what she larnt from old folkses in Africa, and some de Indians learned her." Old March, an enslaved root doctor in nineteenth-century South Carolina, said that he purchased supernatural secrets from "an old Indian" years prior to commencing his career as a supernatural healer. In Georgia, an anonymous "old African or Guinea Negro" was said "to have derived the art form from the Indians," according to several sources, "after he arrived in this country from Africa." Cultural connections between African American Conjure and American Indian spiritual traditions may have been retained by members of a black community in lower Virginia, where one enslaved Conjure practitioner in the mid nineteenth century was referred to as an "Indian Doctor." The writer Charles Chesnutt insisted that black American magic and "goopher" practices had emerged in Africa but over time were "mingled and confused with the witchcraft and ghostlore of the white man, and the tricks and delusions of the Indian conjurer." A famous Conjurer in the early twentieth century, Jim Jordan of Hertford County, North Carolina, considered his powers to be the product of a mixed bloodline, the merging of African and Indian ancestry.[42]

Supernatural traditions among blacks in America thus developed in an eclectic manner. Spiritual healing, witchcraft, and divination were performed by a variety of persons, including professionals who were well known for their expertise and skillful manipulation of supernatural powers, and others who only periodically engaged in magical experiments. The shift from the exclusive role of the spiritual specialist to the practice of a shared tradition, available to all, is difficult to chart. It points to a democratization of spiritual knowledge that typified expressions of the supernatural in America. Nevertheless, even with its diversity in form and style, the core emphasis of Conjure remained substantially the same: Conjure enabled African Americans to gain power in order to address their particular circumstances and effect immediate transformations in an individual's world. For slaves, these traditions provided sources of knowledge that were unavailable to slave masters and offered confidence to those who found themselves in adverse and unpredictable circumstances. Finally, supernatural beliefs enabled black Americans to maintain African-based worldviews.

As the following chapters will make clear, African American conjuring traditions revolved around the issues of control, power, and security that shaped the lives of many black people. After Emancipation, supernatural beliefs and practices emphasized personal well-being and protection for members of the freedpersons' community. Certain practices surfaced primarily in contexts of resistance, at times when individuals used supernatural resources as a direct means of challenging their persecutors. And supernatural practices articulated hostilities within black Americans' own communities. Some of these "harming" traditions also encompassed Afro-Christian religious beliefs and practices. The paradoxical mix of healing and harming, which became a focal point of black American conjuring, is our subject now.

CHAPTER 3

"Folks Can Do Yuh Lots of Harm"

African American Supernatural Harming Traditions

Augusta, Georgia, late 1930s. A few short months after their wedding, a husband begins to leave his wife at home alone at night. He stays out, she says, until early the next morning. According to his spouse, he would "get up fussin' and leave without eating." She is pregnant, and before the birth of their first child he deserts her. She learns that he is having an affair. Tormented, she falls ill, dizzy with headaches, finally she goes deaf. She has been Conjured.[1]

This story not only gives voice to the pain its narrator experiences because of her husband's infidelity and abandonment, it also provides the framework by which she interprets her misfortune. Moreover, the format of this account is not unique. Many others like it can be found in the folklore records of the Works Progress Administration of the 1930s and 1940s, which contain a sizable collection of African American Conjure narratives. These narratives nearly always focus on some sort of human suffering, and they inevitably articulate a link between conflict and supernaturally induced misfortune. Like the account here, they describe sudden illness, with symptoms of headache, deafness, and unusual physical debilitation—all precipitated by conflict or emotional in-

Facing page illustration: nineteenth-century slave religion: African American oathing and divination ritual. From Richard Bridgens, *West Indian Scenery with Illustrations of Negro Character . . . the island of Trinidad* (1836), courtesy of the New York Public Library.

jury. As this victimized wife and mother understands it, the source of her trouble is Conjure.

The use of the supernatural for causing affliction—what I call harming practices—was well known among African American slaves and, later, among their descendants. From devious acts of petty sabotage to organized schemes of collective revolt, blacks utilized Conjure as a form of resistance, revenge, and self-defense. Just as significantly, however, harming magic was a pervasive means to express blacks' hostility within their own communities. This chapter examines these practices, including Conjure, supernatural oath taking, witchcraft, and poisoning. As with benign Conjure, many harming practices were connected to spiritual beliefs. At times people embraced harming practices and religious faith simultaneously, integrating Conjure and Christianity as dual sources of empowerment.

Older approaches to African American religious history link spirituality with acts of resistance. In an essay written in the 1960s, the historian Vincent Harding considered the "significant, identifiable black responses to religion which stormed beyond submissiveness to defiance" sometimes leading to "protest, resistance and death." Far from classifying religion as an opiate of the black masses, Harding held that African American spiritual experiences were characteristically "ambiguous" and "two-edged." While Harding's comments were confined to expressions of Christianity in the nineteenth century, his approach is relevant for studies of black religion in the years outside that period.[2]

In chapter 2 I assessed some of the earliest documented supernatural practices among black people in America—the use of magical charms and talismans, as well as African-based rituals of spiritual protection—which were intended for self-preservation and security. Other supernatural techniques believed to inflict physical injury on others, though diverse, reveal similar motivations. Black Americans employed them in order to punish criminals and wrongdoers; to attack opponents; to combat evil forces; and to retaliate against enemies and perceived adversaries. Conjure harming fit into a broader conceptual scheme by which blacks addressed the presence of misfortune in the world. These spiritual beliefs demonstrate fundamental concerns over the nature of evil that have occupied African American people across place and time.

Some of the earliest accounts of supernatural harming among blacks in America come from the early eighteenth century, when African Americans

took part in strategic uprisings against the institution of slavery. One rebellion, the New York Conspiracy of 1712, drew together a diverse group
of American-born blacks, native American Indians (or mestizos), and
Africans of the "Nations of Carmantee and Pappa." Together, the group
initiated a "riot," with the intent of striking out for their freedom by
"destroy[ing] all the whites in the town." This was, according to later
testimonies, done in retaliation for "some hard usage they apprehended
to have received from their masters." Setting fire to a building in one of
the central districts, the conspirators attacked the inhabitants as they tried
to save the burning structure. After a brief skirmish that left nine white
persons dead, the insurrection was crushed by the local militia, and nearly
all of its thirty-nine participants were condemned by the court and subsequently executed.[3]

Of particular relevance here is the New York account's description of
supernatural ritual activity. One of the insurrectionists' first collective
acts bore the marks of African spirituality. According to a letter written
by the chaplain of the English garrison in New York City, an oath had
been sworn between members of the conspiracy and an African "sorcerer" who had sealed the pact between them using blood and an enchanted powder as a necessary protection that ensured their invulnerability. The oath, by which the group had "ty[ed] themselves to Secrecy,"
involved a ritual in which blood was drawn and shared among members
"by Sucking . . . of each Others hands." Like many African rituals, this
oath was a form of spiritual invocation. The conspirators were bound
together by the act, having sealed a covenant between themselves and
the invisible forces of the supernatural world.[4]

Such rituals were well known in precolonial Africa, where oaths
were administered by priests and other religious functionaries. Oaths
were sworn in order to detect thieves, to find social malefactors, or to
adjudicate cases with conflicting claims. Often, oaths functioned as
sacred ordeals by which a person's guilt or innocence could be determined. Willem Bosman, on the Gold Coast in the seventeenth century,
described Akan oaths as "part of Religious Worship," which dictated
"that their Fetiche may punish them with death" in the event that they
violated the oath. Other African cultures such as those of the
Kongolese, conceived of the oath as a *nkisi,* a spiritual being that attacked witches and human beings who had been cursed. In many
African societies, oaths were administered by appointed religious
practitioners. The oath force, an ancestor or divine entity, was protective and all-knowing and would punish the person who swore,

should the pledge be broken. As in Africa, oaths in the New World worked to solidify unity in moments of upheaval and conflict and, most significantly, to rally soldiers in times of war.[5]

Oath-taking traditions were apparently well known to slaves in the New World. As performed by the New York conspirators, the oath ritual parallels the traditions described among Africans elsewhere in the diaspora. Such rituals were usually enacted by the enslaved as a prelude to rebellion. An uprising on the island of Antigua in 1736, for example, was found to be preceded by oaths that had been "administered in at least seven different places in the island . . . sealed with a draft of rum mixed with grave dirt and cock's blood." Similar rituals were believed to have prefaced a major Jamaican rebellion in 1760, and another in 1777, with the latter described as "an alarming insurrection" involving Africans and Creole blacks who had "taken a blood oath to massacre all the whites." Utilized by Africans of diverse ethnic backgrounds, an oath gave the gathered participants spiritual sanction. While its precise religious meanings had eroded over time, the oath evoked sacred authority and instituted bonds of fidelity among human beings and between them and the spirits of the supernatural realm.[6]

In America, oath-taking rituals were transformed as blacks incorporated new elements into their practice. In antebellum South Carolina, an ordeal for discovering theft among slaves was noted as making use of the dust "from the grave of a person who had died last" and an incantational formula with explicit Christian referents. Mixing the grave dust with water, an examining committee offered the concoction to the accused individual while uttering the appeal, "In the name of the Father and the Son and the Holy Ghost, if you have taken Sam's chicken don't drink this water, for if you do you will die and go to hell and be burned in fire and brimstone, but if you have not, you may take it and it will not hurt you." While ingestion of the grave dirt as a sign of solidarity with the supernatural realm remained consistent with African beliefs, this Afro-Christian version of the ritual replaced the oath spirits with biblical characters who assumed the roles of the otherworldly arbiters of divine judgment.[7]

In the United States, the perceived power of collective rituals aroused great misgivings among slaveowners and members of the slaveholding establishment in the nineteenth century. Worried over the implications of providing Christian religious instruction to bondpersons, slaveowners blamed Conjurers and other supernatural practitioners for organized transgressions and subversive activities. "Ignorance and superstition render them easy dupes to their teachers, doctors, prophets, conjurers;" wrote Charles Colcock Jones in 1842. "When fairly committed to such leaders, they may be brought to the commission of almost any crime."[8]

Were such fears justified? While revolts in mainland North America were far less extensive when compared to other slave societies in the New World, many possessed a spiritual dimension. Native-born Africans and second- and third-generation black Americans transcended their differences when they were drawn into the vortex of African supernaturalism and evangelical Christianity, potent cultural forces in nineteenth-century America. Two of the best-known slave conspiracies in the United States, that of Denmark Vesey in Charleston, South Carolina (1822) and Nat Turner in Southampton County, Virginia (1831) gave expression to powerful impulses of supernaturalism and spiritual harming.

The successes of Vesey and Turner hinged on their abilities to channel racial discontentment while arousing chialistic expectations in their followers. Their actions were consistent with those of other spiritually influenced radicals in America prior to that time. For instance, in eighteenth-century South Carolina, three blacks—a slave and two freedmen—plotted an insurrection in St. Helena Parish, with the intent to kill the "Buckras." The governor accused the trio's leader of trying to "stir up Sedition among the Negroes" after he received an apocalyptic vision in which he had fellowshiped with "God Almighty . . . in the Woods." These prophetic, visionary strains of religious radicalism were also in evidence among black insurrectionists in North Carolina and Virginia at the turn of the nineteenth century.[9] What was distinctive about the Turner and Vesey uprisings, however, was the rebels' perception of African-based supernaturalism as an additional weapon in their arsenal of resistance. In these conspiracies, Conjure harming beliefs and practices would play indispensable roles.[10]

A confluence of Christianity and African-based spiritual traditions linked Turner and Vesey. Turner, a self-styled prophet, was believed to have interspersed the famous *Confessions* with divine pronouncements, otherworldly revelations, and graphic apocalyptic visions. Although he was said to have eschewed the practices of "conjuring and such like tricks," he shared dramatic traits with other African American supernatural practitioners and Conjurers who were his contemporaries. In fact, the fusion of Christianity and supernaturalism in Nat Turner's life has led one historian to conclude that "religion and magic sustained Nat Turner's rebellion."[11]

The particulars of Turner's 1831 conspiracy and the ensuing events that resulted in the bloody deaths of fifty-five whites in the environs of Southampton County, Virginia, have been fully investigated elsewhere. While there is general historical consensus on the details of the revolt's planning and execution, there is less agreement about the person of Nat Turner, particularly the spiritual beliefs that may have played a part in his mission. Scholars have portrayed Turner both as a ruthless fanatic with messianic aspirations and as a martyr in the black Christian tradition of heroic protest. And yet it can be argued that neither model adequately represents him. As a religious figure, Turner had more in common with African-based spiritual practitioners than with black plantation preachers. Turner, one biographer has written, epitomizes two "overlapping strands in a single story." Nat Turner was the product of a dual heritage, an African American who drew on both Christian and non-Christian cultural sources.[12]

Apart from what is revealed in secondhand reports and official documents, there are limited details on Nat Turner's spiritual development. Turner's two most formative influences were his paternal grandmother, whom he described as "very religious," and his mother, an African-born slave who arrived in Virginia in the late 1790s and was given the name Nancy. Nat was born in 1800. Recognizing precocity in her son, Nancy predicted that he was destined for "some great purpose" that was yet to be revealed. Distinguished in his youth by an ability to receive revelations from the spirit world, Turner enjoyed something of a seer's reputation among the local population. His gift at interpreting esoteric signs confirmed his status as a holy man. According to one commentator, "Nat was no preacher, but . . . he had acquired the character of a prophet . . . he traced his divination in characters of blood, on leaves, alone in the woods; he would arrange them in some conspicuous place, have a dream telling him of the circumstance . . . and he would interpret their meaning . . . by means of this nature, he acquired an immense influence, over such persons as he took into his confidence."[13]

Turner adopted ascetic behaviors that gave outward witness to a devout Christian life: no drinking, no swearing, extended periods of prayer and fasting. Guided by the same "spirit that spoke to the Prophets," he was led to expect a sign that would direct him to the fulfillment of some hidden divine purpose. The awaited epiphany occurred in a series of visions in 1822, 1825, and 1828. These successive revelations—relayed in

Turner's *Confessions* with profoundly esoteric imagery and occult symbolism—communicated the objective of his final, fateful mission. In August 1831 Turner struck out in one of the boldest uprisings of slaves ever to occur in the United States, with a violent force that reverberated throughout the entire South.[14]

Like Nat Turner, Denmark Vesey was a religious person. Vesey organized an extensive insurrection plot in Charleston, South Carolina, a city that in 1820 possessed a majority of about fifteen thousand slaves and black freedpersons to eleven thousand whites. In that year, the city's governing authorities had taken steps to curtail the emerging political power of the African American population, using legal repression, harassment, and threats of violence. It was within such an atmosphere of racial discord that the conspiracy developed. As a freedman in the Society of black Methodists, an independent African American church, Vesey was positioned to tap the spiritual resources of the black community for the advancement of his cause.[15]

Accounts of the events leading up to the discovery of the plot reveal that Vesey, a well-to-do carpenter who had purchased his freedom from a slaveowner, began recruiting participants from the city and the outlying lowcountry regions as early as 1818. By the summer of 1822 the conspiracy had taken shape. It involved perhaps as many as nine thousand persons, who—according to the trial report—intended to carry out "an insurrection among the blacks against all the whites." Organizationally, the conspiracy was significant for the manner in which it galvanized participants from a variety of class and ethnic backgrounds. Vesey gathered about him several "lieutenants" or co-organizers who recruited blacks from an assortment of occupations. The ranks of rebels included urban Creole artisans, black American laborers, and rural African field hands. Persons of diverse religious positions, including Methodist deacons, Methodist class leaders, and congregation members were enlisted by way of the extensive infrastructure of the African Methodist Church, which became the strategic center of the movement.[16]

Using religious faith to consolidate his sympathizers, Vesey provided the Charleston uprising with a spiritual impetus that secular ideology did not supply. Religion became both a tool and a motivating force. But while Christianity gave justification to the noble but dangerous cause of freedom fighting, ritual action was the catalyst. Combining biblical rhetoric and antislavery discourse to inspire his followers, Vesey utilized the Old Testament trope that identified the slaves with the Israelites, portraying blacks as freedom fighters in a decisive struggle that had already

been foretold in sacred history. As described in the confessions of Rolla
Bennett, a slave of the former governor, Vesey held secret gatherings in
which he planned strategy and shared his revolutionary ideas. In a meeting at his home, Vesey gave a militant exegesis of the Exodus story of
the deliverance of the Hebrew slaves, a favorite biblical account for
African Americans in the nineteenth century. According to Bennett's confession,

> At this meeting Vesey said . . . that we ought to rise up and fight against the
> whites for our liberties . . . he read to us from the Bible, how the Children
> of Israel were delivered out of Egypt from bondage. . . . He then read in the
> Bible where God commanded, that all should be cut off, both men, women
> and children, and said, he believed, it was no sin for us to do so, for the
> Lord had commanded us to do it.[17]

Ultimately the uprising failed when an informer betrayed the conspiracy. Vesey, his lieutenants, and eighty of the plotters were captured;
all were jailed, executed, or deported. In the aftermath of the trials, state
legislators enacted a series of laws that severely curtailed the movement
of slaves and free blacks by restricting their right to organize, thereby
forcing many church leaders and religious functionaries underground or
out of the South entirely.[18]

Although it is difficult to ascertain precisely how spirituality influenced
the acts of those involved in the Vesey conspiracy, it is clear that for some
participants, African-based beliefs and practices were integral to the success of the plan. Most significant was the role of Gullah Jack Pritchard
(or Purcell), an African-born ex-slave who has been characterized as "the
religious embodiment of the movement." Jack, one of Vesey's lieutenants,
was a leader in the Gullah Society, a church-based association comprised
of blacks from the remote plantation regions of the Carolina coast and
the Sea Islands. Ethnically distinctive, the Gullah had maintained many
African cultural practices, developed its own systems of community reg-
ulation and governance, and instituted its own traditions of worship.
Authorized to command the Gullah company, Jack Pritchard was acknowledged as a priest-figure of the African tradition. Known among
the conspirators as "the little man who can't be killed, shot or taken,"
Jack adopted conventions of ritual that were characteristic of *obeah* rebels
in the Caribbean. "He had a charm, and he would lead them," claimed
Vesey. It was believed that Jack had carried his conjuring implements
"with him in a bag which he brought on board the [slave] ship." He dis-

tributed crab-claw talismans he called *cullah* for invulnerability, and poison, which was to be used in a preemptive attack on the enemy. Jack also conducted African-based rituals of oath taking among his Gullah Society members, who read psalms, prayed, and swore their allegiance to the movement. A fowl, eaten half-raw and shared among them, was their "evidence of union."[19]

Within the trial accounts and in subsequent interpretations of the events, Gullah Jack is referred to as a "sorcerer," a "doctor," a "necromancer" and a "Voodoo" practitioner, but never as an African Christian. Given his affiliations, however, he might have qualified for this status. Gullah religiosity combined missionary Protestantism and African-derived spirituality, producing "a syncretic blend" that included "belief in the efficacy of Christian salvation, the prevalence of the living dead, and the awesome powers of Conjuration." The prominence of Gullah Jack and several other Conjure practitioners as leaders in the Vesey plot suggests that African-based spirituality and supernatural traditions did not present a conflict for the other conspirators.[20]

In the cases of the Nat Turner and Denmark Vesey conspiracies, we find evidence in the New World of a spiritual orientation that is reminiscent of African traditions. It is survivalistic and militant; it emphasizes empowerment, manifestations of supernatural force, and collective rituals of protection and self-defense. Its leaders are believed to possess visionary gifts and miraculous abilities. These resistance movements sometimes occur in contexts where indigenous African religions and Christianity converge, and the interface of "magic" and religion, exemplified by Conjurers like Gullah Jack and holy men such as Nat Turner, is a natural outgrowth of Afro-Christian spirituality.

What *kind* of Christianity do they represent? The indigenization of Christian beliefs in the African diaspora produced a spectrum of variations, with African-based religions developing not only in relation to Catholicism (as with *santería* in Cuba, or *vodou* in Haiti), but also as offshoots of the Protestant faith. The merging of African-inspired practices and Protestantism shows affinities with, as well as departures from, universally held Christian traditions. In the British Caribbean, for example, Christian traits prevail within sects such as the Spiritual Baptists of Trinidad and Guyana, and in the ceremonial practices of Shakers of St. Vincent, which all maintain strong African elements. In Jamaica, the

Africanization of belief persists in the Protestant churches of the Zionists and the Native Baptists. And in other West Indian revival movements such as Convince, Kumina, and Pocomania, a synthesis of ancestral rituals and Protestant worship styles can be seen. Within the indigenous African churches themselves, evangelical Christianity began to take root in the western, southern, and central regions of the continent during the nineteenth century. There, the rise of new independent African churches and revitalizing prophet movements was the product of the melding of traditional religion and the spiritual imperatives of biblical Christianity. All of these bold, Africanized forms of Protestantism shared characteristics with African-based religions elsewhere and put great emphasis on ecstatic behaviors, spirit revelations, supernatural healing, and antisorcery ritualism.[21]

The persistence of elements such as these in black religion in the United States may be the consequence of similar developments. African American spiritual traditions are properly located on a continuum encompassing both African and Christian sources. The combination of supernaturally oriented black Christianity and African-derived ritual was typified in the activities of Conjurers, who, as we have seen, fraternized with Christian converts, were Christians themselves, or drew power from the symbols of Christianity. What is distinctive about these practitioners in the United States is that few of them were able to establish sustained movements that outlived them. Some were like Turner, individualists outside the leadership structures of the organized churches. Others were like Vesey, churchgoers with limited impact on the formation of new movements within the churches themselves. For many black supernatural practitioners in the United States, spiritual power—especially the power to do harm by supernatural means—was largely uninstitutionalized.

Black Americans have historically utilized supernatural harming more frequently in personal acts of defiance than in collective confrontations. As evidence of the fragmented manner in which African culture was maintained on the American mainland, their acts also typified the ways that enslaved peoples conceptualized the modes of resistance that were available to them. Some, viewing slavery through the lenses of sorcery and witchcraft, used supernatural harming to make lone, disabling attacks on the slaveholder's person and property. For examples of the latter, we turn to an especially subversive harming practice—poisoning. Poisoning was a potent outlet of slave aggression that emerged as a weapon of choice

in the plethora of conflicts that engaged blacks and whites in eighteenth-
and nineteenth-century America.[22]

Since slavery, many African Americans had viewed poisoning as a form
of spiritual affliction. Consider the following remarks from an article published in the nineteenth-century *New Orleans Medical and Surgical
Journal*. The author was Samuel A. Cartwright, a renowned Louisiana
physician and champion of the "scientific" management of plantation
slaves. Cartwright described Negro Consumption, a disease he believed
to be rampant among black bondpersons in the South.

> The seat of Negro Consumption is not the lungs, stomach, liver or any
> organ of the body, but in the mind . . . the patients themselves believe they
> are *poisoned;* . . . they are right, but it is not the body, but the mind that
> is poisoned. Negroes . . . fancy that their fellow servants are against them,
> that their master or overseer cares nothing for them . . . and that some
> enemy on the plantation or in the neighborhood has tracked them, that
> is, laid poison for them to walk over, or given it to them in their food or
> drinks.

Cartwright believed that the slaves saw certain illnesses as deriving from
a mysterious deadly force, what they thought was a kind of supernatural poison. Certainly, African Americans' interpretations of poisoning
were constituted by a nexus of spiritual ideas and beliefs. Although tech-
nically distinguishable from harming practices that operated solely by
supernatural agency, the secretive nature of poisoning, and its tendency
to inflict sudden, inexplicable illness and death, led many persons to con-
nect them.[23]

Legal records illuminate a network of incidents of poisoning involving both Africans and Anglo-Americans, slaves and freedpersons, that
reach back to the eighteenth century. In many instances poisoning and
supernaturalism were seen as twin evils. Within trial accounts, deposi-
tions, and court reports spanning the Chesapeake region and the lower
South, Conjurers were regularly identified as responsible for creating and
administering poisons. In fact, the roles of poisoners and that of supernatural practitioners appear in some cases to be identical.

Poisoning was an aggressive response by enslaved blacks to the pervasive power that whites yielded over their lives. In 1795 two Virginia
slaves who were otherwise "Orderly well behaved fellows," were implicated in a scheme to murder a slave master with poison, although a
"Negro Wench, or Conjurer" was suspected as the primary instigator of
the crime.[24] In 1771 a "Valuable man Slave named Sharper" of Stafford
County, Virginia, was accused of attempting to procure "Poison from a

Negroe Doctor or Conjurer as they are Call'd," with the purpose of "de-stroy[ing] White People." Slaves convicted in a 1779 trial in Johnston County, North Carolina, were accused of giving "powder" and "at-tempting to Conger *[sic]*" by unknown means. In a 1783 case in Louisa County, Virginia, a slave was found guilty of "poisoning and Conjuring" but was eventually pardoned by the governor on the grounds that the court had been deceived by his white accusers.[25]

Poisoning incidents culminated with the vigorous prosecution, con-viction, and punishment of numbers of blacks in the eighteenth century. From the mid-1700s to the turn of the century, proceedings against poi-soners constituted some of the most frequent actions taken against African Americans by local courts in South Carolina, Maryland, North Carolina, and Virginia. From 1715 to 1785 in North Carolina, thirteen separate indictments were given in slave trials for poisoning. In Virginia between 1740 and 1785 more slaves stood trial for poisoning than for any other crime except theft. Criminal indictments in Virginia in 1772 and 1810 alone resulted in the execution of some twenty slaves for poi-soning. The occurrence of poisonings of whites by black bondpersons stimulated such anxiety that lawmakers in the South moved swiftly to enforce statutes that called for the strictest punishment. Legislation from Georgia required the death penalty for anyone convicted of poisoning, including doctors and healers. Clauses in South Carolina's 1751 Negro Act were also extreme. This law provided, "That in case any slave shall teach or instruct another slave in the knowledge of any poisonous root, plant, herb, or other poison whatever, he or she, so offending, shall upon conviction thereof, suffer death as a felon." Acts of poisoning by blacks were considered seditious and were usually treated with the utmost sever-ity by authorities or with violent public reprisals.[26]

Perhaps as much as the members of Anglo-American communities, many African Americans themselves feared the poisoners. Their con-cerns were not without foundation, for a great proportion of cases in-dicate that poisoning flared within racial boundaries, with blacks harming other blacks. In the North Carolina slave court of 1761, for example, several bondmen were implicated for poisoning other mem-bers of the African American community. It was determined that a slave called Toby had visited an African American "doctor" for treatment of what he believed was poisoning. Toby suspected that the near-lethal dosage had been provided by another slave. In another case in Virginia a black bondman, Peter, was paid by other slaves to "Destroy . . . their

Enemies," but was later betrayed for his work and indicted for poisoning and conjuring. One study of slavery has characterized the extensive occurrence of intrablack poisonings in the eighteenth century as "a prime example of the black community ministering to its own needs." Poisoners were viewed by many African Americans as arbiters of justice and, certainly, revenge.[27]

Many cases underscore the cultural and social divisions that existed within enslaved populations. An investigation involving the poisoning death of a black servant named Crusquet on a Louisiana estate in 1728 showed that the motive behind the murder was enmity arising out of ethnic rivalries among the African slaves. "Among the plantation Negroes," stated the report, "witchcraft is supposed to be the weapon of Crusquet's poisoner's tribe." A case from Illinois in 1779 involved Moreau and Manuel, two bondmen who plotted successfully to poison some slaves and their owners. The narrative of this affair, abstracted from testimony that chronicled details of a "buried poison," a ritual with a horn filled with "boiling blood," and statements given against the accused by several "Negro countrymen," is especially interesting for its revelations of divided loyalties among Africans and African Americans in the early national period. Black intraracial tensions were also noted by Pieter Kalm, a Swedish visitor to the republic. Kalm described the "dangerous art of poisoning" he believed to be prevalent among North American blacks, observing that "the negroes commonly employed it on such of their brethren as behave well [toward the whites], are beloved by their masters, and separate, as it were, from their countrymen," and on those who shunned or did not speak to other slaves.[28]

Conjurers who were able to induce poisonings were taken very seriously by both blacks and whites and greatly feared for their powers to inflict supernatural harm. A dispute occurring at the turn of the nineteenth century illustrates the intimidation that the occasional poisoning specialist/Conjurer could produce both within and outside their immediate communities. John, a North Carolina bondman, was brought to trial in the General Assembly in 1800 for the murder of a white slaveholder. In damaging testimony against him, other slaves "told of being rubbed by John and falling ill, of resorting to an 'old Negro conjurer' to ward off John's powers," and "of hearing John wish for a Rattle snake's head," after boasting that he could create a toxin that "one of the most skilful [sic] doctors" of Conjuration could not counter. Because of the fear he aroused among his fellow slaves and the strength of the evidence against him, John was found guilty and ultimately executed for his role in the affair.[29]

African American supernatural practitioners were known to use their reputations as poisoners for personal advancement and occasionally did so in decidedly intimate ways. One unusual case in North Carolina raises the possibility that blacks were not above manipulating fears of occult powers and poisoning for sexual gain. An account of a trial of infanticide involving a white woman in the late eighteenth century, in which the defendant justified her actions in the murder of her illegitimate mulatto infant by saying that a "Negro Fellow," Will, made her drink "under a pretence of Curing her," and thus "by that means had Carnal knowledge of her body." Will threatened her, she claimed, after she was found with child, saying that "he would poison her," or "do something to her that would kill or otherwise destroy her" if she revealed to any other person the details of their cohabitation.[30]

The cultural background of poisoners played a significant role in their identification as supernatural practitioners. In particular, "saltwater" Africans and recent arrivals from the West Indies were thought to possess the accumulated wisdom of Old World poisoning techniques. It was frequently reported that native African slaves carried Old World knowledge of herbs, roots, and other preparations necessary for creating toxic substances with them to the New World. Alexander Garden, an English commercial botanist in colonial South Carolina, asserted that Africans were uniquely adept at extracting lethal substances from local vegetation. "I greatly . . . suspect that the Negroes bring their knowledge of the poisonous plants," he pondered, "which they use here, with them from their own country." Some blacks were believed to have learned poisoning abilities as a supplement to a larger complex of ritual talents; others were regarded as innately "gifted" at harming and poisoning practices. In a notorious plot in Louisiana, conspirators apparently assumed that African ancestry alone guaranteed one slave's access to poisoning skills. In 1731 a rebellious Creole overseer in New Orleans enlisted an accomplice to murder a slave driver, choosing a "native of Guinea" to create a poison from the "gall and heart" of a crocodile, a secret formula known only by African priests. "As a Creole he knew nothing about how to make such drugs," the case report states, "but the lately imported negroes knew these arts." When the scheme was exposed, the "Mandringa-speaking" Guinea Negro who was implicated in the conspiracy was thrown in prison, and there he eventually died. The case was closed, with the records acknowledging that the unfortunate convict "never fully understood the importance of [his] offense."[31]

The antecedents of poisoning practices among blacks in America are found in indigenous African traditions. Olaudah Equiano, the eighteenth-century autobiographer and abolitionist, explained how the Ibo were "extremely cautious about poison," regularly consulting specialists in order to detect its presence. "The magicians were also our doctors or physicians," he reported, "They practiced bleeding by cupping; and were very successful in healing wounds and expelling poisons." Thomas Winterbottom, a British physician on the windward coast of Africa in the early 1800s, found that "active and fatal poisons" were used in conjunction with magical ceremonies and in the composition of *gris-gris* by religious specialists in Shebro, Sierra Leone. Job Ben Solomon, an African nobleman whose life and adventures were popularized in a 1734 narrative, described the cultivation and use of a poison that was extracted from a locally grown root in the Senegambia. The plant produced "so deadly" a poison, he explained, "that one pint of it will soon kill any creature that drinks it." Utilized in Africa as a lethal weapon, poisoning techniques survived among blacks in the diaspora.[32]

In America, poisoning methods usually involved herbal preparations. In 1761 a North Carolina bondman named Sambo was found guilty for conspiring to administer "touck," a harmful substance, to the wife of a slaveowning planter in order "to make her better to him." The potion was derived from the juice of a wild plant that was known to African and native American peoples of the region. One physician, describing poisoning practices, characterized such harming traditions as "Indian or Negro poison[ing]." Court records referred variously to the "poisonous powders, roots, and herbs" utilized by Conjure practitioners. As with other African traditions, Old World ethnomedical lore was adapted to black botanical practices in the New World.[33]

The creation of poisons could involve a combination of ingredients. In addition to plants, poisons were made with minerals, animal parts, blood, or other organic materials. Many of these substances were also essential for creating harming implements such as charms and "trick bags." At a 1766 trial in Maryland, one "Negro Nero" was found guilty and sentenced to death for attempting to poison with "groundpuppies," or dried salamanders, which would become a staple in the ritual formulae of African American Conjurers in the post-Emancipation era. In eighteenth-century Virginia, a slave was charged in a conspiracy to kill a slaveowner by exposing him to a potent mixture. "Dick was a superstitious fellow," the record states, "and believed that he could accomplish his purpose by beating up leaves with snake heads, and leaving the combination at the door of his master." The bondman's concoction also resembled the *materia maleficia* that were routinely utilized by African American supernatural specialists in later decades. Poisoning materials consisted of two types: substances that were activated by ingestion, and artifacts that were activated by invisible forces, requiring no contact with the intended victim.[34]

Related to African supernatural poison traditions was the use of harming "medicines" that could bring about physical affliction as well as alleviate it. The use of medicines required the skills of practitioners who were knowledgeable regarding the correct combination of ingredients, and who were empowered to manipulate the spiritual forces needed to assemble them. These individuals were sometimes described as ritual specialists, either "poison-doctors" or "Negro doctors," who were sought out by the sick and afflicted for medical treatment. Perhaps recalling these traditions, blacks in the United States during later periods would refer to individual acts of Conjure poisoning as "medicating" their enemies.[35]

A combination of elements linked African American poisoning with magico-religious ritual. The select persons who controlled poisoning consolidated the arts of herbalism and ritual expertise into a single practice. They were often considered authorities in the spheres of health and religion in black communities.[36] The juxtaposition of poisoning with "medicine" and "doctoring" also underlies the philosophy of African American harming. Healing and harming specialists did not perceive an ethical contradiction in the performance of these two activities. The categories of healing and harming were morally neutral attributes of the same powers of predisposition and control. The Western idea of delineating good from evil as "obverse and reverse" concepts has no parallel in the African tradition. A more accurate dichotomy for characterizing the amoral principle underscoring such practices might be "powerful" versus "powerless."[37]

Spiritual power, therefore, was viewed as neither absolutely good nor absolutely evil, but "potentially either and often complementary to one another," and thus obtainable for all purposes. In America, conjuring specialists both cured and caused injury. For the slaves, as Albert Raboteau has observed, "the primary categories were not good and evil but security and danger." In contexts of resistance, supernatural ritual was a viable countermeasure against oppressive forces, involving practices that sometimes prescribed violence. For black bondpersons, malign forces might be embodied by slaveholders, brutal overseers, or other slaves. Embedded within African American understandings of harming was the notion that evil was not theoretical but situational, immediate, and located in the domain of human actions and relationships.[38]

After the turn of the nineteenth century, magical poisoning practices came to be widespread among African American slaves. According to Irving Lowery, a former bondman who became a minister in the Methodist Episcopal Church in South Carolina, black "voodoo" practitioners and poisoners, as he called them, shared the same terrifying status. "It may appear strange," wrote Lowery, "but it is true, nevertheless, that in some way or other the slaves very often connected sickness and death with voodooism or conjuration." Supernatural specialists, he explained, were the most intimidating of all persons in black communities, "the voodoo 'doctor'" being an "almost omnipotent individual in the estimation of his fellows." Lowery remarked that "some of the 'voodoos' were skillful poisoners, and while the great mass of their professed art was a rank imposture, still they possessed enough of the devilish skill to render them objects of wholesome dread." Although skeptical of the veracity of Conjurers' claims to power, Lowery detailed a case of poisoning by "voodooism and conjuration" involving a female plantation slave in South Carolina who had been in a "love scrape" with another bondwoman. "Some conjurer of the neighborhood prepared the dose for her, so it was said," he explained. When the white physician who attended blacks on the plantation was brought in to help the fatally afflicted woman, the slaves summoned their own "voodoo doctor," who determined that she had been Conjured by a jealous rival.[39]

This account highlights the dual emphasis on harming and healing that was characteristic of black American supernatural traditions in the slave period. In some cases Conjure "doctors" offered the only effective therapies for victims of poisoning. In South Carolina, one white physician noted that black patients who were suffering from "African poisoning and tricking" were cured by the "art" of an "old African," rather than more conventional medical techniques. When the father of James Lindsay Smith, a bondman in early-nineteenth-century Virginia, became critically ill, a slave doctor treated him successfully after diagnosing his ailment using divination and determining that he had been poisoned by a vengeful neighbor. In another case from the 1830s, the Virginia slaveholder-planter John Walker cited the failure of a white physician to restore a slave who had become "almost blind" after being poisoned. It was only when "an old Negro" named Doctor Lewis treated the bondman with a "special decoction of herbs" that he recovered. These examples of "doctoring and curing," typical of slave narratives, demonstrate the two-sided nature of supernatural belief, which, as we have seen, encompassed practices in which spiritual power could be utilized to work for or against an individual.[40]

Belief in the power of magical poisons and poisoners was not confined to African Americans. On occasion whites were known to exploit black practitioners for their own illicit interests. In the case of *The State v. Martin Posey,* heard in the South Carolina Court of Appeals in 1849, a white yeoman was convicted for his wife's murder. The farmer, Martin Posey, was found guilty after it became known that he had hired a bondman, Jeff, to "doctor some of his Negroes." Posey, according to the report, had discovered that Jeff "was a Conjuror, and . . . could do something that would secretly cause his wife's death." Although the slave was not implicated in the murder by the court, Posey's willingness to solicit an African American Conjurer to commit the crime demonstrates that supernatural specialists like Jeff may have possessed a reputation for harming that was recognized—and accessible—to whites as well as blacks.[41]

In fact, it was well known by whites, according to one nineteenth-century source, that slaves on antebellum plantations were well acquainted with a "genuine African poison" that was implemented for acts of harming. "No person who has not lived in the South can form any adequate conception of the effects of African poison, or the frequency of its use," wrote Daniel Robinson Hundley, an Alabama-born scholar of southern history. Similar concerns over the "diabolical practices" of poisoning among blacks were voiced by other white authorities. "Their skill in poisons is something fearful, and baffles the most expert practitioner," asserted the poet Sarah Handy in 1891. Conversing with a physician in James River, Virginia, Handy recalled the man's frustration with the numerous claims of Conjure poisoning among blacks in the area. "The Negroes themselves think they are tricked," he complained, "and I feel sure they are poisoned; but how in the world is anyone to prove it?" Likewise, a study of supernatural traditions in Mississippi, Alabama, and Georgia at the turn of the century concluded that "to the rural Negro, as to the African," poisoning and conjuration were "identical." Well beyond the slavery era, the combined forces of supernatural belief and poisoning exerted powerful influences in African American life.[42]

Whereas the alliance of Conjure and harming was well known, comparatively fewer incidents of poisoning of whites by African Americans were reported after the start of the nineteenth century. Although whites continued to be apprehensive of black supernatural specialists, documented cases of interracial harming showed a decline in the 1800s. More typical were instances of *intra*racial harming in which blacks were believed to have worked harming magic against other blacks. They point to a shift that transformed African-based beliefs and made older norms for regulating the social order obsolete. A new, contemporary outlook, informed in part by Christianity, replaced the archaic worldview of ancestral authority, with its sacred sanctions and conservative vision. No longer were neglected spirits and the troubled dead the sole supernatural forces that carried affliction into the world; often it was evil from within a community's midst that produced the gravest harm. As African Americans created a new world, they sometimes found enemies that lived very close to home.

Since slavery, practices of supernatural harming in the African American community had been known by many names such as Hoodoo, root working, tricking, and Voodoo. Although these terms are distinguishable, there was considerable overlap in their use. *Hoodoo,* for instance, alluded to the practice of spells and other forms of magical manipulation, but could also refer to healing and harming traditions. *Root work* characterized the style of utilizing certain natural objects in the performance of ritual. In black American oral traditions, both terms were used interchangeably. *Voodoo,* a term that was adopted by blacks and whites, properly described a religion of Haitian origin *(vodou)* that flourished in Louisiana from the late eighteenth to the early nineteenth century. However, in the African American vernacular, Voodoo was often applied, as were tricking and Hoodoo, to describe any exercise of spiritual powers for malevolent purposes, the so-called practice of black magic, or maleficia.[43]

The pervasiveness of Conjure harming and the terms for describing such practices raise questions regarding the significance of the supernatural in the lives of black Americans. Albert Raboteau has argued that Conjure served as an alternative religious theory of misfortune for the slaves. He explains that in black folk traditions "the concept of suffering for the guilt of the father is biblical; the concept of being victimized

by a 'fix' is Conjure." He adds, "both attempt to locate the cause of irrational suffering." For bondpersons and later, for freedpersons, Conjure
identified sources of evil and provided explanations for the occurrence
of misfortune. Conjure and supernatural harming beliefs therefore helped
define all manner of afflictions, from unanticipated maladies and tragic
accidents to consistent bad luck.[44]

For black Americans, victimization was sometimes viewed as a consequence of supernatural harming. Claims of supernatural injury were
constantly voiced in narratives by slaves and former slaves. In considering stories of supernatural Conjure harming, we sift through charge after charge leveled by blacks against other blacks for malevolent spiritual
practices. Far from a picture of fraternal solidarity, Conjure beliefs de-
pict black Americans as living in a world of dissension and discord.
Jealousy was often cited as a chief motivation for supernatural attacks.
Mary Jackson of Atlanta, Georgia, related the tale of a woman who became convinced that her entire neighborhood was resentful of her financial success. This woman, she claimed, became stricken by a mysterious illness sent by those who thought she had become "more than
anyone else," because, in her words, "she worked hard and got something for herself." In an account from the Sea Islands at the turn of the
century, a missionary teacher on St. Helena reported that an African
American woman found herself ill from what she believed to be a supernatural poison. The affliction had been sent, she explained, because
others had "wished some evil" on her because she was particularly independent. Another example concerns a woman who was accused of "fixing" her neighbor and was said to have been envious of another woman,
who had provided "nice clothes and dancing lessons" for her child.
Conjure-related conflicts could also turn on resentments involving the
aesthetics of racial identity. In one such account by an African American
writer in the South, a black woman was believed to be Conjured by another who disliked her "straight hair," "this being the one thing," it was
noted, "most ardently desired by most females."[45]

Supernatural harming was also adopted for coercion and intimidation, used by rivals in the economic sphere. The schoolteacher Mamie
Garvin Fields met a Conjurer on John's Island, South Carolina, during
her sojourn there between 1906 and 1908. The Conjurer's many clients,
she found, included a "successful businessman" who sought magical
assistance in order to "play root against his competition." Similar reports abound in black American narrative accounts. Avarice led one

woman to Conjure another so that she could corner a greater share of the neighborhood washing trade, according to one writer, describing Conjure among African Americans in urban New York at the end of the nineteenth century. Numerous accounts of Conjure-related conflicts over property, employment, and money illustrated some of the consequences of poverty and economic discrimination in many black Americans' lives.[46]

Stories of supernatural harming also provide glimpses of the conflicts that divided blacks across time and place. A range of accidents, losses, and problems were blamed on Conjure. Some explanations were illustrative of the hazards of rural agricultural life. The white sheriff J. E. McTeer, the chief law enforcement officer of Beaufort County, South Carolina, in the late 1940s, told of a case in which witchcraft was cited as the force that caused the children and the mule of one black farmer to sicken and die, made his hens produce eggs with double yolks, and ruined his crops. Correspondingly, a nineteenth-century plantation owner in Georgia explained how the rivalries between his African American workers, Jane and Anna, were linked to a series of farm mishaps. Undergirding these problems, he noted, were very real conflicts between the women.

> Though Anna milked, Jane churned, and every effort to make butter failed. Jane said that Anna had put a spell on the milk. Anna retorted by saying that Jane put something in the milk to prevent the butter coming, so that she, Anna, could be discharged. Chickens about the yard began to die, the water in the well had a peculiar taste. . . . Negroes would use neither axe nor hoes kept at the yard. . . . When a hen was setting, she rarely brought off chickens. . . . It can be well understood from the foregoing, how this matter of "cunjer," in designing hands, can work evil to the innocent.[47]

Other harming charges speak to the personal interests of individuals in black communities. Attributions of supernatural harming often had sources in conflicts of a sexual or romantic nature. In an example dating from 1878, the Hampton Institute administrator Alice Bacon recounted the story of a Conjure victim who was "suffering from a sore and swollen foot," said to be inflicted upon her by "an old man who wanted to marry her," who conducted his evil work "in church one night." Another incident of "tricking" was brought about by a young woman's mother who decided to punish the haughty suitor who had spurned her daughter. Some practitioners specialized in such matters. The anthropologist Zora Neale Hurston recounted her experiences as an apprentice to African American

Hoodoo doctors who dealt solely with romantic entanglements. She recalled one episode in which a client came to one specialist in order to
"fix" her partner. "I went to study with Eulalia," Hurston wrote, "who
specialized in man-and-woman cases. Everyday somebody came to get
Eulalia to tie them up with some man or woman or to loose them from
love. . . . So one day a woman came to get tied to a man." The distraught
woman who requested assistance from Eulalia declared that a man she
desired would not marry her because his current wife had "got roots
buried" and was keeping him under her power. She believed that the ties
between them could be undone if she could "work roots" of her own.
She approached the Conjure woman for supernatural assistance for re-
solving the situation. In Hurston's account, "Eulalia sat still and thought
awhile. Then she said: 'Course Ah'm uh Christian woman and don't believe in partin' no husband and wife but since she done worked roots on
him, to hold him where he don't want to be, it tain't no sin for me loose
him.'" In the end Hurston and her teacher devised a ritual that effectively
banished the man's spouse, and nuptials between him and his new para-
mour were ultimately performed.[48]

Sexual competition sometimes had tragic results that were ascribed
to harming magic. "Deah wuz somebody wut want muh huzbun tuh leab
me an go off wid um, so dey hab me fix," complained Dye Williams, an
ex-slave and a resident of Savannah, Georgia. She explained, "Whoebuh
fix me fix muh huzbun too, cuz he go off an leab me an I know he
ain nebuh done dat lessn he bin fix." Williams not only attributed the
abandonment of her husband and her own sickness to Conjure, but also
the death of a baby, and another child's fatal illness to the intentional
workings of an individual using harming practices against her. "Muh son
die wen he wuz twenty-tree. . . . Deah wuz so many women attuh him,
lots uh people tink one uh dem fix 'im, but duh doctuh say he die from
pneumonia."[49]

For some black Americans, violence followed love-and-Conjure rivalries. A late-nineteenth-century Georgia folklorist recounted a well-
known incident in which two men sought "to win the affections of a
young negress" by employing enemy conjuring specialists. After a bitter campaign of supernatural warfare with charms, spells, "cross marks
and graveyard dirt," one of the suitors found himself "fearfully muti-
lated with an axe," while the other "suffered a fearful beating with
sticks." In a later period, the folklorist Richard Dorson related a story
involving two African American women who waged a bloody knife fight
over a man but were compelled to make up following the ministrations

of a New Orleans "Two-Head" doctor. Sometimes severe emotional injury could result from the incendiary combination of supernatural harming and sexual rivalry. In a instance from Charleston, South Carolina, in 1884, a young black woman was admitted to an insane asylum for hysteria: "it was generally believed by the girl's colored friends that her insanity was caused by a 'spell,'" asserted the author, "laid on her by [a] rejected lover." The woman's belief in the power of supernatural harming necessitated her confinement and institutionalization. She was eventually cured, however, after a "Voodoo Doctor" removed the spell from her.[50]

Violent or unaccountable death was sometimes explained as the result of Conjure "fixes." The murder of an African American woman in a Savannah, Georgia, community in the 1930s led some frightened members of the local population to speculate that malign supernatural forces were involved. Their shared belief in Conjure reinforced their opinion that the woman's death was the result of harming magic. Similarly, folk beliefs provided an explanation in one community for the loss of a child. "Some time ago my son, my only chile, wuz drownded," asserted the mother, Katie McCarts. "Every time I turn roun some of my neighbuhs wuz tellin me my son's death wasn't fair. They say 'somebody hoodooed yuh child an cause him tuh git drownded.'" The issue of "fairness" raised by McCarts elucidates the explanatory power of supernatural harming beliefs. To persons who faced hopelessness and utter despair, Conjure traditions provided a framework for tragic and inexplicable events.[51]

Like witchcraft allegations in many cultures, accusations of supernatural harming in African American life reveal stress points in the fabric of social relations. Allegations of Conjure often erupted as individuals grappled for power in circumstances of finite resources and limited autonomy. Concerns for economic and social mobility, health, and safety were foremost for blacks, in slavery and freedom, and harming accusations were often allied with these issues. Conjure accusations were also directed at those who were perceived as attaining opportunities at the expense of others. These overly successful individuals may have represented a discomforting threat to tightly bonded communities in which all were expected to share their resources as they struggled for advancement. Ambition itself was not an evil, but striving for individual, selfish gain—as opposed to group uplift and communal progress—fostered the kinds of resentment that brought about supernatural harming charges. Conjure may have functioned as an internal process of social control in

African American communities where personal aspirations vied with collective interests.

White observers generally linked supernatural harming beliefs with what they considered to be the social deficiencies of black people. "Negroes are not necessarily loyal as a race," remarked Myrta Avary, a southern historian in the early 1900s. "They fear each other, dread covert acts of vengeance, and being conjured." Philip Bruce asserted that African Americans had "no compunction about inflicting injury" on each other and were "always suspicious that their enemies have turned the black art against them in the same spirit that they themselves have sought to turn that art against their enemies." Bruce, a Virginia historian, commented on African American life in the tobacco plantation regions of the Chesapeake in the 1880s. There he claimed to have found "a notable increase of quarrelling and wrangling" with an atmosphere that was "alive with anger and terror" when Conjure practitioners were about. "A neighborhood in which a trick doctor may happen to be, is sometimes thrown into a state of general turmoil by his presence," he wrote. "It then resembles a community of personal enemies whose hands strike at each other either directly, or through the medium of his supposed power." Bruce's attitude was mirrored by other white observers of black life after the turn of the century. "In the conduct of plantations, difficulty and annoyance were not infrequently experienced," wrote Charles Colcock Jones, a Georgia historian in the early 1900s, "from the interference of [the] old negro women—Conjurers,—who, in plying their secret trade, gave rise to disturbances and promoted strife and disquietude."[52]

According to some accounts, Conjure practitioners could throw entire neighborhoods into a frenzy of paranoia by their very presence. Cain Robertson, a successful Hoodoo doctor and "two-head nigger" in antebellum Georgia, was threatened with arrest if he came to town. The arrival in a South Carolina community of "a peculiar-looking genius" who had the power to "unfold the secrets of the past and present" caused many African Americans to act on their suspicions. With his powers of divination, this Conjurer apparently tapped into deeply held misgivings among domestic partners. According to one, "he improved the opportunity of telling the fortunes of several of the heads of families and their wives." "To some husbands he unfolded the infidelity of their wives, and then he, in turn, revealed to the grief-stricken wives all the mysteries of their husbands' guilty loves. The result of all this . . . was that there were few cabins . . . where peace and quiet prevailed." Citing similar disruptive influences, authorities occasionally forced Conjurers to abandon the premises. "When their work becomes known and its effect felt, for the peace of all, master as well as man," remarked one writer, "it is necessary to remove them from the place."[53]

The pervasive fear of victimization reflected people's sensitivity to potentially treacherous persons. Katie Sutton, a former slave living in Indiana, took her suspicions of supernatural harming to an extreme: "there are folks right here in this town that have the power to bewitch you," she claimed. Refusing to lend her personal goods to neighbors, Sutton explained that some individuals were able to "hax" (hex) others through borrowed items. "Evil spirits creeps around," she warned, "and evil people's always able to hax you." Like others she swept her tracks obsessively to cover her footprints, avoided having photographs taken, and pursued numerous countermeasures to divert the effects of supernatural harming. Similarly, the remarks of a former slave in Augusta, Georgia, who, having been Conjured by persons who were known to her, epitomized this suspicious outlook. "People is mean in dis world," she said, "Don't let 'em get mad wid you 'bout nothin', 'cause dere ain't nothin' too low for 'em to do to you." Black folk wisdom taught that awareness of one's enemies and the evil potential of others was vital in order to survive in the world. This "mother wit" was summarized in the pronouncements of "Ma" Stevens, a 103-year-old ex-slave in Savannah, Georgia, who acknowledged the power and pervasiveness of Conjure by noting that "folks can do yuh lots of harm."[54]

A discussion of spiritual harming would not be complete without a comment on the numerous African American beliefs surrounding witches and witchcraft. Accepted by Europeans and Africans, witchcraft beliefs were carried by black slaves and white settlers arriving in the New World. The obsession with witchcraft in colonial American has been well documented, especially in New England, where witchery was seen as a religious threat to the covenanted community of Puritan saints. The witchcraft persecutions and trials that extended over several generations in early America revealed deep fissures that divided communities along the lines of gender, class, and race, where those most likely to be suspected witches were Indians, slaves, disorderly women, or bad neighbors, and not the benign cunning persons whose skills extended to healing, captivating reluctant sexual partners, or guiding wayward ships safely home.[55]

Blacks who were believed to practice witchcraft were not usually identified in these early American prosecutions, although some Africans were
among the first to be accused. Sources do not give voice to the witchcraft fears of black people at this time. Instead, African American witchcraft beliefs were manifested in folklore, and the products of these beliefs were transmitted in oral traditions. Many of these African American
oral traditions merged with Anglo-American visions of spirits, ghosts,
and other supernatural beings.[56]

European and African-derived witchcraft traditions evolved as a dual
presence, confirming their significance to Anglo- and African American
folk beliefs. But conceptions of the witch differed dramatically for both
peoples. In the Western Christian tradition of which Anglo-Americans
were inheritors, witches were seen as disciples of the devil, and theologians viewed witchcraft practice as a form of heresy. In contrast, black
American ideas of witchcraft sprang from traditional African beliefs in
the mixed potential of good and evil. "Negroes . . . seemed not to as-
cribe any undue wickedness or malevolence to the [witches]," noted
one nineteenth-century reporter, "as they tend to think him or her gifted
with unusual capacity for either good or evil." Witches in black
American folklore were sometimes depicted as persons who were in the
service of Satan; but this devil was more deviously mischievous and
magical than absolutely evil, more of a trickster than an archenemy.
Witches (or "hags," the more frequently appearing ghosts of witches)
in black American folklore were subversive characters whose harming
actions usually revealed some hidden, didactic purpose or moral
lesson.[57]

African witchcraft beliefs intersected with black American harming
traditions in several ways. As with indigenous African beliefs, black
American ideas of witchcraft maintained strong explanatory functions.
Studies by the early-twentieth-century British anthropologist Edward
Evans-Pritchard demonstrated that witchcraft accusations were integral
to the cognitive understandings of the Azande, an East African people.
Witchcraft beliefs among the Azande, Evans-Pritchard found, were part
of a philosophical framework that made intelligible the causes of affliction in human life. For the Azande, witchcraft beliefs provided a self-
sustaining theory for understanding coincidence, as witchcraft "participated in all misfortunes," as the means by which all misfortunes were
comprehended. Witchcraft explained *why* events happened in a certain
way, and *why* harm came to one person and not another, because, according to Evans-Pritchard, witchcraft was a "causative factor in the pro-

duction of harmful phenomena . . . in particular places, at particular times, and in relation to particular events."[58]

Other academic theories have proposed that the witchcraft beliefs of traditional peoples provide an arena for the enactment of grievances, an idea that would appear to be supported in black American Conjure practices. The anthropologist Clyde Kluckhohn, researching native North American witchcraft beliefs in the early twentieth century, found that witchcraft functioned as a medium of social control in Indian cultures. The witch, he concluded, was an antisocial character who embodied danger, promoted evil, and encouraged unnatural acts—an inversion of normative behavior in the Navajo world. Kluckhohn also believed that witchcraft beliefs permitted "socially legitimate hostilities" to emerge within Navajo Indian society. "The witch," he stated, "is the person whom the ideal patterns of the culture say it is not only proper but necessary to hate." In other words, witchcraft provided an outlet for the aggressive scapegoating of persons who were hated and feared.[59]

As with the Navajo, indigenous African cultures tended to articulate conflict in witchcraft accusations. Some of these conflicts were channeled along the lines of economic competition or sexual rivalry. "The witch . . . stands for the subversive norms, the impulse to disorder," notes the Africanist Basil Davidson, "for the antimoral which supposes the moral." Whereas spiritual power ultimately derived from life-giving forces, witches and witchcraft were also perceived to be spiritually destructive, the "eaters" of life and spirit. Intrinsically harmful, the African witch represents "all that is anti-human and threatening within the general category of the Other."[60]

These beliefs intersected with African American witchcraft traditions in the expansive complex of black American conjuring practices. In some cases Conjurers and Hoodoo practitioners were also known as witches. "A witch is a cunjuh man dat somebody paid tuh tawment yuh," explained Christine Nelson, a descendent of slaves in coastal Carolina and Georgia. In many accounts the terms "witchcraft" and "conjuring" are interchangeable. "Dey's sho' hoodoos," remarked an ex-slave informant, elaborating on the harmful practices of witches, "Mos gen'ally dey rides you in de shape uv a black cat, an' rides you in de daytime too, well ez de night." Other interpretations suggest a blurred distinction between witchcraft and conjuring. "The Negro poisoner is nearly always a great Conjurer, or witch, in the estimation of the other blacks," wrote one southern historian in 1860. At the turn of the twentieth century Tom Peete

Cross, a philologist, asserted that "the means by which southern witches
. . . attain their ends are many." He explained, "They vary all the way
from incantations . . . to cheap 'conjer' or 'tricks,' the rationale of which
is difficult to determine." In the late 1800s the folklorist Mary Owen
claimed that the Voodoo practitioners she met in Missouri's border regions "invariably [spoke] of themselves as Witches, men or women, or
as Conjurers."[61]

The witch and the Conjurer possessed similar attributes. Each was believed to have the ability to harm others with lethally potent substances,
or with the malevolent exercise of spiritual power. "Witches an' root
men," stated one informant, "hab duh same magic powuh." Like many
Conjurers, a witch was an anomalous being with supernatural abilities,
such as the capacity to undergo physical metamorphosis or to become
invisible. The witch or Conjurer was described as a solitary being who
consorted with animal familiars or congregated with like practitioners
in secret associations. But the similarities between witch and Conjurer
went only so far. Unlike the Conjurer, who chose to attack his victims,
the witch had involuntary power. A Conjurer often manipulated supernatural forces using charms, roots, or other handmade articles, whereas
a practitioner of witchcraft was believed to bring about harm solely
through spiritual means or by psychic or spiritually projected powers,
without rituals or created objects. Witchcraft harming was arbitrary, but
Conjure harming was consistent with a human need for vindication or
revenge.[62]

Conceptually, African and African American witchcraft beliefs overlapped in cases where victims of witchcraft and Conjure believed themselves to be the casualties of supernatural harm. Both African-based
witchcraft beliefs and Conjure required a scapegoat—a known or unknown member of the community. Both traditions also assigned the
causes of misfortune to spiritual agents, even though human beings in-
stigated it. African Americans portrayed witches as otherworldly beings
dwelling liminally between the realm of human persons and the wilderness. Impetuous and wicked, they slipped through keyholes and windows,
mounting "nightmares," their dream horses, the unfortunate individuals whose sore muscles and tangled hair remained the sole evidence of
their victimization when they awoke. Such accounts were told and re-
told, with slight variation, among black Americans for generations.

African American witch stories, or witch tales, were distinguished by
several consistent themes. The motif of the skinless witch was one of the
most popular accounts in the slavery era and persists to the present day.

In this particular format the witch sheds her bodily covering as she embarks on her nocturnal rampage but is detected before she is able to move back into her skin. The discarded flesh has been tampered with while the witch is off engaging in mischief. In the following, most frequently recounted version of this story, the skin is addressed by the witch when it refuses to recognize its owner despite her miserable pleas:

> Once there was a woman that could turn into a witch. When the husband would go to bed, she would slip out. . . . While she was gone, the husband missed her and got up. He saw her skin lying by the fire. He got some red pepper and put it inside the skin. Then he locked the door to keep her from coming into the house that night. When she came back, she slipped through the keyhole and went to get into her skin. Everytime she went to get in, the pepper would burn her. She would say, "Skinny, skinny, don't you know me?" Then she would try again: it would burn her still. She would say, "Skinny, skinny, don't know me?" The husband woke up. She got into it, but could not stay. Then she was tarred and burnt to death.[63]

Another familiar theme is "witch-riding," the witches' practice of clambering on a sleeping human at night and riding him to exhaustion. The belief in riding also appears in European contexts with minor variations—sometimes the witches ride humans who are transformed into animals—but the human-as-mount motif in the tale has been related in black American folklore since the early 1800s. Other European witchcraft traditions such as broomstick riding, for example, are negligible in African American folktales.[64]

Among African Americans, beliefs in witches and witchcraft were accompanied by numerous practices designed to prevent the malice of the witch. Anti-witchcraft precautions and remedies became standard in black supernatural traditions. Prophylactic measures such as the scattering of salt, for example, in areas believed to be plagued by witches and ghosts were widely practiced and can be seen in the South even today. The witch, known to be a hopelessly compulsively creature, would pick up and examine any object set before her. Accordingly, persons sprinkled grains of sand and seeds or displayed sieves or newspapers with tiny printed characters—any material with minute form or detail—in order to deter the witch from her destructive ways.[65]

Witchcraft beliefs underwrote a good number of African American folk customs as well. "Jumping the broom" in celebration of slave marriages was said to protect husbands against witches. It was believed that the uncontrollable instinct of the witch to count each straw would foil her disguise as a human bride at the crucial moment. The well-known

practice of hanging an inverted horseshoe above the door in some black
and white southern households found justification in the idea that
witches would flee on viewing it, reminded that they too could be captured and shod by wary humans. Suspending empty bottles from tree
limbs drew on the idea of trapping the offending spirit of the witch within
a glass enclosure as she came and went during the night. Many anti-
witchcraft techniques may have become detached from their specific purposes, but they retained their significance as folk practices that mitigated
misfortune and bad luck.[66]

Not only were witch tales relayed as folklore within African American
communities, but witch beliefs were also recorded in the writings of some
early black autobiographers. Jacob Stroyer, an ex-slave and deacon in
the African Methodist Church, attested to the beliefs that prevailed
among blacks in his hometown in South Carolina. "The witches among
slaves were supposed to have been persons who worked with them everyday," he wrote, "and were called old hags or jack lanterns." Stroyer told
how witch beliefs were confirmed by others within the slave community.
"The Negroes," he wrote, "would gather in each other's cabins which
looked over the large openings on the plantation, and when they would
see a light at great distance and see it open and shut, they would say,
'there is an old hag.' They claimed that witches rode human beings like
horses, and that the spittle that ran on the side of the cheek when one
slept, was the bridle that the witch rode by." To Stroyer and other bondpersons, witchcraft beliefs were normative. "I held the idea that there
were such things, for I thought that the majority of the people believed
it," he wrote, "and that they ought to know more than could one man."[67]

Some accounts of witchcraft illuminate the dark dimensions of the
world of the imagination of the enslaved. William Grimes, a fugitive
bondman, recorded with frank conviction his belief that a witch occupied the very household in which he was employed. "I slept in the same
room with [the slave woman, Frankee] under the kitchen," claimed
Grimes in his autobiography. "I was convinced that this creature was a
witch, and would turn herself into almost any different shape she chose."
To Grimes, little distinguished the realm inhabited by human beings and
that of supernatural beings. To him, both were real, and both were in-
disputably dangerous.[68]

Whether viewed in historical documents or in folklore narratives, African
American witchcraft beliefs had concrete implications for the everyday

world in which blacks lived. Although the witch was as proximate as the realm of dreams and spirits, the threat of harm loomed in the next tragedy or undeserved misfortune. African American witchcraft traditions collapsed supernaturalism into folklore, and conjuring practices brought the powers of the witch into the arena of human relations and conflicts.

For many black Americans, supernatural harming practices were protective. Conjure provided individuals with the means by which to defend themselves against afflictions that were both seen and unseen. It set up a self-perpetuating cycle: causing harm and curing it. Conjure was therapeutic, but Conjure also often caused the afflictions that needed curing. But how did Conjure protect as it informed black American spirituality? We now turn to supernatural healing traditions, to deepen our understanding of how conjuring beliefs and practices operated in African American life and culture.

CHAPTER 4

"Medical Doctors Can't Do You No Good"

Conjure and African American Traditions of Healing

In the mid twentieth century the Reverend Addie Battle, pastor of the Mount Zion Holy Trinity Spiritualist Church of Cleveland, Ohio, rendered an account of her life. "I was born of farming parents on January 15, 1903, near Tuskegee, Alabama," she began. "I had three older brothers and five older sisters." Toiling in the rugged cotton fields of the Alabama black belt, Addie and her family saw few material returns from their labor. "Most of the time we had almost nothing to eat because our crops failed," she recalled, "and the man who owned the farm, he was white, would not pay papa and then we was destitute." When Addie was seven, her mother died and her siblings, older and more independent than she, left her with her father, a violent alcoholic. During this trying period she began to reflect on spiritual matters. "I guess I just had a 'natchul' calling then. I didn't know it but I was always praying."[1]

At the age of fifteen Addie became pregnant and suffered a miscarriage while she was working in the fields; at seventeen she left Alabama with an older man, whom she later married. In an anecdote that is typical of Conjure narratives by women, Addie described being "hoodooed" by her husband's "other woman" and then falling ill. She sought the as-

Facing page illustration: founder of the Church of God in Christ (Pentecostal), Bishop C. H. Mason, with "God's handiworks in nature," early twentieth century. Photo courtesy Sherry Sherrod DuPree Collection, University of Florida, Gainesville.

sistance of a Conjurer who eventually cured her. "I sent my husband a telegram and he sent for me. He was still running around. Then *he* "hoodooed" *me* so that I couldn't leave him." Then, one night, she recalled, "something" told her to look inside of his pants pocket. There she discovered the conjuring charm that she believed had captured her will. Destroying it, she was able to leave her husband. Addie made her way to a church. It was a Spiritualist congregation, a sanctuary where divine spirits and the invisible dead regularly fellowshiped with believers. "I fasted and prayed two days and on the second day I was praying . . . when the Holy Ghost came upon me and I spoke in tongues. I felt so glad and pure and clean that I just had to tell it." Thus Addie began her life anew as a preacher, prophetess, and healer. "God was really working through me," she exclaimed, "the Spirits have been working wonders through me and I'm trying to do all I can while I live."[2]

Addie Battle's oral history is a drama, with its devastating losses, its self-discoveries, and its crowning achievements. Stylistically, it is reminiscent of the Afro-Christian testimonial, as it is a story of redemption. It is also a story of healing, for at its heart it is a narrative of recovery from emotional and physical affliction. Addie's healing hinged on her belief in the efficacy of Christianity against the threat of Conjure and supernatural harming. The themes of supernaturalism, healing, and spiritual power are woven through her life like threads in a tapestry.

This chapter highlights supernatural healing beliefs and practices among black people in the United States from slavery times and after. Throughout their history, African Americans have retained distinctive ideas concerning sickness, its causes, and cures. Affliction expressed disorder in the physical body and conflict in the social body. Disease could be physiological, or it could reflect the onslaught of malign spiritual forces. As we will see, African Americans viewed healing as an integral part of the ongoing struggle of good against the evil that plagued humankind.

Using a language of invisible causes, African Americans articulated health concerns by incorporating spiritual healing practices and beliefs into their therapies. Two religious groups, the black Pentecostals and the black Spiritual churches, also promoted ritual healing, actively conjoining supernaturalism and Christian piety. With the rise of Pentecostalism in the late 1800s, and the black Spiritual churches after the turn of the twentieth century, healing became a central concern in African American religious life.

Certain parallels between the healing practices of black Conjurers and those of black Pentecostals and black Spiritualists point to common sources. Practitioners of all three traditions held similar assumptions about the body and embraced analogous visions of misfortune, conceptions of disease, and the uses of spiritual power for extraordinary cures. These traditions emerged in response to the intractability of black oppression in the United States, and all drew momentum from cultural sources that had roots in indigenous African spirituality. The task remains of examining the dynamics of these beliefs. In what ways was affliction addressed by African American spiritual traditions? To answer this question we must focus on the environments in which black supernatural healing practices developed.[3]

⚜   ⚜   ⚜

Given the harsh conditions under which most black persons lived in the United States both before and after Emancipation, it is not surprising that an emphasis on alleviating suffering emerged in African American culture. The centrality of healing in slave and postslavery narratives demonstrates the priority placed on collective responses to the diverse forms of affliction that blacks experienced. Manifested as illness, bad luck, or inexplicable misfortune, affliction was often viewed as an imbalance in the otherwise harmonious social order on which a healthy existence depended.

African American healers utilized a variety of therapies. Sources from the late nineteenth and early twentieth centuries show a convergence of spiritual beliefs, supernatural traditions, and practical techniques in black healing practices. For many blacks, the distinction between spiritual healing and other forms of healing was often blurred. In order to be successful, a healer needed to be familiar with spiritual interventions as well as conventional techniques such as herbalism and traditional "doctoring." The overlap of these approaches reveals the pragmatic strain that has characterized African American healing traditions.

Herbalism was a healing practice that evolved out of African Americans' assimilation of native African, native American, and Anglo botanical techniques. "Root and herb" systems of medicine had been preferred by bondpersons. " 'Twan't no used to send fo' a docta," recollected one former slave, " 'cause dey didn't have no medicine. My grandmother got out in de woods and got 'erbs." Some herbalists shared similar perspectives on affliction with Conjurers. Ex-bondwoman Patsy Moses recalled a "Dr. Jones," a Conjurer who first learned " 'bout de medicine w'en he wuz a slave boy in de piney woods from his ole granny" in Texas. "De

Conjure doctor, old Doctor Jones," she explained, "walk 'bout in de black coat like a preacher . . . and uses roots and such for he medicine." Many blacks found the herbal system to be superior to the medical care offered by the slave masters. "We didn't go to no doctor," claimed the ex-bondwoman Janie Hunter of South Carolina, "My daddy used to cook medicine—herbs medicine." For Mrs. Hunter, botanical cures were a sound therapeutic option in the absence of other alternatives: "All this from old people time when they hardly been any doctor. . . . Those old people . . . worked their own remedy and their own remedy came out good."[4]

After Emancipation, blacks continued to turn to traditional healers as they had done in slavery. Impoverished freedpersons usually lacked access to formally trained medical practitioners, or, when they were available, patients were unable to afford the exorbitant fees that physicians charged. By contrast the relatively low cost and easily acquired formulations of herbalists and Conjure doctors were a sound medical alternative. "People couldn't afford doctor," recollected Mrs. Hunter. "Dey only had homemade medicines," asserted a former Alabama bondperson, "and dat is unless dey got sho nuff powerful sick an den dey would to see a doctor."[5]

African Americans also had other reasons for seeking out their own healing practitioners. White doctors often treated blacks with contempt. The attitudes of many southern physicians reflected ideologies of nineteenth-century racism.[6] Blacks also tended to mistrust white physicians, who, they believed, were disinclined to sufficiently serve the needs of African American patients. These suspicions sometimes reached folkloric proportions. A newspaper report from Columbia, South Carolina, in 1889 stated that black patients in three counties were convinced that sinister practices were being carried on by a local physician:

> They claim that there is a white man, a doctor, who can make himself invisible, and who then approaches some unsuspecting darkey, and, having rendered him or her insensible with chloroform, proceeds to fill up a bucket with the victim's blood, for the purpose of making medicine. After having drained the last drop of blood from the victim, the body is dumped into some secret place where it is impossible for any person to find it.[7]

Frightening stories of physical mutilation, bodily theft, and other diabolic acts by white doctors circulated in black communities for generations after slavery. Their consistent theme—that of health authorities who deliberately harmed or experimented on unknowing patients—demonstrated the acute misgivings of African Americans toward the "white" medical establishment.[8]

Blacks also had little confidence in the invasive techniques and heroic procedures that were common in nineteenth-century medical practice, preferring the more benign treatments of root doctors and herbalists. "duh root doctuh was all we needed," explained William Newkirk, an ex-slave in Georgia, "Dey wuz bettuh dan duh doctuhs now-a-days. Deah wuzn all uh dis yuh cuttin an wen yuh sick, duh root doctuh would make some tea an gib yuh aw sumpm tuh rub wid an das all." Blacks utilized root doctors and Conjurers for their medical needs not only because there were few alternatives, but because these persons shared their perspectives on sickness, therapy, and the sources of affliction in their lives.[9]

For all their service to black communities, African American traditional healers were often scorned by whites, who derided their "quackery" and "superstitious" practices. The former bondwoman Mildred Graves, a midwife in Hanover County, Virginia, described how she was ridiculed by two white physicians when she was called to attend a difficult delivery. "Something was all wrong wid dat chile an' dey didn't know what. . . . I tell dem I could bring her 'roun', but they laugh at me an' say, 'Get back darkie, we mean business an' don' want no witch doctors or hoo-doo stuff.'" Yet, although whites generally had no respect for the effectiveness of black healers, some were impressed by the breadth of their experience. "The knowledge which some of these Conjurers possess of the properties of every herb and tree of field and forest is positively uncanny," wrote one author, at the turn of the nineteenth century. "They have a tea or ointment for every ill that flesh is heir to, and some of them would make the fortune of every dealer in patent medicines." A few white doctors derived benefits from the botanical cures and treatments of African American slaves. The famous South Carolinian physician and botanist Francis Porcher, for example, acknowledged that some of his medical discoveries were obtained from the healing knowledge of enslaved blacks. This appropriation of African-based medical knowledge by Anglo-American practitioners had historical precedents in cases that dated back to the colonial era, where black healers had been consulted by white professionals for medical assistance and doctoring expertise.[10]

Black-white healing interactions sometimes went both ways. A few

Conjure practitioners were admittedly influenced by techniques such as homeopathy, an Anglo-American sectarian healing movement that challenged the excesses of professionalized medicine in the United States in the nineteenth century. The educator Daniel Webster Davis visited the office of a popular "Voodoo doctor," as he called him, in Richmond, Virginia, in the late 1800s. He recalled the signboard, which bore "the inscription, '*j.t. shelton, h.p.;*' the h.p. being supposed to stand for homeopath." Black patients sometimes viewed Anglo-American medicine as a complex with multiple meanings. Laura Towne, a white Pennsylvania teacher who made her residence in the Sea Islands in the 1870s, was trained as a nurse, specializing in homeopathy and herbalism. The Gullah residents welcomed her medical skills but reinterpreted her healing practices with a cultural framework that was more familiar to them. Acknowledging the success of her treatment of an elderly woman for dysentery, Towne found that they believed she had "neutralized" the ailment by means of witchcraft.[11]

Although many utilized spiritual sources of knowledge in their treatment of affliction, not all African American healers were supernatural specialists. Many did not perform rituals or use charms and healing devices, as did the Conjurers. "Ole Doctor Jones," commented Patsy Moses, referring to a local practitioner, "used roots an herbs fer his medicine an' did not cast de spells like de Voodoo doctor did." Zora Neale Hurston found that a hierarchy of healing roles operated among African American workers in southeastern mining and turpentine camps in the early twentieth century. "Nearly all of the Conjure doctors practice 'roots,'" she noted, "but some of the root doctors are not Hoodoo doctors." The former, Hurston found, "make medicine only, and white and colored swarm around them claiming cures." Another popular class of healers specialized solely in herbal remedies. Homeopaths like James Still, for instance, the renowned nineteenth-century black doctor, used neither Conjure nor spiritual cures, according to his famous autobiography. Some African Americans considered the healing work of the Conjurers to be fraudulent, even as they acknowledged other traditional healing practitioners. "I don't believe in Conjurers," asserted a former slave. "because I have asked God to show me such things—if they existed. . . . I believe in root doctors because . . . we must depend upon some form of root or weed to cure the sick."[12]

Nevertheless, many African Americans saw the roles of "natural" healers and supernatural doctors as overlapping, even as they drew a distinction between natural and supernatural forms of illness. In general, healing with herbs, roots and other organic substances was implemented for common physical ailments, but supernatural healing was utilized for illnesses that were not responsive to other methods. Hurston concluded that there was little difference between the two types: " 'Roots' is the southern Negro's term for folk-doctoring by herbs and prescriptions," she observed, "and by extension, and because all Hoodoo doctors cure by roots, it may be used as a synonym for Hoodoo." Another African American writer distinguished between Conjurers and Root Doctors according to their healing and harming roles. "the way I see it, a Conjurer, they mostly jus' put it down for you, and you be sick if you step over it," she declared, "a root doctor, he jus' fix up medicines for you ... maybe in bottles, or put it in little sacks for you and things like potions or charms."[13]

The relationship of these diverse styles of healing practice is complicated by the fact that some black herb doctors were identified with the unusual attributes that were normally reserved for supernatural practitioners. Henry Lewis, a former slave living in Beaumont, Texas, acknowledged the healing abilities of his companion, Ada, noting that the unusual signs accompanying her birth were special portents. "she got a gif," he insisted. "She know kinds of herb am good for medicine for different ailments. She born with a veil over the face and am wise to dem things." A practitioner's ability to heal was often associated with his or her spiritual power.[14]

Many healers were believed to possess supernatural insight and knowledge. "They say root-doctors have power over spirits, who will tell them who does the Conjuring," declared Braziel Robinson, a slave in nineteenth-century Columbia County, Georgia, "they ginerally uses yerbs gathered on the changes of the moon, and must be got at night." Healers such as Aunt Darkas, a blind root worker in McDonough, Georgia, maintained that she was blessed by God with healing knowledge. "She always said the Lord told her what root to get," explained one of her patients, "Old Aunt Darkas said the Lord gave her power and wisdom, and she used to fast for a week at a time."[15]

Some African Americans acknowledged the supernatural sources that enabled them to perform healing works. Mrs. Emma Dupree of Fountain, North Carolina, had been known since in her youth as "that little medicine thing." Mrs. Dupree ascribed her skills with healing plants to the "power of Christ," who she believed was the source of all healing, and to the special events that accompanied her birth. Her words recall folk traditions that can identify a healer according to a supernatural lineage:

When I was born, I was the seventh one, the seventh sister. And they say
the seventh one will be over-endowed in everything. Well, I was the seventh
child. . . . And my daddy went for the doctor. . . . When he got back it had
got day just like early in the morning. They had a glow—the yard, leaves
and the house glowed—and that light stayed until 10 in the day, and it was
brighter than the sun when I was born. [My mother] says that's why I was
so different.[16]

Many healers repeated the claim that their knowledge was a spiritual
gift. "Some people calls 'em *two-headed* doctors," explained a black
woman in early-twentieth-century Washington, D.C., using a common
term for specialists who cured using natural remedies and spiritual power,
"That's because they knows two kin's o' medicine. They can see both
ways." "Two kinds of medicine" were also acknowledged by one African
American healer who considered herself "an instrument in God's hand."
"Often I have gone to work and pray for patients and seen them through
after the doctors have given them up for dead," claimed the woman, a
trained nurse. "I always take Dr. Jesus with me and put Him in front and
if there is any hope He lets me know." Many African American healing
practitioners, whether herbalists or Conjurers, considered themselves vessels through which supernatural power was channeled.[17]

Some black healers credited their skills to unseen personalities, such
as Jesus and the Holy Ghost, who guided them in dreams, visions, and
other divine revelations. "Dr. Jesus tells me what to do," explained one
woman who had been directed by the "Spirit" to seek a specific herbal
cure. A song offered by a black woman at an early-twentieth-century revival meeting, conveyed a similar sentiment:

I know Jesus am a medicine-man,
I know Jesus kin understan'
I know Jesus am a bottle uv gold
He takes jes' one bottle ter cure a sin-sick soul.[18]

Thus for many black people, the healing experience encompassed religious dimensions. Narrative accounts that relate healing to religious
conversion confirm the bond that exists in African American culture between spirituality and physical well-being. A sixty-year old ex-slave in
Georgia told how he had become "sin-sick" and remorseful over the state
of his soul, as a young man. "One day while I was very sick," he recounted, "I saw the heavens open and [a] voice said to me, 'If you are
sick, behold I am a doctor!' " After receiving his healing this man "prom-

ised to serve the Lord and try to become a Christian." Similar accounts of supernatural healing characterized the ministries of African American religious practitioners, to be discussed below.[19]

Black Americans drew from a broad selection of meanings in their interpretations of affliction. Their attitudes were sometimes strongly predestinarian. "Disease and death were unalterably fixed in the plans of Providence," observed W. S. Harrison, a white commentator on black southern life in the nineteenth century. "The Negroes rarely ever looked to imprudence or local causes to account for these things. God willed it so, and they could only submit." In the Sea Islands after the turn of the twentieth century, white teachers and missionaries were struck by the fatalistic attitudes of blacks toward physical ailments and disease. The experience of one teacher, Grace Bigelow House, on visiting an elderly black woman in the Gullah community, was not unusual. House could not see that the woman's conceptions of healing and therapy fit into a more comprehensive perspective that viewed affliction as having both human and spiritual sources:

> One of the older women . . . had an affliction which she said no "medical doctor cayn' cure." "I had dis affliction before," she said, "and I ben to Parris Island doctor and all de doctors, an' dey say it could do no good."
> "But you can tell me what the sickness is like?"
> "Hump, hump!" shaking her head, "dey is some illness come from God, and some come from man!"
> "Do you think this sickness came from God?" asked Miss House.
> "No," she whispered, "No, no! Dishyuh sickness came from man."
> "Do you think some one wished some evil on you?"
> "Yes," came back the expected answer in a whisper.

In a parallel case, when a white doctor visited smallpox-infested areas on St. Helena Island after the turn of the twentieth century, he found that some persons there were hesitant to take inoculations because they thought that such treatment would be with "going against God." He reported that African Americans there feared that the smallpox plague was divine retribution. "Fever was God's method of punishing his people," one woman explained, "and if we went against it, He would punish more!" In an article written nearly twenty years later, tuberculosis was said to be viewed by blacks in Jacksonville, Florida, as a "favorite form of punishment meted out by God for one's sins." African Americans placed great emphasis on the conduct of individuals in relation to the moral codes of a community in their consideration of probable causes of affliction. This perspective can also be seen in African Americans' assessments of epidemics and other outbreaks of pestilence as manifestations of divine judgment, the belief that individual actions could result in sickness extended to the collective community.[20]

In their characterization of disease, blacks paid particular attention to supernatural causes. This does not mean that they dismissed physical or organic etiologies in their quest for explanations for disease; it is just that their views of illness were more inclusive of external agencies. The body was the bridge that linked physical disorder and spiritual imbalance by its mediation of the two worlds. Affliction was much more than the physical symptoms that were so incisively described by victims as bodily states. It was viewed as a kind of attack by an invisible agent, motivated by human intent.

Adopting an idiom of the spirit to interpret affliction, African American healers used both conventional techniques and magical ritual to treat their patients. "There's a cure for every disease, and I can cure most anything," asserted one female healer who came of age in Reconstruction Virginia, "but you have got to talk with God and ask him to help out." The North Carolina Conjure doctor Allen Vaughn's patients received physical and psychic treatments for their ailments. The doctor, according to one patient, would "give them medicine to ease the pain, and *pull the tricks* to ease the mind." Combination remedies were often successful. Govan Littlejohn, who was emancipated from slavery as a youth during the Civil War, believed that he had been conjured when he began to have difficulties with his foot. He called the local physician for help. "He lanced my foot three times," he claimed, "but nothing but blood would come." Littlejohn suspected that the source of his ailment was the work of a jealous rival. He was healed when a herbalist administered an effective treatment. "One day an herb doctor came to see me and said he could cure my foot. He took corn meal poultices, rhubarb roots and some other things, and it wasn't long before my foot got well." His suspicions of Conjure were confirmed, however, when he found a bag of "pins, feathers and something else" buried at his front door.[21]

Govan Littlejohn's comments are indicative of the logic that underlay African American interpretations of affliction in the nineteenth and early twentieth centuries. For Littlejohn, the painful symptoms of an inflamed foot were linked to a larger complex of beliefs. Each of the stages in the healing process—the defining of the illness, its cause, and its treatment by the healing practitioner—connected to specific notions of explanation, prediction, and control of affliction. For Littlejohn, illness was not solely a matter of physical disorder. Because he believed that he was the object of another's enmity—in this case, malice conveyed through a hidden "trick"—the combined power of the charm and the evil intentions of its creator had direct consequences on his physical person. Conjure healing was therapeutic, but Conjure also caused the afflictions that necessitated treatment.

Black slaves and ex-slaves, as did their African forebears, connected physical suffering with the spiritual forces around which their lives revolved. Personal affliction was rarely attributed to chance. Rather, illness, and misfortune were seen as the outcome of malicious human actions or destructive powers. Disease had moral implications; a life-threatening illness could derive from an individual's own sinful deeds, or it might evolve from the ill will of an enemy. Unanticipated misfortune could be a consequence of witchcraft or the evil thoughts of a mean-spirited person. In the cosmology of supernatural affliction, misfortune was never random or abstract.

In order to identify the sources of affliction, some healers resorted to divination. Divination ritual was essential to the diagnostic process that began the healing process. Using clairvoyance and prediction, Conjurers were believed to be able to locate the direct sources of spiritual misfortune that had occurred, whether they were the destructive practices of another Conjurer or the deleterious effects of an enchanted object. Others used more idiosyncratic methods. The avid scratchings of a wildly feathered, "frizzled" chicken in the earth, for instance, revealed that some dangerous, unknown maleficence lay beneath the surface. Discarded grounds in an otherwise ordinary cup of tea or coffee also gave forth hidden facts. Other healing experts gazed at cups, gourds, and crystals for camouflaged signs. Others read mysteries in a deck of cards. "I remember once of being at a woman's house," wrote a correspondent in the late nineteenth century to Virginia's Hampton Institute publication, the *Southern Workman*, "and a Conjurer came there . . . and he threw his cards to the top of the room and called them out one by one until he called them all down." The practitioner told her that she needed to be saved from a "fix."[22]

Practitioners often combined techniques in order to detect harming magic, as described by Virginia Hayes Shepard, an ex-slave in Virginia. "When you sent for the Conjure doctor he always brought a pack of cards and a bottle with a live bug in it—a string tied around the neck of the bottle," declared Shepard. "He shuffles cards, you cut them, and he calls them off. All the time he is watching his bottle with the bug in it called a 'walking boy.'" According to Shepard, when the insect shifted in the underside of the bottle, the specialist was able to determine the direction in which the victim's enemy went. Another healing practitioner used the "walking boy" to uncover a charm believed to be hidden beneath the grass in someone's yard. "After he had walked over and around the yard several times," related an observer, "the "boy" fluttered and kicked as though he would come out of the bottle." A person was ordered to dig quickly in that spot, for a "trick bag" could be found. Divination with a silver dime was one of the more popular practices that was used to determine the presence of malign Conjure for blacks in the early-twentieth-century South. "A dime will turn black or blue in the presence of evil," noted an anthropologist in North Carolina. Dimes could also be boiled with potential tricks and charms, and if the dimes would "jump around" or become discolored, it was seen as a sign of maleficia. A dime placed under an individual's tongue would also reveal if that person had ingested magical poisons. These diverse, esoteric techniques for discovering the causes of affliction served to reinforce African American patients' confidence in supernatural healers.[23]

Through divination, African American healers distinguished between sicknesses that were the result of natural causes and those that involved supernatural forces. "Well, dey's some believe in cunjuh an some would don't," stated Charles Hunter, a son of slaves on St. Simons Island, Georgia. "Dey's lots would say sickness ain natchul an somebody put something down for you." The frequency with which life-threatening disease struck was, for some, a sure sign of evil magic. "Everytime somebody gets sick it ain't natchel sickness," observed a black woman in Richmond County, Georgia, in the late 1930s. "I have seed folks die with what the doctors called consumption, and yet they didn't have it. I have seed people die with heart trouble, and they didn't have it. Folks is havin' more strokes now than ever but they ain't natchel."[24]

Conjure was suspected when an ailment was chronic or unresponsive to treatment; when sickness manifested especially unusual signs and symptoms; or when illnesses were dramatic and unanticipated. Afflictions that could not be corrected by conventional medical means were often believed to have been caused by Conjure, and these necessitated special care. "They's lots of those kind of cases the ord'nary person never hear about," said the ex-slave William Adams when questioned concerning such ailments. "You hear of the cases the doctors can't understand, nor will they 'spond to treatment." "The medical doctors aint no good for nothing lak that," asserted Jasper Millegan, whose uncle had been poisoned by supernatural means, he claimed. "He nebber did get any better and he died." A former bondwoman in Yamacraw, South Carolina, argued for the effectiveness of supernatural remedies in especially stubborn cases. She believed that she had been Conjured, and ordinary medicine had failed her: "I call a regluh doctuh, but he didn seem tuh do no good." She was encouraged by the treatment that was offered by the Conjure practitioner. "three weeks ago I went tuh a root man," she stated, "I guess I soon be well."[25]

In some instances a previously sick patient would relapse under the ministrations of regular physicians. "I knew an old lady that had not been able . . . to even sit up in bed," stated a letter in the *Southern Workman* journal in 1878, "She was pronounced incurable by all the other doctors." Called at the last minute, a Conjurer restored her health. "How he managed to do it," the writer pondered, "I do not know." The administrator Alice Bacon, who collected folk beliefs from over twenty years at Hampton Institute, observed that among blacks "the surest sign that [a] disease [was] the result of a spell or trick" was that a patient would grow "worse rather than better under the treatment of regular physicians." The *Southern Workman* also printed a letter describing an old man who was "ill with palsy," who "after spending much money employing medical doctors and getting no relief," sought a Conjurer, a specialist who "found the cause of his illness." "Not many days elapsed," the account concluded, "before he was walking as well as ever." It appears that from the perspective of many African American patients, conventional medicine was inadequate because it did not consider the spectrum of possible causes in its diagnosis. "Let me tell you right here, when you done been Conjured, medical doctors can't do you no good," claimed Rosa Millegan, a daughter of slaves in Atlanta, Georgia, "you got ter get a nudder Conjur doctor ter get it off you."[26]

A range of physical afflictions were treated with conjuring methods. Pneumonia, rheumatism, and arthritis were included among the infirmities for which blacks described supernatural cures. The black novelist Charles Chesnutt observed that Conjure-related ailments among African Americans accompanied hard lives, worn bodies, and old age. "To many old people in the South . . . any unusual ache or pain is quite as likely to have been caused by some external evil influence as by natural causes," he wrote. "Tumors, sudden swellings due to inflammatory rheumatism or the bites of insects, are especially open to suspicion. Paralysis is proof positive of Conjuration." Other ailments that were sometimes believed to be caused by Conjure included anemia, boils, chills, and depression.[27]

Some illnesses manifested distinctive characteristics that were specifically associated with Conjure. Pellagra, a respiratory disease that afflicted many African Americans in the South in the nineteenth century,
was accompanied in its late stages by symptoms of dementia and insanity, which was seen as a sign of supernatural harming. Another affliction
was neuralgia, a nerve disorder that was frequently attributed to the work
of witches. Some Conjurers acted as disease specialists who treated particular disorders. The talent of one root doctor in Alabama lay in curing venereal disease. And because supernatural afflictions were usually
portrayed with specific physical symptoms, healers were called on to treat
a substantial number of the ailments that affected members of African
American communities.[28]

Persons with unusual symptoms were prime candidates for Conjure
healing. When the ex-slave Alex Johnson experienced an unbearable
burning sensation in his feet, as if there was "a fire in them," he immediately surmised that he had become a target of malign conjuring. "It
struck me in the right foot, and then in the left, but most in the right
foot," he explained, "then run over my whole body, and rested in my
head; I went home, and knew I was cunjered." Even more frequently,
African Americans described Conjure sickness as an intrusion of entities
within the body. In these narrative accounts, physical affliction is portrayed as a state in which the body becomes a living menagerie. "In 1873
I was going down the street and came across a Conjure doctor, and he
asked me where did a certain lady live, and I told him and he went there,"
related one witness, "the woman told him she had some kind of pain in
her head and side and told him something kept coming up in her throat."
The Conjure doctor discovered that she had been fixed by a cup of tea
that she had been offered. According to the witness, he gave her his own
formula, told her to drink it, and "in five minutes a scorpion came out
of her mouth." Nathaniel John Lewis of Tin City, Georgia, was another
witness to such a bodily intrusion. "My wife Hattie had a spell put on
her for three long years with a nest of rattlesnakes inside her," he insisted.
"She just lay there and swelled and suffered." Another story was related
to Hurston in 1928 by Rachel Silas, of Sanford, Florida. "Ah seen uh
'oman wid uh gopher in her belly," she asserted. "You could see 'm movin'
'round in her. And once every day he'd turn hisself clear over and then
you could hear her hollerin' for more'n a mile. Dat hard shell would be
cuttin' her insides." Such descriptions, related in grim detail, graphically
conveyed the powerlessness and agony of Conjured victims.[29]

Accounts of reptiles and small animals circulating throughout the internal system are peculiar to African American sickness narratives. George Little, a root doctor in Brownsville, Georgia, described the deadly consequences of this kind of Conjure attack. "Frawgs an lizuds and sech tings is injected intuh people's bodies an duh people den fall ill an sometime die," he maintained. Usually, these stories were relayed with the firm conviction of their veracity. "since I came to talk with such good old Christians who I known would not tell a lie," declared one unidentified writer in a letter to the *Southern Workman,* "they told me they have seen ground puppies jump out of folks feet, and lizards and snakes." Another account described a man that had been made sick by another's malicious "work:" "Everytime they tried to give him soup or anything to eat, something would come crawling up in his throat and choke him," stated one onlooker. "This fortuneteller said it was a turtle in his throat." After the man died, it was explained that the "turtle come up in his throat and choked him to death," although most around him believed that the *cause* of his suffering was the deadly, malevolent power of Conjure.[30]

Since the Conjurer was a diagnostician and healer, he or she was able to relieve afflicted persons by removing the invading creatures and determining the precise origins of the malady, thereby treating the symptoms and their source. Some of their techniques were intense and dramatic. In 1919 a folklorist in Virginia reported that he had seen a black Conjure doctor use a cow horn to treat his patient, a device that closely resembled the cupping and blood-letting instruments of practitioners in traditional Africa and premodern Europe. Summoned to attend a desperately ill woman, the Conjurer "pricked the back of the woman's neck, drew blood, and put his cupping horn to it," according to the account. "He took it off, and dropped out of it a young snake and a lizard. 'From dishyere on you gwine to be a well woman,' he said. And she was." Another specialist who was paid to treat a sick patient "took out of her right arm a spool of thread, and out of her leg a lizard," stated a letter in the *Southern Workman.* "This is the truth, what I saw with my own eyes," the correspondent professed. Chesnutt told of a man who had been poisoned when a lizard had entered his system. "This lizard, according to the 'doctor,' would start from the man's shoulder and pass down the side of the body to the leg," he wrote. "When it reached the calf of the leg the lizard's head would appear right under the skin. After it had been perceptible for three days the lizard was to be cut out with a razor, or the man would die." Having no other explanation for the story, Chesnutt turned to evidence from his observations of the natural world. He guessed that the tradition of bodily intrusions may have "derived its existence

from the fact that certain tropical insects sometimes lay their eggs beneath the skins of animals, or even of men, from which it is difficult to
expel them until the larvae are hatched." He concluded that blacks drew
these ideas from their observations of subcutaneously burrowing insects
and parasites.[31]

The usual species of animal invaders in Conjure accounts included reptiles, turtles, spiders, scorpions, frogs, groundpuppies (salamanders),
worms, and snails—all creatures associated with mud, water, or slime.
Whether the aftermath of poisoning, where the creatures were believed
to be introduced by way of ingestion, or just as often the result of a
charmed object somewhere in the proximity of the victim, complaints of
bodily invasion were always accompanied by great physical suffering.
Their presence—beneath the skin, infiltrating the cavities, spilling
throughout the body without restraint, overwhelmingly present in the
body but very clearly not of the body—conveys the image of a human
container. The narratives suggest porosity of the inner person.[32]

The traditional cultural association between lower animals and pollution indicates that African Americans might have interpreted some afflictions as a moral sign. Descriptions of creatures whose presence engendered an unclean inner self may explain the regular identification of
the animal invaders as serpents or crawling, serpentlike reptiles. The subsequent release of the creatures could denote an individual's freedom from
corruption, or sin. When the Georgia ex-slave Ellen Dorsey called a specialist "to wawd off conjuh" in her legs, the practitioner who treated her
described "a big black snake" that slithered out of her foot. As the snake
retreated the Conjurer remarked, "Deah goes duh devil," and Dorsey
later recovered. Sarah Handy noted that one doctor's treatment included
the burning of "various vile-smelling powders" in a patient's room, followed by his opening a window "to let the devil out." The devil was incarnated in the form of a snake, an archetypal symbol for evil in the biblical tradition.[33]

These accounts offer numerous possibilities for understanding physical affliction among African Americans. Some patients and practitioners balanced multiple ideas in order to interpret the causes of sickness
and misfortune in their lives. A late-nineteenth-century ex-slave narrative shows how individuals might propose a variety of reasons for their
victimization. In this case, an African American woman explained the
causes of her sudden onset of blindness by positing divine judgment, her
own immorality, and evil Conjurers, as potential sources. Her story, like
most other Conjure narratives, begins with an account of her relation-

ships with other persons and provides evidence of the social nature of supernatural harming:

> a man and he wife and I was workin' as woodchoppers on de Santa Fe route up Beaumont to Tyler County. After us git up and I starts 'way, I . . . hear somethin' say, "Rose, you done somethin you ain't ought." I say, "No, Lawd, no." Den de voice say, "Somethin gwine happen to you," and de next mornin I's blind as de bat and I aint hever seed since. . . . Some try tell me snow or sweat or smoke de reason. Dat aint de reason. Dey a old, old, slewfooted somethin' from Louisiana and dey say he de Conjure man, one dem old hoodoo niggers. He git mad at me de last plum-ripenin' time and he make up powdered rattlesnake dust and pass dat through my hair and I sho' ain't seed no more.[34]

As victims so often did, the narrator made sense of her affliction by looking at others within her immediate environment as possible perpetrators. Conjure harming, as we have seen, was a vehicle of conflict, and hence bodily infirmities originated at the site of human intention, where fear, greed, and anger pitted person against person and ensnared victims in a cycle of pain and suspicion.

Turning from the multifaceted complex of Conjure beliefs to explicitly religious understandings of affliction and healing, we find similar ideas with no clear provenance. Some blacks may have reconfigured healing beliefs and practices to fit within the framework of institutionalized Christianity. Not only does it appear that some black Christians reinterpreted the older Conjure healing traditions, but the corresponding experiences of many religious healers and Conjure practitioners suggests that they drew from a common cultural vernacular.

One of the most significant events in American religious history at the end of the nineteenth century was the formation of the Holiness-Pentecostal movement. The modern Holiness movement had roots in the perfectionist strands of Wesleyan Methodism, which taught that a life of complete righteousness, called sanctification, was available to the believing Christian through a "second work of grace" by the indwelling Holy Spirit. Sanctification began with the conversion and justification of the individual and continued as a process in which the Christian was empowered in a baptism of the Spirit that allowed him to live a devout, sin-free life. Holiness practitioners believed that sanctification was achieved by God's grace, although they differed in their ideas of what the human role in this process would be. Various doctrinal views concerning the attainment of sanctification developed in the mid-1800s and were complemented by the establishment of a number of new churches that embodied various wings of the Holiness movement.[35]

Although the movement became increasingly middle-class in its orientation after the turn of the twentieth century, African Americans of the poor and working classes were some of its most active early participants. The attraction of blacks to the Holiness tradition, it has been argued, had to do with its espousal of values that harked back to traditions and forms of worship that had been disavowed by upwardly mobile freedpersons after Emancipation. Holiness churches represented a "conservative counterweight" to Christian liberalism, for Holiness practitioners sought to keep alive the "old-time religion" that seemed in danger of dying out. African American Holiness churchgoers revived the spirited practices of the slave church, including its inspired preaching and song, its shouts, ecstatic devotionals, and visionary experiences. In their pursuit of a folk primitivism, blacks in the Holiness movement rekindled the embers and traditions of a religious culture that belonged to the past, which had been abandoned by many mainstream African American Protestant churches.[36]

The blossoming of the African American Holiness movement initiated, in part, an institutionalization of the folk traditions of the former slaves. Pentecostalism, which emerged as its outgrowth, also expressed strong affinities with some ex-slave traditions. Two of the pioneers of Pentecostalism, William J. Seymour, a black preacher from Texas with Afro-Baptist roots, and Charles F. Parham, a white Methodist evangelist hailing from Topeka, Kansas, had carried forth the old-time practices and biblically fundamentalist beliefs of their forebears. Yet their particular innovations regarding the sanctification doctrine marked a departure that ultimately was to shape the course of modern Christianity. Both Seymour and Parham insisted that the sanctification experience should be accompanied by a manifest sign of the baptism of the Holy Spirit, glossolalia, or speaking in tongues. They began to popularize this "third blessing" of the gift of tongues. While Parham is credited with having introduced the practice in his bible school as a "formally stated doctrine," it was Seymour who is considered responsible for its institutionalization in the public revival that inaugurated the Pentecostal movement at the Azusa Street Mission in Los Angeles, California, in 1906.[37]

Divine healing became a cornerstone of Pentecostal theology. The conviction that physical healing, along with unknown tongues and other gifts of the Holy Spirit such as prophecy and miraculous signs and wonders, existed in the present-day church stemmed from the Pentecostals' emphasis on biblical authority. For Pentecostals, physical affliction ran counter to God's will for the faithful Christian. In this tradition, cause of all disease was sin, which had originated with the fall of humanity. Underlying the Pentecostal faith healing doctrine was the establishment of a "healing contract" with God, in which the health of the believer was linked to a biblical promise that was accomplished through Christ's redeeming work of atonement. Thus encapsulated within the Pentecostal healing process was the entire experience of repentance, conversion, salvation, sanctification, and baptism by the Holy Spirit. As Seymour wrote in a publication from the Azusa Street revival, "Thank God, we have a living Christ among us to heal our diseases. . . . We that are the messengers of this precious atonement ought to preach all of it, justification, sanctification, healing, the baptism with the Holy Ghost, and signs following." Faith healing, which vied against tongues and Holy Spirit baptism for preeminence in the early stages of Pentecostal revivalism, emerged as the dominant focus of the movement by the mid twentieth century.[38]

Early African American Pentecostal traditions show similarities with many of the supernatural traditions that were prevalent among the slaves and their descendants. Pentecostal belief revolved around invisible forces, beings, and powers in the spiritual realm, and like the Conjure practitioners, Pentecostalists viewed unusual events as signs of divine or satanic intervention in the physical realm. In a sermon, for example, entitled "Storms—Storms—Storms," Charles Harrison Mason, founder of the largest black Pentecostal denomination, described some of the miraculous activities that he attributed to "God's strange work:"

> in His strange act He put a woman in a well and the water felt as cotton under her feet, then in His strange way lifted her out, unhurt. . . . It is said in one home a lady had lately installed a new gas range but God came and swept it out of the house and set a coal stove in its place. Was that not one of God's strange acts? . . . In a little town . . . where there was so much race hatred, I am told that a sign bearing these words was raised, "Negroes, read and run." God performed another one of His strange acts. The town was completely destroyed.[39]

Healing testimonials by black Pentecostals described similar acts of supernatural intervention. "He reveals to me the revelation of his mysteries," wrote C. S. Reese of Memphis, in the Church of God in Christ magazine. "He gives me power to cast out devils, to lay hands on the sick, and they recover." Other Pentecostal testimonies emphasized visionary experiences and acts of supernatural healing. "I saw a man standing near my bedside, who said to me, 'you have a very bad stomach and you will have to have an operation,'" stated one account. "Then suddenly the man disappeared. I then turned to the Lord and began to pray." After praying for "ten days," claimed the writer, "God truly healed me of my infirmities." Reports of Pentecostal faith healing highlighted its supernatural dimensions. "Some of the miracles which God performed in healing," wrote Mason, were "the extraction of the jawbone of a woman who came to the meeting in Memphis, Tennessee, a few years ago. . . . Another who was suffering with toothache came up. . . . The tooth came out of her mouth and she showed it to all who were present." Such accounts resonate with the African American conjuring narratives of supernatural healing by slaves and ex-slaves.[40]

Pentecostals employed techniques such as prayer, the "laying on" of hands, and anointing with oil, as prescribed in the Bible, for healing. These practices may have revalidated older African American beliefs in the efficacy of special material objects as sources of supernatural power. Blessed cloths and handkerchiefs, for example, popular with both black and white evangelists in the early twentieth century, were standard accoutrements in African American Pentecostal healing services. A notice in *The Whole Truth* magazine, the newspaper of the Church of God in Christ, illustrates the currency of these traditions among black American Pentecostals in the early twentieth century. "Sister Larry of Columbus, Mississippi, writes . . . that God has so wonderfully healed her son through the prayers of Elder Mason and others. He was very sick with appendicitis. She wrote to Lexington to Elder Mason to send her an anointed cloth, which he did send, and today her son is at work." Another testimonial, published more than twenty years later, related an account with a similar emphasis on the efficacy of certain materials for healing. "My little granddaughter was totally blind. . . . I told Elder Samuel to pray for her. He sent an anointed cloth. I put it on her eyes and her sight came back. Glory!" Articles of spiritual potency, cloths and handkerchiefs embodied divine grace. "My heart rejoiced and the power of God came upon me as I applied the cloth to my breast," read one account, "I could feel the affected part being drawn, and when I applied the second cloth it completely left. I have not felt the hurting any more. I thank the Lord for being healed."[41]

"Casting out" various ailments from the bodies of the sick was another practice that was widely utilized in the ministries of Pentecostal faith healers. Elder Lucy Smith, a preacher in depression-era Chicago, told how she once rebuked the "death demon" of a woman who was "past talking or seeing." The performance of this "work of deliverance," as such spiritual traditions came to be known, strongly resembled the ritual gestures of Conjurers, who made a common practice of extracting afflictions in the form of small animals or objects from their patients. Similarly, Pentecostal healers claimed power over diseases that they literally delivered from the bodies of the sick, which were sometimes manifested in visible malevolent tumors or growths.[42]

Some Pentecostal healers personified the anomalous traits of supernatural practitioners. Bishop Mason, for example, was said to have been endowed with visions and remarkable gifts at an early age. During his ministry he had demonstrated such talents as "spiritual" writing and singing, and had once levitated, according to his own account. Mason owned a collection of unusually formed objects including roots, branches, and vegetables that he consulted as "sources for spiritual revelations," revisiting the tradition of conjuring charms. Mason would illustrate his sermons by referring to these "earthly signs" and "freaks of nature," as he called them. "When scriptural texts seem to fail and audiences seem to tire of the monotony of sermons," wrote C. G. Brown, a secretary of the Church of God in Christ in the early twentieth century, "the Spirit directs Elder Mason's mind to a sign. As he turns it over and from side to side, God's mystery comes out of it." Mason delivered divine interpretations while meditating on misshapen tree limbs, stones, or the entrails of chickens. "It appears that he is reading one of the recesses of the object from which he is preaching," commented Brown.[43]

The accent on magic-as-miracle figured in the practices of other popular healing practitioners who were influenced by the Pentecostal tradition, such as Charles Manuel Grace, the African American sect leader who attained prominence in the 1930s as "Sweet Daddy Grace." Grace, a former member of the Church of God in Christ, tapped a potent vein in black supernatural culture by infusing Christian practices with biblical magic. Grace attained a loyal following by promising salvation, good fortune, and physical wholeness to his devotees. A stream of enthusiastic letters in his *Grace Magazine* attested to the spontaneous healings that resulted from his touch, the sound of his voice, or meditation on his portrait. Bishop Grace's followers also used the *Grace Magazine* as a charm: chewed and swallowed, its pages remedied internal ailments and diseases of the vital organs; made into a poultice or bandage, they rehabilitated fractures and wounds. A patch of "Grace healing cloth," tucked away or worn about the neck like a Hoodoo bag, provided special blessings and supernatural protection. A marketplace of Grace products, including soap, lotion, toothpaste, coffee, writing paper and other accessories, brought the supernatural into the everyday lives of persons whose physical and spiritual needs were experienced as a single condition. As one testimonial exclaimed, "there is healing power in the Grace Magazine and the products is [sic] my doctor. I use them for medicine, and I be healed both soul and body. Thank God for that, and for Daddy Grace, for he is the cause of it all."[44]

Paralleling the Conjure doctors, religious leaders such as Mason and Grace established their approaches to healing within the cultural worlds of their patients. As religious practitioners, they affirmed and acknowledged the divine sources of their power. And in Indianola, Mississippi, the anthropologist Hortense Powdermaker located several sectarian preachers who were known as "Voodoo doctors," including a "Reverend D.," who likewise claimed that his power came from God and that his ability to heal was "learned by listening to the 'old folks'" as a young man. "In addition to curing illness, he gives advice and aid in any sort of predicament," wrote Powdermaker, "instructing people how to act and giving them a charm to insure success." Reverend D.'s clients included women seeking mates, businessmen involved in lawsuits, and others who sought to retrieve stolen property, attain money, or locate sources of livelihood. "His practice and his religion are firmly interwoven," concluded Powdermaker, "so that each is reinforced by the other." Like the slave Conjurers, Reverend D. helped alleviate physical afflictions while addressing the salient conflicts in his clients' lives.[45]

Other African American healing practitioners such as Madam Truth, a professed "fortune-teller and clairvoyant" and member of the early-twentieth-century Holy Sanctified Church of Sandfly, Georgia, combined religious piety with supernatural artistry. Madame Truth identified the causes of clients' afflictions that came about from conflicts over money, work, and the interpersonal relationships. "I advise on business and love affairs," she maintained. "Deah's a remedy fuh ebry trouble and I hab dat remedy, fuh a spirit hab brung it to me." Madam Truth's healing practices extended to social and emotional distress as well as physical disorders that were perceived to possess spiritual origins.[46]

Even as they offered a variety of possibilities for addressing affliction within an individual's life, black sectarian healers, Pentecostalists, and Conjurers all shared fundamental beliefs concerning the underlying sources of affliction. To African American Pentecostal Christians, disease was a manifestation of God's judgment, or evidence of a demonic spiritual assault upon the body. Immoral behaviors such as fault-finding, jealousy, and criticism were conceived as forms of sin and deemed responsible for bodily afflictions as well. Pentecostalists understood healing as an exorcism of evil spirits. In some cases, the healer would speak directly to an offensive entity, rebuking and commanding the presence to withdraw from the body of the afflicted. Similarly, in the Conjure healing tradition, practitioners placed liability on spiritual powers that had operated through the actions of malign practitioners and spiteful persons. Affliction originated in relationships. Furthermore, like the Pentecostal healers, Conjure specialists emphasized the supernatural dimensions of affliction and their own authority over the powers that had brought about sickness and disease.

Even as the spiritual and physical worlds converged in the human condition in these traditions, the supernatural beliefs themselves overlapped and intersected in the lives of the afflicted. Thus victims of untreatable ailments might seek out both for treatment. Conceived as ministry in black churches and as therapy by conjuring specialists, African American healing traditions reinforced the belief in supernatural power and the ability of certain individuals to draw on invisible forces to restore wholeness.

One significant theological difference separated Afro-Christian religious healers from supernatural practitioners like the Conjurers. Pentecostals claimed that God was the vehicle of all miracles and wonders, and all curing rituals were conducted in His name and legitimated by their understanding of sacred Scripture. The nature of the source of spiritual power in Conjure was more ambiguous. Some Conjurers claimed that the origins of their abilities were divine, and others believed that spiritual force emanated from the objects and charms that they had themselves created. Still others were less forthcoming on the origin of their powers. Finally, although black Pentecostalists' supernatural beliefs exhibited significant similarities with those of practitioners in the conjuring tradition, acknowledged practitioners of Conjure were rarely accepted in the Pentecostal churches. Conjure was viewed by many churchgoers as something evil and negative—a danger to be opposed and subdued with a stronger, Christian "magic."

A more explicit adoption of supernaturalism in a religious context occurred within the black Spiritual churches, a network of congregations that emerged within cities in the United States after the turn of the twentieth century. Its earliest officially chartered congregation was the Eternal Life Spiritualist Church, founded in 1913 in Chicago. The city was a veritable mecca for thousands of blacks who left the South between 1914 and 1918, and subsequently between 1939 and 1945, during what became known as the Great Migration. Fleeing labor exploitation, a devastated agricultural economy, and Jim Crow segregation, masses of black southerners poured into Chicago and other northern cities, filling a demand for cheap labor in northern industries. Concurrent with the rising tide of urbanization developed an increasingly diverse religious situation, as African Americans founded and joined Baptist and Methodist congregations, Holiness churches, Muslim temples, Judaic sects, and a host of fraternal and nationalistic associations. The rise of the Spiritual churches fit into a larger pattern of spiritual pluralism that characterized black American religious life in the first quarter of the twentieth century.[47]

The early Spiritual churches have been aptly described as urban "wayside shrines" where persons in black communities sought guidance on a variety of secular and spiritual matters. Many of these churches were actually private venues that offered personal consultations for individuals in need of employment, protection, or healing. Spiritualist advisors sometimes doubled as pastors, forming new congregational bodies with their regular clients. In this manner many new storefront churches were organized around Spiritual ministers.[48]

The decentralized structure of the Spiritual church movement permitted considerable eclecticism in the groups' theology and practices. Although the churches shared a common origin, Spiritual tradition varied from congregation to congregation. The emphasis on church autonomy might have fostered religious syncretism. In New Orleans, for example, home of some of the first Spiritual churches in the country, church practices were shaped by unique regional influences. Even as most Spiritual churches developed as singular entities—with a few mushrooming into national prominence—the culturally distinctive congregations in New Orleans in the first quarter of the twentieth century bore only a slight resemblance to their counterparts in other areas of the United States.[49]

In the New Orleans Spiritual tradition, the integration of Christianity and supernaturalism was openly acknowledged. The churches drew from a variety of cultural and religious sources, including Roman Catholicism, Caribbean *vodou*, Italian American folk tradition, and African American Conjure and Hoodoo. Regarding the New Orleans churches, Hurston wrote in 1932 that "in addition to herbs, reptiles, and insects, [they] make use of the altar, the candles, the incense, the holy water, and blessed water of the Catholic church—that being the dominant religion of the city and state." Another reporter observed of these churches that while they publicly disavowed Conjure and Hoodoo, most of the Spiritual ministers in New Orleans maintained practices that were virtually identical to those traditions. "All present day Mothers [Spiritual church leaders] deny they practice Voodoo, and many of them don't," claimed Robert Tallant, a local writer. "However, others use many of the oils and powders and sell a mild sort of *gris-gris*." Outside New Orleans, in cities like Chicago, Detroit, and Harlem, the supernatural orientation of the black Spiritual religion was also well known. "The attraction of the Spiritualists was their straight-forward utilitarian use of religion," asserts one source, "Magical objects in the form of charms or amulets were used to guard against any possible evil or attain some cherished good."[50]

Despite its highlighting of the supernatural, Spiritual worship was virtually indistinguishable from that of black Pentecostals and Holiness practitioners. Like African American churchgoers in these traditions, Spiritualists participated in expressive singing, jubilant dancing, shouting, and glossolalia. A hallmark of black Spiritual liturgy was possession by the Holy Ghost, an activity demonstrating the dynamic influence of Protestant revivalism. Furthermore, like their Pentecostal counterparts, black Spiritualists incorporated prayer, the laying on of hands, and anointing with oil into their healing services. A primary difference between the Spiritualists and other Afro-Christian churches concerned the emphasis that the former placed on human mediation with the diverse forces of the spiritual world. In the black Spiritual tradition, a pivotal event was the believer's interaction with divinities, sacred entities, persons who had "passed on," Roman Catholic saints, or other powerful beings. While some Spiritual churches instituted public ceremonies for "calling up" the spirits, such rituals more frequently occurred in the context of private séances or in personal sessions with Spiritualist mediums (also known as prophets, divine healers, and advisors) outside regular church services.[51]

The emphasis on supernaturalism in the Spiritual churches can also be seen in particular practices. While retaining the liturgical trappings of Christianity, black Spiritualists put a distinctive accent on devotional spaces, objects, and rituals that facilitated the invocation of "Spirit." Spiritual sanctuaries and altars were filled with statues of saints, photographs of Spiritual forebears and leaders, colored candles, and tall vases with colorful bouquets. Using techniques such as prayer and bibliomancy (guidance through biblical revelation), Spiritualist practitioners addressed clients' concerns. Some Spiritualists embellished older conjuring techniques by utilizing the dramatic visual impact of miraculous healings. For instance, according to witnesses, Mother Catherine Seals, a legendary Spiritual leader in the early twentieth century, removed a black cat, a wasp's nest, and an assortment of other rustic creatures from the bodies of afflicted patients at her church in New Orleans.[52]

African American Spiritualists also stimulated the advent of an active public economy of store-bought supernatural merchandise. Spiritualists and their clients traded and sold amulets, accumulated charms, and created talismans in order to fend off evil forces and ensure the presence of positive spiritual forces. The most popular items of Spiritual practitioners were used sanctify impure environments. Hans Baer, an anthropologist who researched the black Spiritualist movement in the 1970s and 1980s, observed that a profusion of commercial goods that guaranteed prosperity, wealth, and other extravagant promises was bought by believers. "Sprays, incenses, baths, floor washes, perfume oils, special soaps, powders, roots and herbs" were trade items for Spiritualist practitioners. "It was not uncommon," Baer found, "to see 'jinx removing' candles or 'Dr. Japo' anointing oil used in Spiritual churches." The ritual procurements utilized in Spiritual ceremonies were often the same as those obtained in the occult drugstores and religious markets frequented by Conjure practitioners.[53]

A concern for healing was prominent in the ministries of Spiritualist leaders from the beginning of the movement. Like Conjure practitioners, black Spiritual practitioners treated affliction in the context of the conditions that shaped the lives of members of their congregations. In Nashville, Tennessee, where the state's first Spiritual church was established in 1924, narratives by African American practitioners testified of the web of relations that bound family members, neighbors, and acquaintances in sickness and health. These ties encompassed the living and the dead. One man, a seventy-year-old member of the church, told how his mother, his brother, and his spouse, all deceased, frequently visited him and expressed great concern for his well-being. "My wife comes to comfort me," he claimed, "in the spirit, so often . . . she told me to check up on myself in some of the things I was doing. She said, 'you ain't going right, now watch your step, now you must go straight.'" Another woman, an embattled wife in a lover's triangle, spoke of the healing power of a Spiritual minister who cured her of "madness" when she was "hoodooed" by her adulterous husband and his mistress. The minister, she claimed, "had power above. She had a strong power to heal," she professed, "I just . . . thank God that He enabled me to get myself back to be myself from that way they *fixed* me." Another congregant commended a Spiritual medium for helping her after a series of "unlucky" accidents caused her to become sick. "I was nothing but a shell," she declared, "I went up there to [the medium] and she told me to fast and pray on Monday for my health and fast and pray on Wednesday for my strength. . . . She sure has helped me a lot. I tell you I came out." Spiritual churchgoers attested to recovery from ailments that ranged from alcoholism and substance abuse, to crippling disabilities and handicaps. Spiritual beliefs, they acknowledged, had provided an effective system for healing their afflictions.[54]

One of the most important services that Spiritual practitioners provided for clients and congregation members was psychotherapeutic. Their treatment emphasized the active role of the individual in overcoming the inner, self-inflicted obstacles that could hinder one's progression to good health. The faith that believers placed in Spiritual ministers allowed persons to take charge of their own afflictions, and by extension, to take charge of conflicts that had occurred within their lives as well. Spiritualist healers offered valuable counsel to African American men and women whose control over their own environment—often tainted by racism and discrimination, economic inequalities, and damaged interpersonal relations—was uncertain or precarious. By providing remedies and spiritual "work," Spiritualists bolstered individuals' beliefs in their ability to care for themselves. "I tell the people what the spirit directs and they go back to work out their problems," asserted a medium in the Nashville church during the depression era. "So many of them worry about jobs now and that's the thing I try to advise in some way. But you see people must live right and clean to get God's full blessing." A Spiritual minister in Chicago offered similar insights into the relationship between her congregants' afflictions and the quality of their lives. "People around here are very insecure," she claimed. There is nothing so upsetting as fear of losing your job. A lot of people are troubled and nervous, and I'm here to help them. . . . What I do is advise people what to do to better themselves." An ethic of responsibility informed Spiritualists' approaches to healing. Coupled with the emphasis on supernatural empowerment, black Spiritual healing traditions offered a multifaceted approach to affliction in the human condition.[55]

Correlations with other supernatural traditions are rarely acknowledged by ministers in the present-day black Spiritual churches. Like the

Pentecostals, Spiritualists are adamant in denying the similarities between themselves and the Conjure practitioners. In fact, the negative linkage of Conjure and malign supernaturalism has caused wary black Spiritualists to publicly repudiate such practices in connection with their own beliefs. Nevertheless, such a connection may exist; in the early twentieth century, Zora Neale Hurston noted that several Spiritual congregations in the South were "stolen" by Hoodoo doctors who later became ministers. She found what she called "a strong aroma of hoodoo" hovering about the churches that she visited. Still most black Spiritualists continue to view Conjure as contrary to their sacred intentions. "if you believe in Hoodoo, don't come in here," warned one Spiritual minister in Nashville, "If you got dimes in your stocking or bags about your necks, take 'em out of here, *we don't deal in that.*" Others corroborated a genealogical relationship to Conjure, although with some qualifications. "Some branches of the [Spiritual] church are under the influence of Voodoo, or Hoodoo, as some call it," claimed Elder B. S. Johnson, an archbishop in one of the New Orleans churches, "but . . . all my works come directly out of the Bible." Despite a continued emphasis on supernatural healing, séances, charms, divination readings, and spiritual advising, black Spiritualists eluded public disapproval of their tradition by adopting many of the standard worship practices in black Protestant revival churches.[56]

Black Spiritualists established churches that integrated supernaturalism into their practice and theology. Like the Pentecostals and like the Conjurers, Spiritualists utilized spiritual power for healing. Spiritualists and Conjurers alike explained the presence of disease and misfortune as products of both supernatural agents and social actors, acknowledging the human potential for evil and the intransigence of the invisible forces that battered body and soul. Connecting both of these traditions was their promotion of physical well-being through invocation of the supernatural. Supernatural therapy brought resolution in the physical and spiritual arenas and further allowed for the prevention of future afflictions. Through healing, Conjure and spiritualism intersected with the social and cultural forces that shaped black Americans' lives.[57]

As a spiritual practice, Conjure was woven into the fabric of black life. Yet it also inevitably entered the public sphere and colored the sensibilities and convictions of others. As it became more visible in the United States, Conjure took on varied, complex meanings in American culture, meanings that practitioners embraced and questioned. After slavery, and well beyond, as African American supernaturalism revitalized older practices, new traditions emerged. Art, music, and literature, as we will see in the following chapter, were widely influenced by the ferment of African American supernatural traditions that began in slavery. The dramatic urbanization of African American life, and attempts to repress Conjure, would have a powerful impact on these beliefs and practices. We turn then to the rise and fall of Conjure and its transformations in the African American cultural experience.

CHAPTER 5

"We All Believed in Hoodoo"

Conjure and Black American Cultural Traditions

Early in the twentieth century the composer Scott Joplin completed *Treemonisha,* the first folk opera by an African American. Produced in 1915, *Treemonisha* was an original musical whose dramatic plot featured seven characters: Remus, the noble hero; Zodzetrick, Simon, and Luddud, evil Conjurers; Ned and his wife, Monisha, parents of Treemonisha; and the young heroine herself. The events took place on an Arkansas plantation in 1884. In his preface to the opera, Joplin provided the background.

> There were several Negro families living on the plantation. . . . All of the Negroes but Ned and his wife Monisha, were superstitious, and believed in conjuring. . . . One morning in the middle of September, 1866, Monisha found a baby under a tree that grew in front of her cabin. . . . Monisha took the baby into the cabin, and Ned and she adopted it as their own. . . . Monisha, at first, gave the child her own name; but when the child was three years old she was so fond of playing under the tree where she was found that Monisha gave her the name of Tree-Monisha.

Struggling to support themselves, Treemonisha's parents offered the only assets they possessed in exchange for the education of their daughter—their labor. It was a sacrifice that would have significant ramifications. "When Treemonisha was seven years old Monisha arranged with a white family that she would do their washing and ironing and Ned

---

Facing page illustration: a newspaper advertisement for a popular blues Race record with a conjuring theme. *Chicago Defender,* November 12, 1927.

would chop their wood if the lady of the house would give Treemonisha an education, the school house being too far away for the child to attend. The lady consented and as a result Treemonisha was the only educated person in the neighborhood."

As time went by, Treemonisha grew into adulthood and decided to become a teacher. Then three "very old men," Zodzetrick, Luddud and Simon, appeared. They were the local Conjurers, unscrupulous, deceitful magicians who went about peddling "little luck-bags and rabbits' feet" to members of the community and "confirming the people in their superstition." One day Treemonisha chastised them for their exploitation of the townspeople. Vengeful, they kidnapped her and were about to do her harm when Remus appeared, overcame them, and freed Treemonisha. Triumphantly she returned home, and as the town gathered to celebrate her arrival, the people pleaded for her help by raising a chorus of song:

> We ought to have a leader in our neighborhood,
> An energetic leader to follow for our good,
> The ignorant too long have ruled, I don't know why they should,
> And all the people they have fooled, because they found they could.
> Lead us, lead us, and we will surely rise.
> You must lead for you are wise, and we will surely rise.[1]

Scott Joplin's narrative exposes many of the critical concerns of his African American contemporaries. Enduring the scourges of poverty and marginalization, blacks urgently sought opportunities for education and representative leadership. But what conveyed Joplin's bleak assessment of African American culture was the three crude and shameless Conjurers, who epitomized the slave tradition. For Joplin, Conjure was the most conspicuous symbol of the moral impoverishment and backwardness of black people. His contempt for supernatural traditions was shared by other African Americans who aspired to racial advancement. Thus, even as it integrated African American experiences into musical theater, *Treemonisha* frankly depicted the rival forces that engaged—and divided—many black Americans as well.

This chapter explores some of the public impressions of Conjure in the decades between Emancipation and the first half of the twentieth century. After slavery, black supernatural traditions acquired vastly different meanings as they were exposed to forces of change both within and outside their communities of origin. In the 1870s, clergy and educators working among the former slaves in the South attacked conjuring practices. Ostensibly committed to the improvement of freedpersons' lives after the Civil War, these cultural reformers, including blacks and whites from the northern states, called for the repudiation of Conjure and other slave traditions, identifying them with degradation, ignorance, and the demoralizing experience of bondage. But at the end of the century other voices would begin to speak of these same practices and beliefs in more favorable terms. To scholars in the emerging disciplines of anthropology and ethnology, Conjure embodied peculiar mystical traits, an unrefined spirituality, a racial and religious sensibility. African American super-natural traditions contained the essence of the primitive vision, a per-spective believed to be at the heart of the religious beliefs of many of the descendants of Africans living in the United States. Conjure later emerged as a powerful trope in popular culture, representing the exotic but dan-gerous "black magic" of literature and music, including stage produc-tions like *Treemonisha*.

These complex, changing perceptions of conjuring traditions registered slowly and unevenly through the general public. Ideas of African American magic and supernaturalism often followed the lines of social stratification. In the decades after *Treemonisha* was written, conjuring themes were explored by artists, poets, novelists, and musicians as a source of creative inspiration. Concurrently, masses of black Americans moved out of the South in the largest population relocation to take place in the United States. Migrants who flocked into urban centers encoun-tered supernatural practices both familiar and unfamiliar to them. In the cities, Conjure was exploited as a commercially viable and marketable product for blacks, and whites as well.

The transformation of Conjure had special consequences for the de-scendants of Africans. As vernacular expressions of slave culture, magic and supernaturalism reflected the rhythms of black spirituality in par-ticular times and places. When African Americans moved out of slavery and into the social order that freedom offered, they carried their spiri-tual traditions with them. Supernatural beliefs and practices readily in-fused new spaces and places. They were ultimately present in almost every geographical location in which African Americans settled.

Emancipation represented the initial period of transition, for it helped disperse conjuring practices. It brought "educational, occupational and spatial mobility," writes the historian Lawrence Levine. "Underlying all the changes there persisted crucial residues of traditional culture which helped shape expression in every sphere" of the African American ex-perience. Acculturation may have offered possibilities for mobility, but it was slavery that determined the content of the freedpersons' cultural heritage. Slavery culture and slave religion governed African Americans' understanding of the past and shaped their perceptions of the future. Post-Emancipation black culture, with all of its promise and potential, was yet a culture inherited from bondage.[2]

The first generation of freedpersons confronted the perspectives of another world. Some would eschew the styles of conduct they associated with the past, with enslavement. For others, the realignment of values and interests did not entail a wholesale rejection of the older traditions. As a standard of the older ways, Conjure would persist in black life for years beyond Emancipation. And in time, alternative traditions and styles of supernaturalism, magic, and spirituality would take root.

We turn first to Reconstruction in the South, where the "Negro problem" was formulated in terms of African American initiative. The theme of self-help emerged as a practical and ideological strategy by which blacks could achieve racial advancement. Improvement of character, it was believed, would present a strong collective challenge to white perceptions of black inferiority. Thus it was with great ambivalence that African Americans in all walks of life scrutinized the world of their former bondage. As Robert Russa Moton, a student at a freedmen's college and a member of the advancing generation of sons and daughters of the slaves, observed, "The conditions under which we live . . . have created in the race an anxiety and an earnest desire that every effort the Negro puts forth shall be of the best." Undergoing acculturation into a realm of new possibilities, African Americans viewed the future as self-conscious observers as well as participants in the fashioning of their own destinies.[3]

Between the years 1861 and 1875, a great mass of black and white administrators, schoolteachers, and clergy swept into the South, spearheading a vigorous campaign that was directed toward the former slaves. Sponsored by a powerful coalition of religious and secular associations spanning some nineteen states, members of the largest northern benevolent agencies—including the American Missionary Association, the Freedmen's Aid Society, and the American Baptist Home Missionary Society of New England—took part in this redemptive venture. Bound by the tenets of abolitionism and Christian evangelicalism, the Freedmen's Aid Movement provided for the relief, medical care, and supervision of the scores of refugees and freedpersons whose uncertain political and economic status, they believed, presented a potential threat to regional stability. Within a short time, however, the goals of religious uplift had replaced the priorities of material relief. To accomplish the herculean task of spiritual instruction and proselytism, more than one thousand schoolteachers and missionaries were dispatched to the southern states. The cultural welfare of the freed slaves had become the main thrust of missionary efforts in what has been viewed as the "neo-Puritanization" of the South.[4]

When African Americans were declared an emancipated people, their "invisible" traditions—the practices, beliefs, and values of the slave quarters—were detached and analyzed apart from the insular world that fostered them. As whites were exposed to the customs and habits of the freedpersons, many reacted to what they perceived as the moral and intellectual deficiencies of blacks. In the religious arena, clergy attacked the indecorous, enthusiastic styles of worship that were common in many southern black churches. Teachers and administrators assailed spiritual practices like Conjure as evil and irrational superstitions. The ex-slaves' traditions became part of the contested terrain on which missionaries, clergy, and educators waged a struggle for cultural preeminence.[5]

Missionaries and teachers were determined to impose acceptable standards of behavior on the former slaves. "The very temples of the South must be cleansed of their filthiness," demanded a white minister in Beaufort, North Carolina. "The superstitions of heathenism have little less force here, than in the heart of Africa." In 1874 Alexander Weddell, a missionary in Petersburg, Virginia, dispatched a panicky missive to the Protestant Episcopal organ *Spirit of Missions,* claiming, "I desire to raise no false alarm, but I assure you that the religious life of the southern negro is lapsing into the grossest superstition." Attempting to divert funding from overseas missions to the reformers' projects in the United States, Weddell and others presented a grim picture of the religious world in which black Americans lived.[6]

In their spiritual practices, freedpersons exhibited a variety of actions and behaviors. Other than conjuring practices, worship ceremonials such as the ring shout were prominent. The shout was widely reported on and routinely denounced by observers in the South. "I never saw anything so savage," wrote the schoolteacher Laura Towne, referring to the circular, ecstatic dance that she had observed among blacks of the coastal regions of South Carolina. Another missionary, noting the persistence of the shout among Sea Islands blacks, called it a "fetish dance, doubtless the relic of some African rite." The African American educator Charlotte Forten declared the shouting ritual to be a "barbarous" remnant of

African paganism. Teachers and missionaries took great pains to suppress these and other slave practices, going so far as to attempt to ban the freedpersons' exuberant praise meetings. "Many of those old churchgoers still cling to their heathenish habits," wrote Emma B. Eveleth, in Florida. "We speak against it in the school and bible class and we can see the effect of our teaching."[7]

What especially troubled the missionaries was the lack of a "practical" dimension to black religion. Some found their worst expectations confirmed as they witnessed the high-spirited expressions of the freedpersons' religion. "The great mass of the colored people are deplorably ignorant, often sadly immoral, and in their manner of religious worship, wild and extravagant, often mistaking mere animal excitement for true religious emotion and joy," remarked one New England pastor after returning from a visit in the South in 1867. Others bemoaned the day-to-day disruptions that accompanied black spirituality. One Port Royal, South Carolina, schoolmistress was "at her wit's end" when several of her students disappeared unexpectedly for a "seekin'" ceremony, the visionary ritual of passage from justification to conversion in Gullah religion. To many whites, black spirituality was at best distasteful or defective, a product of slave immorality, and at its worst, an outgrowth of African idolatry and heathenism, the result of forces that the elevating power of Christianity had failed to check.[8]

For many white southerners, whose disposition toward African American traditions vacillated between derision and contempt, the practices of the former slaves were familiar. Still, many showed surprise that independence had brought such a powerful sense of religious autonomy to blacks, as was evidenced in their hasty and conspicuous departure from most biracial southern churches. As they wrested control of their own places of worship or withdrew from racially segregated congregations, African Americans publicly acknowledged aspects of their spiritual lives that had been concealed within the confines of bondage. White southerners viewed the independence of the ex-slaves with apprehension and repeatedly voiced their concerns. James Sparkman, a slaveowner in South Carolina, was "astounded" that former slaves, many of whom had been indoctrinated with Christian teachings by white plantation ministers, quickly backslid "into Fetishism and voodooism" when freedom came. Some whites attributed the excesses of black religious zeal to a lack of supervision. "With freedom, the negro, en masse, relapsed promptly into the voodooism of Africa," noted a chronicler in Virginia. "Emotional extravaganzas, which for the sake of his health and sanity, if for nothing else, had been held in check by his owners, were indulged without restraint." The Episcopalian rector Alexander Glennie was genuinely bewildered by the hasty egress of former slaves in his Waccamaw, South Carolina, congregation. "Strange to say," remarked one of his parishioners, "after the Civil War, no negroes listened to his preaching, but would shout and sing after their own fashion, and surround themselves with their old African superstitions." The new spiritual liberty that freedpersons enjoyed had delivered a mortal blow to heretofore uncontested white authority.[9]

Many ex-slaves rejected practices and beliefs that they believed had little meaning to their own experiences. One African American Baptist preacher in Mississippi made this position clear when he declared that whites' religion could provide "a mighty good God for white folks, but de dark poperlation hab no use for such as he." Similarly, a former bondwoman by the name of Aunt Fanny reacted to the criticisms of a plantation mistress after black worshipers performed a healing ritual around her sickbed, rejoining, "Honey, that kind of religion suits us black folks better than your kind. What suits Mars Charles mind, don't suit mine." Others insisted, as had many of their slave forebears, that the dogma taught by whites had no place in the Bible. After the Civil War, when the businessman Charles Stearns attempted to offer spiritual tutelage to the freedpersons on his Georgia plantation, he was surprised that most were indifferent or averse to the lessons he drew from the Scriptures. On questioning them he determined that their lack of interest was attributable to the fact that most of them considered the Bible to be "a slaveholding document" and refused, said he, to "believe in its divinity." Stearns concluded that the blacks had "a religion of their own," as he put it, "which, ignoring Jesus and the Bible," was founded on "their own experience," the witness of the Spirit of God, and "various visions and revelations."[10]

Throughout the South, the freedpersons' teachers were surprised at the tenacity of the former slaves with respect to maintaining their religious and cultural traditions. "Not only do their old habits cling to the freedmen as they rise," wrote one, "but their ignorance will betray them into new and perilous mistakes. We look for slow progress and much disappointment." Another teacher confessed, "I felt that my endeavors to instruct them in the plain and simple duties of a Christian life . . . were altogether vain and futile. The idea seemed to be inherent with them, that the duty of Christians consists primarily in boisterous prayers and weird singing and shouting." Others appeared to have greater confidence that the evangelical undertakings of the missionaries would prevail. "The custom which has been the most trouble to us, is that of 'getting happy,' " noted an educator in South Carolina, "when they have their meetings at private houses, that, I hear, is still the most important feature. Still I am not hopeless . . . but believe they will abandon the foolish custom." Nonetheless many of the ex-slaves continued to explore such traditions privately and in all-black gatherings.[11]

The attempt to honor tradition was at the heart of the freedpersons' desire to maintain many slave practices. Older, entrenched notions of spiritual authority presented a special challenge to the reforming clergy. "The old heathen churches still bear sway, and hinder the moral progress of the race," wrote C. L. Woodworth, a Congregationalist instructor. "Their preachers, ignorant, and many of them vicious, still have a mighty hold upon the race." According to a Baptist missionary in Augusta, Georgia, "The colored people are most devotedly attached to leaders, pastors, and others. The word of their leaders is law, is *everything!* They have almost unbounded influence over their people." Another witness claimed that African American ministers and their congregations were far too tolerant of supernatural beliefs. "I attribute the strength of [the freedpersons'] superstition to their ignorance," he wrote, "and also to the exclusion of negroes from the religious services of white people." He went even further to make an explicit link between practices such as Conjure and the persistence of other black religious traditions:

> Most of their preachers in this region are nearly as ignorant and superstitious as their flocks, and as the church represents all their ideas of public meeting, and their whole social system turns upon it, they talk freely at their religious gatherings of "tricking" and "conjuring" and tell marvelous tales of the power of those endowed with supernatural gifts.[12]

Black teachers and clergy could be equally harsh in expressing their dissatisfaction with the spiritual practices of the former slaves. In 1874 W. A. L. Campbell, a minister at the African American Congregational church in Macon, Georgia, wrote prior to his dismissal that he had become disillusioned with the conduct and "semifetishism" of members of his congregation. "I won't go to the colored churches," remarked one freedwoman, "for I'm only disgusted with bad grammar and worse pronunciation, and their horrible absurdities." Writing from Charleston, South Carolina, the African American educator Thomas Cardozo protested that he "could not worship intelligently with the colored people." Controversies over education and the licensing requirements for illiterate African American preachers in southern churches eventually hardened into bitter denominational disputes. Such conflicts between black elites and uneducated ex-slave preachers reflected deeply held prejudices against the former bondpersons' ways of life that would divide African Americans along the lines of class and caste long after the turn of the century.[13]

Black reformers, many of whom had assimilated the bourgeois values of their white counterparts, were determined to do away with what they viewed as the chronic manifestations of slave superstition. "I fear it may continue to do evil to the cause of the civilization of the Negro in the South," wrote one African American college graduate. In Hudsonville, South Carolina, "a colored man" among black freedpersons during Reconstruction opined, "Let us hope that a brighter day is dawning for the deluded souls in the Sunny South, when intelligence and reason shall prevail, and ignorance shall be dispelled. Then all these superstitious beliefs will be banished." Some African Americans believed that the rejection of Conjure practices and the overall improvement of literacy for black people were related. "Education . . . has thrown the ban of disrepute upon witchcraft and conjuration," wrote Charles Chesnutt. And the black female author Octavia Rogers Albert used an anecdote in her best-selling treatise on slavery, *The House of Bondage,* to condemn magical beliefs. Appropriating the voice of her Christian narrator, Albert admonished her readers: "Yes, the vice of voudouism which is practiced among the colored people is the result of ignorance and slavery. They will, in the course of time, ignore such doctrine, for they are being educated, and the time will come when such simple and nonsensical teachings will find no place among them." To many of these observers, conjuring traditions harked back to anachronistic beliefs that had been carried over from bondage. These cultural reformers hoped that the rites and revels of the slave past would give way to more proper expressions of religious faith.[14]

Implicit in the defamation of Conjure as heathenism was its identification with indigenous African religions, which African American supernaturalism had sustained for more than a century. Octave Thanet, an Anglo-American collector of Negro folktales, articulated this view: "Conjurers are a feature of African life," he wrote, "they probably represent the survival of the old fetich worship, brought from Africa." "It may be worthwhile to mention an old custom of Southern Negroes," stated the folklorist Louis Pendleton, referring to the persistence of Conjure practices in the latter nineteenth century, "the origin perhaps may be traced to the fetichism or worship of guardian spirits dwelling in inanimate objects of their African ancestors." African American writers such as Daniel Webster Davis, a prominent intellectual from Virginia, shared their opinion of Conjure as barbarous—the antithesis of all that the new generation of uplifted black Americans were striving for. Davis called the Conjure practices of southern blacks "a relic, no doubt, of barbarism brought from their native African home." [15]

Concerning African American supernatural practices, members of both races reserved their most uncharitable remarks for the "pagan rites" and demonstrations of "Voodooism" that they witnessed during their sojourn in the southern states. In a letter to the Hampton Institute's *Southern Workman,* one reader detailed the widespread practice of "Conjuring" and "tricks" among freedpersons as one of the "horrible features" of African American life. "It is not only the vile who practice this misdemeanor and believe in the same," he wrote, "but I believe it is safe to say that at least *three fourths* of the mass of Negroes have a tendency to believe in it. . . . It is said to be so common and popular that it is practiced not only by the people of the church, but even that their leaders are often known as Conjure doctors." In Florida, the freedmen's school superintendent C. Thurston Chase, outraged at the number of unqualified black instructors in his state, concluded that most of them "belong[ed] to that class of persons known as 'medicine men' " who were believed "to hold mighty incantations for the benefit of their patients over the 'hind leg of a frog.' " Similar comments made their way into the letters of reformers, the newspapers, and popular literature. To many freedpersons, however, the offense that others took in supernatural practices was of little consequences. Some of the ex-slaves, in fact, appeared to delight in the trepidation that Conjure caused among outsiders. "Some white school teachers from up North came to teach de chillen," declared a former Texas slave, "us have good times tellin' [them] 'bout black magic and de Conjure . . . de teacher from de North don't know what to think of all dat." [16]

The lines of the cultural battle between the reformers and the ex-slaves were most sharply drawn at the freedmen's colleges. These schools had been established by benevolent agencies, missionary associations, and church denominations during the post–Civil War years. One exemplary institution, the Hampton Normal and Agricultural Institute, in Hampton, Virginia, was founded in 1868 for the training of educators. At Hampton, racial betterment was woven into the institutional fiber. Religious and moral training, as well as technical and trade instruction, was emphasized in the curriculum. By inculcating black students with new standards of character, white educators believed that the freedpersons' sons and daughters would become alienated from their own roots and be forced to make a break with the slave background. Administrators at Hampton hoped to propagate a new system of accommodative education for African Americans in the South that would redirect the culture and consciousness of the African American masses.[17] It was therefore fitting that Hampton, one of the most prominent of the new black colleges in the south, would seize on the symbol of Conjure in its attempt to reorient African Americans and their cultural traditions.[18]

Hampton's founder, the former Union general Samuel Chapman Armstrong, tirelessly promoted this mandate. Slave culture, Armstrong believed, was the dual product of social and environmental forces. Having worked among the freedpersons, Armstrong had determined that many of the traditions that blacks adhered to represented a general lack of character, the result of isolation from enlightening cultural influences. Like the other missionaries, he attributed the social condition of most African Americans to a deficiency in their cultural development, rather than innate racial attributes. Blacks, Armstrong argued, were in "the early stages of civilization . . . their moral development could take centuries, as it had for whites." He and his contemporaries strongly believed that the aim and purpose of freedpersons' education was to impart character through the cultivation of responsibility, hard work and "common sense." With this commission, members of the Hampton administration instituted a system that they hoped would reshape the beliefs and behavior of the ex-slaves and their children.[19]

In 1878 Armstrong sent out a circular letter to friends, interested parties, and subscribers of the school's newspaper, the *Southern Workman*, stating his intent to focus on the "curious prevalence of superstition among the colored people of the south." Armstrong requested eyewitness accounts of folk beliefs among blacks, and in particular, descriptions of root doctors and Conjurers. His aim in gathering this material was to "drag [supernatural practices] into the light where they [would] show for what they really are." The son of missionaries who had lived in the Hawaiian Islands, Armstrong was negatively predisposed toward the spiritual activities of non-Christian peoples and drew parallels between his youthful observations of the Sandwich Islanders and the practices of *kahuna* (a traditional Hawaiian system of magic) and the activities of the African American Conjurers. Believing that the continued viability of a society was linked to that society's moral evolution, he concluded that like the South Pacific natives, blacks in the southern United States were jeopardizing their own survival by their continued acceptance of the supernatural traditions. For Armstrong the "growth of superstition as rank and as fatal" as that exhibited by the Pacific islanders was a sure sign of the moral degeneracy and decay of the indigenous population, as it would be for black American ex-slaves in the South.[20]

When he discovered from the letters that supernatural traditions were promoted by some of the students at Hampton, Armstrong posted a notice in the school newspaper that strongly condemned these practices. Armstrong and his colleagues were vitally concerned with what the reports revealed regarding the strength of Conjure and Hoodoo among the "less enlightened" students at Hampton. In his rebuttal, Armstrong singled out one student who had readily admitted his own belief in Conjure:

> It will be noticed that the writer . . . a member of the Junior class—does not hesitate to avow himself a believer in conjuration. Two years more in the school will change his ideas, it is to be hoped. Yet nothing is harder to eradicate from the mind than early-acquired superstition, and there is little doubt that many who are less frank in its acknowledgement are by no means free from it.[21]

Samuel Armstrong was aware that black students and teachers met with Conjure "everywhere as an obstacle to their work," and although they were "newly emancipated themselves from its dominion," had sometimes found its influence to be "too much for them." Under his scrutiny he hoped that Hamptonites would disavow such ideas and develop a deeply critical outlook toward black folk magic.[22]

The collecting of conjuring stories and tales became part of an academic movement for some students and teachers at Hampton. In 1893 Hampton established the first African American folklore society in the country. The society was made up of black students and white staff and administrators who had an interest in connecting "the Negro's African and American past with his present." Under Hampton's new president, Horace Frissell, the Hampton Folklore Society continued with the program of collecting and discussing Conjure lore that had begun during Armstrong's tenure. Frissell, however, encouraged folklore collecting because he believed that certain traditions represented the particular gift of the black race to the world. He noted that Hampton did "not want to make white men of the Indians and Negroes" but did want to "help them rise to the best that is in them." His concern was that the slave culture of blacks, in particular the legacy of the spirituals, was in danger of being discarded. "The children of the emancipated slaves were generally taught to forget all that reminded them of the long years of race bondage," Frissell warned, "and the more enlightened of their children are only just awakening to the fact that in forgetting those old spirituals, or religious songs, they are allowing a priceless inheritance to slip away from them." Within a generation or two, elements of the ex-slaves' culture had been elevated from despised symbols to the cherished tokens of a quaint people.[23]

A number of practical concerns occupied Hampton Folklore Society members. Most were African American educators who were motivated by the cause of social and cultural improvement of black people.[24] Alice Bacon, who was also the director of a training hospital for student nurses, invited folklore society students to interview African American patients and write down their beliefs and traditions that had to do with health, supernatural healing practices, and medicinal Hoodoo lore. Bacon hoped that her students would be sympathetic to the patients who ascribed to magical ideas but critical of the beliefs that they relied on for health care. It was well known to faculty and administrators that members of the local African American community were suspicious of conventional medicine, and many were reluctant to seek hospital treatment. Some of the students who were also members of the Hampton Folklore Society used their contacts with black patients at the hospital not only to collect and contribute to the folklore society's work but also to ease the feelings of intimidation that these patients may have felt in utilizing the hospital as a medical facility. Bacon and the students ultimately trusted that their understanding of folk beliefs would be helpful in aiding the locals in overcoming their "backwardness" with regard to their dependence on Conjure. Bacon was convinced that these relationships could be achieved only by the most motivated African American students. "The work cannot be done by white people, much as many of them would enjoy the opportunity of doing it," she stated, "but must be done by the intelligent and educated colored people who are at work all through the South among the more ignorant of their own race, teaching, preaching, practicing medicine, carrying on business of any kind that brings them into close contact with the simple, old-time ways of their own people."[25]

The experience of the members of the Hampton Folklore Society reveals how the scrutiny of African American conjuring traditions had developed into a source of interest to both black and white Americans. The historian Donald Waters has explored the motivations for Hampton's preoccupation with folk beliefs, an apparently exotic topic of study for students and faculty at a southern freedmen's college in the last quarter of the nineteenth century. Debates over the cognitive capacities of blacks engaged white intellectuals and scientists during this time, and it is likely that some of these ideas intersected with the educational strategies that were being promoted at Hampton and similar institutions. Hamptonites studied folklore because they believed it was a important indicator for gauging the moral progress of African Americans. For them, folk beliefs became a major criterion by which to measure "the mental condition of the masses of [blacks] and the kind of work that is to be done if they are to be raised to civilization or even saved from extinction," in the words of Hampton Institute's founder. Folklore was also a practical discipline with which black students were taught to critique the culture that they were being taught to deny. According to Waters, Hampton Folklore Society members

> associated folklore in general with the ignorant ways of illiterate black folk, and regarded expressions of oral tradition not as instruments of proper education but instead, as "obstacles" to it. . . . They expressed a critical interest in black folklore only to emphasize the pervasive folly of rural blacks, and by contrast, their own wise and discriminating intelligence as educators. In so doing, they joined the growing ranks of an educated, upwardly mobile black middle class whose members behaved so fastidiously that in their collective attempt to create a respectable identity they wanted little to do with the heritage of their people.[26]

The concerns of the Hampton Folklore society reflected the rising interest in black American folk culture that gained momentum in the United States and Europe at the end of the nineteenth century. Officers in Hampton's folklore society initiated contacts with members of the American Folklore Society, a national organization devoted to folklore collection and preservation. The Hampton students were invited to present their research at professional congresses and academic meetings of folklore scholars. By the end of the nineteenth century, the *Southern Workman* had become one of the most important journals for the dissemination of African American folklore, regularly courting distinguished commentators such as Thomas Wentworth Higginson and George Washington Cable, and black notables like Alexander Crummell, T. Thomas Fortune, and Anna Julia Cooper for their remarks and commentary.[27]

The attention given to black folk culture in the United States from the 1890s through the first four decades of the 1900s was stimulated by the work of ethnologists who were active at this time. A new publication,

the *Journal of American Folklore,* became a sounding board for scholarly work on the cultures of primitive "folk" worldwide. The editors of
the journal, William Wells Newell and Franz Boas, were responsible for
cultivating the interest of an entire generation in African American folklore. Boas in particular believed that the study of folklore could be used
to assist blacks in their efforts at social advancement. A former physi-
cist-turned-ethnologist who had been committed to socialist ideals in his
native Germany, Boas's progressive notions of ethnicity and class led him
to the academic investigation of culture. Boas hoped that anthropology
could be useful to society, and hence he sought to contribute to the resolution of racial problems through scientific investigation. He believed
that folklore was a reference point for understanding cultural diffusion,
the unique ways that different races contributed to the development of
civilization. Using folklore studies as a vehicle, Boas hoped that it would
be possible to augment African American racial pride by the study and
interpretation of traditions from the past.[28]

Boas was also responsible for the cultivation of a new generation of
intellectuals who developed scholarship on black American folklore and
examined the cultural relationships between African and New World
Negro societies. During his career, the impact that Boas had on noted
anthropologists such as Elsie Clews Parsons, Melville Herskovits, Zora
Neale Hurston, and Arthur Huff Fauset was considerable; under his tutelage, they would transform the study of African American folk traditions.
Furthermore, partly because of his influence, several southern chapters
of the American Folklore Society were established. Throughout their lives
both Boas and Newell remained enthusiastic in their support of the
Hampton Folklore Society, and Newell gave an address at the society's
inaugural meeting and provided funding and lecture time at professional
conferences for Bacon and her students.

Hoping to elevate Conjure to a viable subject of academic inquiry
among black and white intellectuals, Bacon observed that for African
Americans "the time seems not far distant when they shall have cast off
their past entirely, and stand as an anomaly among civilized races, as a
people having no distinct traditions, beliefs or ideas from which a history of their growth may be traced." Bacon had found it difficult to
gather materials on "any peculiar beliefs or habits" among blacks because they tended to be "looked down upon as all bad, and to be forgotten as quickly as possible" by some black Americans. She expressed
concern that these valuable "relics of the past" would soon be unsal-
vageable. In a late issue of the *Southern Workman,* she wrote, "In the

first opportunity that has come to the colored people of outgrowing their past of ignorance, slavery, and savagery, it is natural that a reaction should occur against even the history of the past; and it is more than possible that in a generation or two those bits of folk-lore peculiar to the negro may be lost entirely, unless caught now by those so situated as to be able to gather them up." Many other academics in the late nineteenth century bemoaned the decline of folk beliefs and defended their preservation. Newbell Niles Puckett, a white sociologist who began to collect Conjure lore for his graduate thesis in the early 1900s, complained that shame, self-consciousness, and a new racial pride among African Americans were responsible for the lapse in many of the old traditions. "How much better it would be," he speculated, "if those who are ashamed of their folk heritage could but realize the truth that folk-beliefs and superstitions are *normal* stages of development through which *all* peoples have passed."[29]

Thus, with the passage of time an entire spectrum of opinions on the worth of African American supernatural traditions had emerged. By the late 1800s representations of Conjure had shifted, from its initial identification as cultural refuse, to its rise among intellectuals as an important artifact. And, as the arenas of art and entertainment appropriated black folk traditions, they found an even wider audience. African American supernaturalism would become a commercial product in a developing marketplace of ideas and spiritual merchandise, available to all.

The greater public impact of black folk traditions in the United States was perhaps first seen in a profusion of stories written in what was considered the "authentic" language of African American southerners at the end of the nineteenth century. Among the most popular of these was a collection of animal parables and fables that the white writer Joel Chandler Harris introduced in a magazine series. His *Uncle Remus* stories helped pave the way for a new vogue in American literature that included anecdotes and sketches of Negro life in dialect form. The establishment of this genre of storytelling resignified the worth of African American "folk" as literary subjects. In part a response to the impending crisis of the conflicted social order in the South, this new plantation literature privileged a nostalgic view of race relations. Recalling the days of white benevolence and domination, many southern writers rendered their representations of African American life against a cultural backdrop of superstition and religious primitivism. Colorful but condescending representations of the black southern "folk" would become embedded in southern literature.[30]

Accounts of African American magic, Conjure, and Hoodoo were common in the works of fiction authors in the late nineteenth century. Writers who employed the "plantation genre" often included stories and vignettes featuring Conjurers and supernatural practitioners. The novelist George Washington Cable, for example, explored the interstices of Creole society and voodoo in New Orleans in his popular 1880 work, *The Grandissimes*. And Chesnutt, who pursued supernatural themes in his 1899 collection, *The Conjure Woman*, used magical spirituality as a source of elderly wisdom and humor. Other writers drew on conjuring stories to explore aspects of African American identity. Some folklore collectors combined supernatural tales and ethnology in their published works, like Mary Owen, who wrote *Ole Rabbit, the Voodoo and Other Sorcerers* and *Voodoo Tales,* causing "a sensation" at the 1893 International Folklore Congress with her genuine Conjure stories. In their use of conjuring accounts, both black and white authors made African American supernaturalism available to a new generation of readers.[31]

At the very time that conjuring was repackaged and reinterpreted for public consumption, the world out of which such traditions emerged underwent a dramatic transformation. Spirituals, for example, went through several stages of stylistic modification between the end of the nineteenth century and the early decades of the twentieth. No longer possessing the power and meaning they once had, the spirituals were "altered, supplemented, and replaced" as new types of black American sacred music developed. The white schoolteacher Elizabeth Kilham commented on this shift in 1870, attributing it to the intellectual progress that had been attained by blacks. "The distinctive features of negro hymnology are gradually disappearing," she noted, "and with another generation will probably be obliterated entirely. The cause for this, lies in the education of the younger people." A 1875 report in the *New York Times* supported Kilham's observations: "as the Negroes are emancipated and become educated," it stated, "they are dropping this old music which belongs to the days of slavery . . . unless they are preserved in type, these sweet melodies are destined to entirely pass away." Diverse witnesses would note a decline in performed spirituals and a general reluctance on the part of blacks to publicly display their sacred music. Popular demand for African American spiritual songs and melodies, however, underwent a resurgence in the early twentieth century.[32]

Religiously based festivals that had been widely observed among the former slaves also declined. John Kunering, also known as John Canoe or John Conny, a popular African-based masking parade that was celebrated by blacks in North Carolina, Virginia, and other parts of the South, was denounced as an inappropriate practice and all but disappeared from local seasonal calendars. Similarly, the ring shout—although it had endured for generations as a cherished ritual—was ultimately displaced from the center of black liturgical life. James Weldon Johnson recalled that when he was a youth in the 1880s, the ring shout was considered "a very questionable form of worship" that was "distinctly frowned upon by a great many colored people." Johnson noted that the "semi-barbaric" practices were already in decline owing to pressures from members of the community who discouraged their practice. "The more educated ministers and members, as far as they were able to brave the primitive element in the churches," he observed, were among those who "placed a ban on the 'ring shout.'"[33]

And yet, despite the concerted efforts of black and white educators and missionaries, African American conjuring practices endured. A possible but unintended result of the efforts of the cultural reformers may have been the assimilation of Conjure and other supernatural beliefs into black Christian traditions, as we have seen. Elsewhere, African American supernatural practices were driven underground or perpetuated by defiant practitioners—but never entirely abandoned.[34]

Ironically, unlike the spirituals, which regained currency as a source of black musical genius in the early twentieth century, Conjure kept its links to black slave religion—seen as a rural, superstitious spirituality—and resurfaced with special force within northern urban areas like Harlem, Chicago, and Detroit. With the onset of the Great Migration and the subsequent arrival of millions of black Americans into northern cities, these traditions underwent a metamorphosis, exploding with a new and broadened appeal that added to the distinctiveness of the metropolis.

By the second decade of the twentieth century almost 5 percent of the black American population had moved into urban areas. The first significant relocations began during the Reconstruction era, when freedpersons from the southern countryside settled within city districts, in search of employment and security within more densely populated localities. Until about 1890 most of these migrations were gradual and included southwestward and intrastate movements. In cities like Birmingham and Atlanta, the influx of African Americans climbed steadily to the turn of the century. It was not until the first decades of the 1900s that the oppressive cycle of tenant farming, exploitation, disfranchisement, and devastating natural mishaps forced masses of black workers northward, where the promise of higher wages and the prospects for better opportunities beckoned the sons and daughters of slaves to new lives.[35]

Between 1915 and 1919 the northern cities became home and haven to nearly five hundred thousand transplanted African Americans migrants. Roughly one million more followed in intermittent waves throughout the 1920s. Looking back at this world, the novelist Richard Wright envisioned what lay before these sojourners as they "headed for the tall and sprawling centers of steel and stone." In an evocative reflection, Wright grieved for the "landless millions of the land" whose "awkward feet" were first "upon the pavements of the city." There, "life would begin to exact . . . a heavy toll in death." To be sure, the hardships of migration for black Americans were compounded by poverty, discrimination in housing and employment, and by the collective antipathy of white city dwellers, which at its worst erupted into explosive outbreaks of racial violence. Segregated, crowded, and concentrated in ghettos in the cities of New York, Chicago, Detroit, Washington, Philadelphia, and St. Louis (where the greatest population gains occurred), African Americans faced especially harsh living conditions. And yet it was under these oppressive circumstances that many of the spiritual practices that had originated with the slaves had an urban rebirth.[36]

Braving the severity of city life, blacks created institutions that helped them withstand the staggering disorientation of relocation. African American churches, fraternal associations, and clubs gave expression to diverse new cultural forms even as they tempered the vagaries of black people's urban existence. Some cultural establishments became important sites for the survival of supernatural practices. Black storefront churches, for example, sometimes served as institutional bases for conjuring traditions. Spiritualist churches, which operated out of individuals' homes and rented commercial spaces, allowed some practitioners to maintain sources of livelihood and to promote their skills as mediums, psychic readers, and spiritual healers.[37]

Aside from the Spiritualists, a variety of supernatural specialists took their places within black American urban communities in the first few decades of the twentieth century. The rise of these individuals marked a shift in the roles of the former slave Conjurer and Hoodoo doctor. For many of these individuals, supernatural work was a ministry, and their titles, recast to reflect a sacred vocation, were transformed into "Reverend" and "Prophet." The practices of these new neighborhood Conjurers were often syncretic, merging esoteric rituals and occult spiritualities with older supernatural traditions. A 1936 report lists concise descriptions of such practitioners in one major city. These professionals are given titles such as "God sent healer," "clairvoyant," and "witch-doctor," demonstrating the variety and eclecticism of the new Conjurers in the urban context.

> Mrs. Emma Ethridge . . . makes "spiritual" predictions by consulting "Bob," which is nothing more than a conjure ball attached to the end of a strong cord. "Bob" is suspended over an open Bible and consulted on matters of importance to the client, while the latter concentrates on the question asked.

> Mrs. M. L. Harris . . . "divines" the troubles of her clients with an ordinary deck of cards, then prescribes the wearing of conjure balls on their person and sprinkling of dust in the corners of the house. Her usual line is to point to, or describe some friend of the client and credit him with bringing about present conditions by conjuration.

> Mother Turner . . . ascribes the ills of her clients to the working of little devils who are supposed to inhabit their persons and homes. . . . Charms are given to wear on their persons.

> Ben Session . . . tells fortunes by the use of a lighted candle and three glasses of water. . . . Sick clients are anointed and given medicine concocted by the "doctor." Those with other troubles are given lucky charms made of crosses.

> Professor Anthony George . . . attracts large crowds to his "spiritual" meetings. . . . He works his audience into frenzied enthusiasm by a recital of the people he has cured or given lucky numbers and often these individuals come to the meetings and give verbal testimonies of his powers. . . . He also gives lucky charms and clairvoyant interviews.[38]

While many urban supernatural practitioners were not associated with churches, their shared emphasis on healing, coupled with their diversity in style and approach, exemplifies what one historian of African American religion has termed "therapeutic pluralism." Supernatural specialists who viewed healing as a sacred duty solidified the link between spirituality and the body that had long characterized African American perspectives of health and affliction.[39]

Urban Conjure reflected African American styles and interests. The experiences that brought clients to these city practitioners, however, were similar to those that had prompted their enslaved predecessors in the south to seek Hoodoo doctors and root workers. Black urban dwellers utilized Conjure for personal protection, for good luck, and for settling conflicts and grievances. The harsh character of the urban milieu may have intensified a need for supernatural solutions that conjuring traditions offered.[40]

The press played an important role in publicizing Conjure and its practitioners. Between 1903 and 1933 an explosion of print advertisements crowded the pages of major black newspapers. Initially, such advertisements were simple offerings for alternative doctoring and medical treatment. One early advertisement in an African American newspaper promoted the services of a psychic who also attended to mundane foot ailments:

> Professor White. Psychic and Scientific Palmist. Read over 20,000 people. Don't fail to call and see me. Chiropodist work also done here. Corns, Bunions, Callouses and Ingrowing Nails Treated.[41]

In time a growing number of Conjure practitioners, spiritual advisers, and mediums offered and exchanged their services, using print advertising as their primary vehicle. Representing themselves as healers and doctors rather than as Conjurers, these specialists solicited customers independently through the classified sections of the newspaper rather than relying on the strength of their reputations or on word-of-mouth referrals. As a consequence, the intimacy and familiarity that had characterized contacts between Conjure practitioners and their clients in the past shrank in the relatively anonymous medium of print.[42]

Advertising copy drawn from a sampling of black newspapers in the 1920s and the 1930s demonstrates how supernatural practitioners accommodated themselves to the increasingly specialized needs of city dwellers. Press advertisements publicized the special skills and embellished credentials of supernatural practitioners, stressing their professional training or mastery of some esoteric school of thought. Techniques such as numerology, palmistry, hypnotism, and astrology gave a veneer of legitimacy to these supernatural professionals, as did their titles: "Professor" or "Doctor." A 1924 notice in the African American weekly the *Chicago Defender* described "Edet Effiong, West African scientist and herbalist," a "Mohammadan Native of Africa and Oriental Science," who provided "luck and advice . . . as to the whereabouts of lost friends or stolen articles, love, finance, etc., to those who desire it." Effiong also claimed to have the ability to "Cure all kinds of diseases, drunkard [sic], by Oriental Science."

With the allure of their professional credentials came a new emphasis on the ethnic and international backgrounds of practitioners. Often, representation of the "East" created a geographical association with ancient spiritual mysteries. Advertisements for specialists hailing from India or Asia, possessing "Hindu" or "Oriental" secrets, became especially frequent in African American newspapers. In New York City, one could turn to "Oku Aba," a psychic who practiced the "mystical science of Africa," or Professor Domingo, "African Spiritualist and Occultist, Mohammedan, from Kano, West Coast Africa." As urban Conjure matured, it began to reflect influences from theosophy, astrology, and European spiritualism. While it is possible that the cosmopolitan nature of city environments yielded a greater number of practitioners who were familiar with these occult traditions, it is also likely that the influences of various Asian philosophies in American culture at the turn of the twentieth century stimulated the public's fascination with eastern-styled mysticism.[43]

A fierce competition for clients engaged supernatural practitioners in urban settings. Strategies for promoting Conjurers' services veered from outrageous claims to blatantly coercive endorsements. Advertisements also offered the services of specialists who declared their abilities to cure all sorts of social afflictions by supernatural means and provide happiness, well-being, and good fortune as the guaranteed consequences of their supernatural therapies. "Spells of all kinds released and broken," read one prominent display in a city newspaper, "medicinal preparations for Conjured pains, sufferings . . . High John the Conqueror, Adam and Eve, all kinds of highly appreciated roots and herbs." In this instance, the use of magic as a resource for turning back spells of harm recalls the protective duties of the old-style Conjure doctor.[44]

Print advertising also created new stereotypes of black American spiritual traditions. Newspapers and catalogs publicized certain geographical regions such as New Orleans, Louisiana, and other parts of the Deep South as sites of supernatural distinction, the epicenters of Conjure lore. For example, some shrewd mail-order suppliers extolled "the South" as the birthplace of "genuine hoodoo specialists," the only authentic vista from which city dwellers could find the most potent Hoodoo items. This busy marketplace of charms, amulets, and magical products encouraged the further commodification of Conjure. Advertisements for supernatural goods and services appeared each week in the *Chicago Defender*, the nation's largest African American newspaper, where readers could choose from a variety of efficacious products that assured a multitude of solutions for infirmities of body and spirit, often juxtaposed against blurbs for hair straightening preparations and skin whiteners. Esoteric occult literature and magical manuals were also peddled in print, as was other merchandise normally found in the emporium of the old-fashioned root doctor, such as powders, roots, and potent oils.[45]

The shift from an oral dissemination of conjuring lore to print media accompanied a shift from natural and organic supplies such as herbs and roots to new, mass-produced merchandise. Efficient production also allowed for greater sales of spiritual merchandise in a commodity culture that was becoming increasingly undifferentiated. Conjure practices became less specialized, more accessible. The requisite patient-doctor consultations that had defined the relationships between Conjure professionals and their patrons in the earlier context gradually gave way to new relations which were determined by the commercial transactions of mail order agents and their clients in the urban arena. When the trade in mail-order Conjure expanded in the early twentieth century, so did the production of standardized novelties and supernatural "curios." Catalogs for spiritual merchandise in the early 1920s touted novelty talismans such as "good luck" rings and "lucky" amulets as effective icons of magic power that effectively displaced the more labor-intensive charms and hands of the Conjure practitioners.[46]

In the cities, Christian ministers and religious practitioners sometimes doubled as proprietors of magic and occult businesses. Most mainstream Christian denominations distanced themselves from the surfeit of supernatural merchandisers and spiritual shops that sprang up in the shadows of urban black churches in the early twentieth century. On occasion, however, magic entrepreneurs were able to form unusual alliances with members of the churches. In one instance, officers in one of the more conservative black Protestant denominations found themselves playing host to a popular Conjurer-magician during a time of severe fiscal crisis. In 1927 members of Mount Zion African Methodist Episcopal Church in Philadelphia sponsored a series of performances by a shrewd and independent peddler of magical goods, known as Black Herman Rucker, a famous faith healer, Conjurer, and vendor of lottery predictions. Black Herman's highly successful "voodoo campaigns" brought much-needed funds to the black Methodists, as he rented church space and charged admission fees to his public lectures, with audiences that included as many as fourteen hundred persons at one time.[47]

The rise of urban magic also brought about new specialized forms of gaming activity. The advent of the underworld gambling industry, known as the Policy racket, Bolito, or the numbers game, exponentially influenced the growth of Conjure and folk supernaturalism within cities. The early-twentieth-century period also saw the rise of dream books that were connected to the numbers game, texts that elaborated a complex interpretative system of symbols and images and promised successful numeric combinations.[48]

The commercialization of African American supernaturalism spurred the simultaneous publicizing of conjuring traditions by the entertainment industry. The emergence of "Race records," popular music that was marketed specifically to black buyers, provides examples of the broad influence of supernatural themes in the repertoire of African American musical performers. A number of blues titles from the 1920s such as "Louisiana Hoodoo Blues" by Gertrude "Ma" Rainey, "Hoodoo Blues" by Bessie Brown, and "Low Down Mojo Blues" by Blind Lemon Jefferson show a pattern of Conjure topics. As we will see, not only did the migration of the blues parallel the progression of black cultural traditions from rural to city contexts, but the content of the blues themselves—as lyrical expressions of supernatural belief—articulated a profound kinship between Conjure and this distinct form of African American music.[49]

The blues were the first commercially produced music to explicitly embrace the culture from which conjuring traditions emerged. Historians and musicologists have offered various explanations for the emphasis on supernaturalism in the blues. Paul Oliver, a scholar who has written extensively on the subject, claims that magic in the blues lyrics reflected the "superstitions" and "unsound beliefs" of "simple and uneducated persons," those blues performers who migrated from the rural South to the cities in the early twentieth century. Other writers have viewed Conjure and religion as intrinsic to the origins of the blues themselves. The music historian Julio Finn has portrayed the magic of the blues as a legacy of African-derived spiritual traditions in America. Jon Michael Spencer has identified an African-based theological structure in black blues styles. Spencer views blues performers as "express[ing] their cosmology and religious ponderings in the blues." He and others have argued that the blues are an African American form of theodicy that attempts to reconcile the existence of evil in a world ruled and controlled by God, who is good.[50]

It is often assumed that the blues originated in the "downhome" milieu, what one author has called a "place and time and a state of mind," the "land of Jim Crow and lynch law . . . of good music and getting religion . . . the smell of soil and farm." Sharply countering this nostalgic, bittersweet vision of the South is the blues' articulation of the psychic pathos of African Americans in confinement and yearnings for freedom in one form or another. Like the spirituals created in the period of slavery, the blues bore witness to African American thought *after* Emancipation. "The blues and the spirituals flow from the same bedrock of experience," writes the theologian James Cone, for they "formalize a mood already present in the spirituals." Conventionally interpreted as a "worldly" or "profane" music, the blues are more adequately defined as "secular spirituals," for they also delivered sobering reflections on the human condition. In this respect, the blues were the result of African Americans' creative attempts to come to terms with the existential dilemma of human suffering.[51]

While the blues captured the black experience in song, they also served as a prime conduit for African American supernatural beliefs. Conceived in the blues as Hoodoo or Voodoo, Conjure was a constant inspiration of blues composers. From the country styles of the Mississippi delta songsters to the urban blues performers of the post–World War II era and beyond, black bluespeople utilized the rhetoric of Conjure in their songs. Blues records, made popular in the first few decades of the twentieth century, contained direct and oblique references to Hoodoo talismans, spiritual signs, and magical mysteries. In her 1928 song "Shootin' Star Blues," for example, Lizzie Miles, a New Orleans-born blues queen, alluded to the obscure but grisly technique by which individuals could acquire an all-powerful black cat bone, a highly sought-after supernatural artifact:

> I done crossed my fingers, counted up to twenty-three
> I seen a star falling, that means bad luck done fell on me
> A black cat bone's a-boiling, I put it one at half past twelve,
> Tie it in a sack, walk off talking to myself[52]

Blues performers revered figures from the traditions of conjuring, divination, and root working. Aunt Caroline Dye, a famous healer and fortune-teller in Newport, Arkansas, was immortalized in a succession of popular recordings in the first quarter of the twentieth century, begin-

ning with W. C. Handy's "St. Louis Blues" for Paramount in 1922.
Handy's orchestra would elaborate on the Aunt Caroline tradition later
in "Sundown Blues," written in 1923:

> I'm . . . goin' . . . to see Aunt Car'line Dye
> Why she's a reader, and I need her
> Lord, Lord, Lord
> She reads your fortune, and her cards don't lie
> I'll put some ashes in my sweet Papa's bed
> So that he can't slip out, Hoodoo in his bread
> Goopher dust all about
> I'll fix him![53]

Other blues performers, like Texas bluesman J. T. "Funny Papa" Smith,
enshrined the legendary New Orleans Conjure women Seven Sisters in
his "Seven Sisters Blues" (1930). Whether articulated implicitly, as in
Charley Patton's early country blues ("I woke up this morning / jinx all
around my bed"), or explicitly, as in the life and lyrics of the legendary
guitarist Robert Johnson, magic and supernaturalism were potent forces
in African American bluesong.

The blues articulated blacks' experiences of alienation, victimization,
and loss and, as such, like Conjure, became existential appeals for control in an uncontrollable universe. Blues lyrics gave voice to suffering by
describing both personal and collective afflictions. Blues of the "downhome" genre, in particular, were sagas of disaster and tragedy, including
chronicles of floods, the impact of the devastating boll weevil in the South,
natural calamities, migration, or other historical events that had an impact on the blues singer or on black life. Other blue narratives were pre-
occupied with individual misfortune or illness or the furtive quest for
sexual fulfillment—all familiar motifs in Conjure, which was utilized for
these very same purposes. Thus, while the blues most assuredly embodied mythologies of evil, they were also attentive to the ways of addressing affliction by immediate, practical means.[54]

References to Conjure in blues lyrics often consisted of erotic allusions
that bespoke a boastful masculine virility or cunning references to a
woman's sex appeal. Blues men sang of the virtues of femininity that
rested in a woman's possession of the right combination of secret ingredients, like the mysterious contents of a Hoodoo charm. Texas country
songster Blind Lemon Jefferson was one of the earliest commercial blues
artists to impart sexual connotations to the mojo charm, as in his sug-
gestive "Low Down Mojo Blues" (1928):

My rider's got a Mojo, and she won't let me see
Everytime I start to loving, she ease that thing on me
She's got to fool her daddy, got to keep that mojo hid,
But papa's got something for to find that mojo with.[55]

It was common for blues singers to identify the mojo with female sexuality, a powerful, valued "charm" that all women owned and all men wanted. In the 1930s, a popular recording by Leola B. and "Kid" Wesley Wilson on Okeh Records, contained the blueswoman's admonition to

Keep your hands off a' my mojo, 'cause it sure is lucky to me
Keep your hands off a' my mojo, I wish I had two or three
I wear my mojo above my knee,
To keep you from trying to hoodoo me
So keep your hands off a' my mojo, go away and let me be[56]

For blueswomen, charms, Conjure, and Hoodoo practices provided last-resort antidotes for loneliness, despair, or betrayal. Female blues singers insisted that magic had the power to "bring that man home" and "treat me right." Hoodoo was also healing, depicted as a potential cure among cures, as in Clara Smith's 1924 "Prescription for the Blues," on the Columbia label:

Let me tell you doctor, why I'm in misery
Once I had a love and he went away from me
Been to see the Gypsy, Hoodoo Doctors too
Shook their heads and told me, nothing they could do[57]

Supernatural healing and harming were also thematic constants in the blues, as they were in conjuring traditions. However, blues healing was primarily focused on the fixing of relationships that had gone awry, and the resolution of oppressive romantic entanglements. Blues poets wove personal lyrics about heartache, lust, and unfulfilled longings for love. The blues and Conjure often converged in the strident declarations of men and women whose worlds revolved around their attempts to establish intimate bonds. Hoodoo was both a punishment and cure, the supernatural force that ignited the passions of desperate suitors and frustrated paramours, who wielded *goopher* dust or High John the Conqueror roots in their pursuit of satisfying outcomes. It was a surrogate for personal design, an invisible stand-in for the power and will that the blues poets lacked, lost, or wanted, especially in matters of the heart.[58]

Although the blues evolved into a popular form of entertainment, as

African American music and like the spirituals, they shared elements with
other aspects of black culture, especially black religion. They were a powerful medium by which performers articulated personal tribulations and
conveyed them to a receptive audience. Blues singers were storytellers
whose listeners affirmed and participated in the black experience. In this
manner blues men and women depicted the intimate realities and afflictions of black American life, using modes of delivery that resonated with
the prayer, testimonial, and preaching traditions in many African
American churches. The "Hoodoo blues," as the historian Julio Finn describes supernaturally themed blues, were also "songs of power." For
their audiences they could "set off a reaction and bring about a desired
effect." Like conjuring practices themselves, the effects were transfor-
mative. And like preachers or gospel singers, blues performers "conjured"
their audience, evoking collective responses and bringing about cathar-
tic release.[59]

Even with the similarities in their styles, blues performers were never
acknowledged as musical ministers by black churches and churchgoers.
Because they incorporated Conjure sensibilities into their performances,
they were relegated to the margins of institutionalized religious life. Many
of the more conservative black churches would reject the blues as "the
devil's music," for like Conjure itself, the blues tended to foster a deep
ambivalence among Christian believers. Bluespeople sang freely of the
pleasures and perils of erotic love, alcohol, gambling, and fast living. They
flaunted the unseemly behaviors that black elites had repudiated in their
quest for social respectability. In bold defiance of middle-class standards,
bluesmen and women engaged in many of the illicit practices of the culture of the lower classes. Blues singers promoted, in frank and often
graphic terms, attitudes that were considered immoral and inappropriate by pious, churchgoing persons. Defiantly, some of them incorporated
African American supernatural beliefs into their repertoire. Like their enslaved forebears who had stubbornly maintained the traditions of their
African ancestors, black bluesmen and women reclaimed a heritage that
had been denied by the upwardly mobile.

The acknowledged paradigm of kinship between the blues and African
American spirituality will serve as the bridge that allows us to bring this
discussion to a close. Because it is a history of decline and descent as well
as renewal and transformation, it extends, indefinitely, into the future.
The blues, like African American supernatural traditions, have evolved

into a multifaceted faith with many devoted followers. As declared by the great bluesman Muddy Waters (McKinley Morganfield), "We *all* believed . . . in Hoodoo." Muddy Waters spoke of himself and so many other performer-practitioners who lived along the continuum of blues culture and supernatural spirituality. Like Conjure, the blues encircled their practitioners' experiences, mediating the fragile boundaries between magic and religion, between spirituality and material promise. And Conjure, like the blues, although reshaped, reinterpreted, and ultimately dispersed into new venues, belonged to the worlds in which black Americans had always lived.[60]

Conclusion

African American magic is all around us. It resonates in contemporary manifestations of Hoodoo, in the ritual creations of African diasporic religions, and in the vibrant artistic forms that utilize conjuring themes. Even as numerous black American supernatural traditions are fully alive in the twenty-first century, their sources are not readily apparent. Theirs is not a pure, unmediated connection to an essentialized African origin, but a hybridized lineage, one that is additive, constantly recreated, and shaped according to circumstance.

In this book I have argued that African American supernatural traditions, as dynamic products of black spirituality, are best understood within their actual social contexts. These traditions can open a window onto the many levels at which black life has been suffused with religious meaning. Historically, many black Americans have not separated magical beliefs from religion, seeing that the two exist as necessary counterparts. Beliefs in Conjure have not precluded an acceptance of Christianity as a complementary system of practice. Conjure coexists with Christianity because it is an alternative strategy for interacting with the spiritual realm.

For some, conjuring has become a paradigm for understanding the cultural experiences of blacks in the United States. The writer Ishmael

Facing page illustration: an American devotee of *santería* praying before a Shango altar. African diaspora religions evoke older styles of supernatural practice. Photo by Rick Bowmer courtesy of Wide World/Associated Press.

Reed declared that Conjure is the "forgotten faith" of African American people, with its own institution: the "church of neo-Hoodoo," whose emanations in poetry, dance, jazz, and literature demonstrate an aesthetic in which "every man is an artist and every artist is a priest." Reed conceived of conjuring traditions as metaphorical representations of a resilient African spirituality. Similarly, Theophus Smith, a theologian of black religion, identifies "conjuring culture" as the impetus for a biblical hermeneutic, a source for envisioning the ways that black religion "reenvision[s] and transform[s] lived experience and social reality" in creative expressions of ritual, speech, and writing. Conjure, in this latter instance, possesses figurative and symbolic significance.[1]

In this book I have highlighted the origins of Conjure and its role as a means of healing and harming. In the present day, African American conjuring traditions have given way to more diverse forms of supernatural practice. For most persons spiritual healing is a private matter, but its material products are visible in the nearest Botanica, where charms, multicolored candles, efficacious oils, and sacred implements are sold. Linked to the avid commercialism of contemporary spiritual merchandisers is the burgeoning enterprise of New Age therapies that offer self-healing, prosperity, and success to an upscale client base. Scholars are only beginning to assess the meaning of these trends in America today. Factors such as the growth of diasporic religions like *santería,* as well as a current appreciation for miracles, angelic visitations, and life-after-death experiences in popular culture, may signal a new openness to forms and expressions of the supernatural in everyday life. Or it might be that new varieties of magic serve to channel the atavistic desires of contemporary seekers for authentic "traditional" spiritual experiences.[2]

African American magical spirituality retains strongly negative meanings as well. "MISSISSIPPI TOWN IS ALL SHOOK UP OVER VOODOO PLOT," blares a headline. "PROSECUTORS SAY PAIR TRIED TO HAVE JUDGE KILLED USING HAIR, PHOTO, HEX." Two brothers in Tupelo are charged with conspiracy to murder a court judge. The plan, hatched in retaliation for the conviction and sentencing of one of the brothers for armed robbery, unravels when the men try to obtain a photograph and a lock of hair from the intended victim for use in a "Voodoo death curse." As reported in a 1989 *Wall Street Journal,* such strange occurrences can initiate public anxiety, fear, disgust, or ridicule. Although we acknowledge ours as a culturally plural society, African-based supernatural practices often reach the acceptable limits of tolerance for "other" religions in the United States.[3]

Conjure and its associated traditions continue to be much maligned, in part through inadvertent association with harming practices. Today, as in the past, ordinary persons turn to spiritual powers as covert agents of revenge, retaliation, and protection. "A policeman who is unable to arrest an individual in the course of his duty, a jailer who cannot keep a given prisoner locked up, or a judge who cannot convict an obviously guilty person," notes one anthropologist, "are all said to have been *rooted*." While investigating African American supernaturalism in Piedmont Village, North Carolina, in the mid twentieth century, Norman Whitten found that some police officers were reluctant to arrest individuals who carried charms and Hoodoo bags overlaid with threatening spiritual symbolism, for to them it was well known that "malign occult" practices were dangerous and should be respected, even by those in roles of authority.[4]

Today, persons who employ Conjure may do so to challenge a system that they believed has mistreated them. The forces they come up against might include powerful institutions as well as powerful individuals. Back in the 1940s, Zora Neale Hurston identified an old-fashioned "root-and-conjure doctor" in Louisiana whose specialty was "winning law suits." This man, she claimed, prepared charms that enabled the wearer to "keep the court under his control." This example also recalls a time when black Conjurers were so favored by recalcitrant criminals that they were nicknamed the "po' man's lawyers." In the twenty-first century, the trend continues as African American supernaturalism is brought to bear in litigious matters. Some practitioners—such as the infamous "brothers from Tupelo"—might defiantly acquire supernatural agents in order to intimidate judges, prosecutors, witnesses, and juries. Others might surreptitiously utilize magical substances such as "goopher dust" and "uncrossing" powder or "chew the root" to secure favorable court outcomes. These practices evoke the ancient supernatural "work" in the African-based religions *santería* and *vodou*, which is sometimes conducted on behalf of clients with legal problems. This "work" might include private, focused ceremonies of spiritual cleansing, or the exacting rituals of animal sacrifice—even within courthouse spaces.[5]

The persistence of supernatural traditions in the present day illuminates the pervasive pragmatism that is characteristic of African American spirituality. In earlier periods, conjuring provided a conceptual and practical framework by which enslaved blacks confronted misfortune and evil in their lives. Supernaturalism spoke directly to areas that Christian theology did not clearly address, the indeterminate territory between right and wrong, the hazy, gray field of situation-specific ethics and actions.

Although Christianity provided its own set of moral guidelines with which individuals could address the misfortunes that occurred in life, there were other, non-Christian notions that informed blacks' responses to affliction.

Although supernaturalism has become universalized in recent years, the genealogy of Conjure shows some of the important differences between Anglo-American and black American beliefs. An important contrast can be seen in the manner in which magical traditions were used in order to resist the conditions of oppression that African people encountered. Ever conscious of the fundamental power of their ancestral beliefs, black men and women grasped what they could of their spiritual heritage as a lifeline. In this regard, it is noteworthy that Conjure was initially utilized as a means of resistance for slaves. Employed to challenge the cruelty of harsh slaveholders and to deflect the ruthlessness of a system that oppressed them, supernatural power was a weapon of the weak. As did their African ancestors, black Americans made critical distinctions between spiritual activities that were conceived with the intent to injure and harm, and those that were meant to restore and heal. Illicit and socially unacceptable uses of supernatural power were motivated by immoral motives such as selfishness, greed, and jealousy. Beneficial uses of supernatural power were directed toward the preservation of life. Harming practices—protective acts of aggression and retaliation—were attempts to channel spiritual forces defensively. Conjuring also enabled individuals to focus hostility and vent anger against their opponents and rivals, as well as heal the sick and disabled.[6]

As we witness convergence between Conjure and Christianity, we can see tensions as well. I wish to underscore the fact that even though conjuring practices were compatible with the religious beliefs of many black Americans, these two traditions were not identical. Conjure did not develop into a comprehensive system of tenets and doctrines, as did Christianity, nor was it concerned with the larger questions of salvation, eternal life, or destiny. Rather, conjuring tended to supplement the traditions that many African Americans had adopted. Conjure practitioners did not eschew Christianity but often accommodated Christianity within their own complex of supernatural beliefs.

With its diverse sources of inspiration, Conjure, like Christianity, offered power to the powerless. And today, it figures as a relevant force in the lives of many. Evidence of such diversity in spiritual practice and belief should challenge us to rethink the categories that we use for looking at religion in the United States today. Rather than considering supernaturalism apart from a social and cultural mainstream, I have placed it at its center. The verdict is still out on whether it is methodologically sensible to separate magic from religion. While this book does not ultimately resolve this problem, it does suggest that there are alternative ways to view the complex of practical strategies by which human beings interact with the invisible realm.

I still believe that fixed assumptions constrain attempts to understand religious life. Spiritual practices and beliefs are dynamic and possess their own autonomy. Religion helps human beings make sense of their world, even as it explains why things might happen in that world. This much is also true of the tradition known as Conjure. Despite its "magical" orientation Conjure has maintained a strong relationship to its sacred origins. Observers of African American religion should pay careful attention to the ways that new worlds—and new meanings—can be created by religion in various contexts. Whether expressed in Conjure, Christianity, or both, African American spirituality provides power to its practitioners in ways that are both highly responsive and profoundly creative.

Notes

INTRODUCTION

1. Julie Dash, "Screenplay," in *Daughters of the Dust: The Making of an African American Woman's Film* (New York: The New Press, 1992), pp. 74–164.

2. Suzanne Preston Blier, "Truth and Seeing: Magic, Custom and Fetish in Art History," in *Africa and the Disciplines: Contributions of Research in Africa to the Social Sciences and Humanities,* ed. Robert Bates, V. Y. Mudimbe, and Jean O'Barr (Chicago: University of Chicago Press, 1993).

3. James G. Frazer, *The Golden Bough* (London: Macmillan, 1922), p. 59. Following Frazer, a number of writers have given attention to the magic-religion dichotomy. Emile Durkheim and Marcel Mauss placed magic and religion within distinctive social contexts, while Bronislaw Malinowski emphasized the functional elements that distinguished magic from religious ritual (Durkheim, *The Elementary Forms of Religious Life,* trans. Karen E. Fields [New York: Macmillan, 1915]; Mauss, *A General Theory of Magic,* trans. Robert Brain[London: Routledge and Kegan Paul, 1972]; Malinowski, *Magic, Science and Religion, and Other Essays* [Garden City, N.Y.: Doubleday, 1948], and *A Scientific Theory of Culture* [Chapel Hill: University of North Carolina Press, 1944], p. 200). In his formulation of a "workable dichotomy" between magic and religion, Mischa Titiev argued that supernatural practices can be distinguished on the basis of their "calendrical" functions and "critical" functions, the latter referring to those practices that are engaged "when an emergency or crisis seems to have arisen" (Titiev, "A Fresh Approach to the Problem of Magic and Religion," in *Reader in Comparative Religion: An Anthropological Approach,* ed. William A. Lessa and Evon Z. Vogt [New York: Harper and Row, 1972], pp. 335–37).

4. On the category "vernacular religion" see Leonard Primiano, "Vernacular Religion and the Search for Method in Religious Folklife," *Western Folklore*

54 (January 1995): 37–56. I identify as "vernacular" those traditions that are typically associated with African American "folk" religion, including those values and styles by which black Americans have formulated shared understandings of community and spiritual identity. Historically such traditions emerged from the culture of southern black Protestantism, but they are not necessarily limited to institutional expressions. In his study of slave religion, Albert Raboteau argues that folk traditions include "institutional and non-institutional, visible and invisible, formally organized and spontaneously adopted," practices and beliefs, transcending religious affiliation, creed, and denomination (Raboteau, *Slave Religion: The "Invisible Institution" in the Antebellum South* [New York: Oxford University Press, 1978], p. 212).

5. Charles Long, *Significations: Signs, Symbols and Images in the Interpretation of Religion* (Philadelphia: Fortress Press, 1986), p. 7.

6. David D. Hall, ed., *Lived Religion in America: Toward a Theory of Practice* (Princeton: Princeton University Press, 1997), p. vii.

7. Henry Mitchell, for example, writing in 1975, argued that Conjure represented the "low religion" of black America, as it was "contrary to the belief system and ethical rules of the higher tradition" of Christianity. More recently, a historian of slavery has argued that Hoodoo, the vernacular term for black supernatural practices, "represents the legacy of the African worldview divorced from its proper religious context." The magic-religion dualism is also reflected in the work of African American theologians. Dwight Hopkins states that Conjure is a "non-Christian reality of God's freeing representations." For these and other comments, see Henry H. Mitchell, *Black Belief: Folk Beliefs of Blacks in America and West Africa* (New York: Harper and Row, 1975), p. 31; Michael Gomez, *Exchanging Our Country Marks: The Transformation of African Identities in the Colonial and Antebellum South* (Chapel Hill: University of North Carolina Press, 1998), p. 284; Dwight Hopkins, *Shoes That Fit Our Feet: Sources for a Constructive Black Theology* (Maryknoll, N.Y.: Orbis Books, 1993), p. 73. See also Dwight Hopkins and George C. L. Cummings, eds., *Cut Loose Your Stammering Tongue: Black Theology in the Slave Narratives* (Maryknoll, N.Y.: Orbis Books, 1991), p. 93.

8. George Rawick, ed., *The American Slave: A Composite Autobiography* (hereafter cited as *American Slave*), Texas Narratives (Westport, Ct.: Greenwood Press, 1977), vol. 2, ss. 2, pp. 16–17.

9. William D. Piersen, *Black Legacy: America's Hidden Heritage* (Amherst: University of Massachusetts Press, 1993), p. xi; Lawrence Levine, *Black Culture and Black Consciousness: Afro-American Folk Thought from Slavery to Freedom* (New York, Oxford University Press, 1977), p. 389.

10. Theophus H. Smith, *Conjuring Culture: Biblical Formations of Black America* (New York: Oxford University Press, 1994).

CHAPTER 1. "OUR RELIGION AND SUPERSTITION WAS ALL
        MIXED UP"

1. Zora Neale Hurston, "Father Abraham," in *The Sanctified Church: The Folklore Writings of Zora Neale Hurston* (Berkeley: Turtle Island Press, 1981),

pp. 15–18. In addition to his career as a hoodoo doctor, Abraham became one of the most highly successful strawberry farmers in Florida. After his death in 1937, his daughter carried on his ministry for five years. For further sources on Abraham see Sherry Sherrod duPree, *African-American Holiness Pentecostal Movement: An Annotated Bibliography* (New York: Garland Publishing, 1996), pp. 366–67.

2. For recent discussions of Conjure as a religious complex, see Theophus H. Smith, *Conjuring Culture: Biblical Formations of Black America* (New York: Oxford University Press, 1994); and Albert Raboteau, *Slave Religion: The "Invisible Institution" Among Blacks in the Antebellum South* (New York: Oxford University Press, 1978), pp. 275–88.

3. Jeanette Robinson Murphy, "The Survival of African Music in America," *Appleton's Popular Science Monthly* 55, 1899, reprinted in *The Negro and His Folklore in Nineteenth-Century Periodicals*, ed. Bruce Jackson (Austin: University of Texas Press, 1967), p. 335. While this story may be a case of folkloric invention, the retelling of such incidents as "real" events underscores their use as historical sources for important values and beliefs in black communities. On factual truth and moral truth in African American folklore sources, see William D. Piersen, *Black Legacy: America's Hidden Heritage* (Amherst: University of Massachusetts Press, 1993), pp. 35–50. For a conjuring formula for a preacher to "hold" a congregation, see Zora Neale Hurston, "Hoodoo in America," *Journal of American Folklore* 44 (1931): 375.

4. William Wells Brown, *My Southern Home, or The South and Its People* (Boston: A. G. Brown, 1880), p. 70. John Blassingame, *The Slave Community: Plantation Life in the Antebellum South* (New York: Oxford University Press, 1972), p. 45.

5. Rawick, *American Slave*, Mississippi Narratives vol. 6, pt. 1, s.s. 1, p. 271; Frederick Law Olmsted, *A Journey to the Seaboard States in the Years 1853–54, with Remarks on their Economy* (New York: Dix and Edwards, 1856), p. 114; William Owens, "Folklore of the Southern Negroes," *Lippincott's Monthly Magazine*, December 1877, reprinted in *The Negro and His Folklore in Nineteenth-Century Periodicals*, ed Bruce Jackson (Austin: University of Texas Press, 1967), p. 146; Charles Raymond, "The Religious Life of the Negro Slave," *Harper's New Monthly Magazine*, August 1863, p. 816.

6. William Webb, *History of William Webb* (Detroit: E. Hoekstra, 1873), pp. 20–22.

7. Mary Livermore, *The Story of my Life, or The Sunshine and Shadow of Seventy Years* (Hartford: A. D. Worthington, 1899), p. 254. Raymond, "Religious Life of the Negro Slave," pp. 820–23; Rawick, *American Slave*, Florida Narratives vol. 18, pp. 184–88.

8. Elwyn Barron, "Shadowy Memories of Negro Lore," in *The Folklorist* (Chicago: University of Chicago Press, 1982), p. 50; Frederick Douglass, *Narrative of the Life of Frederick Douglass, An American Slave* (1846), reprinted in *Autobiographies* (New York: Library of America, 1994), p. 280; Henry Clay Bruce, *The New Man, or Twenty-Nine Years a Slave, Twenty-Nine years as a Free Man* (York, Pa.: P. Anstadt, 1895), p. 56.

9. Louis Hughes, *Thirty Years a Slave: From Bondage to Freedom* (1897;

reprint, Milwaukee: Southside Printing, 1969), p. 108; Rawick, *American Slave,*
Arkansas Narratives vol. 11, p. 21. See also Lawrence Levine, *Black Culture and
Black Consciousness: Afro-American Folk Thought from Slavery to Freedom*
(New York: Oxford University Press, 1977), p. 72. On supernatural practices and
slave resistance, see especially Elliot Gorn, "No White Man Could Whip Me:
Folk Beliefs of the Slave Community" (master's thesis, University of California,
Los Angeles, June 1975).

10. Brown, *My Southern Home,* p. 75. On black folklore traditions and su-
pernatural figures, see Zora Neale Hurston, *The Sanctified Church: The Folklore
Writings of Zora Neale Hurston* (Berkeley: Turtle Island Press, 1981), pp. 69–78;
John Roberts, *From Trickster to Badman: The Black Folk Hero in Slavery and
Freedom* (Philadelphia: University of Pennsylvania Press, 1989), pp. 65–66.

11. Elliot Gorn, "Black Magic: Folk Beliefs of the Slave Community," in *Science and Medicine in the Old South,* ed. Ronald L. Numbers and Todd L. Savitt
(Baton Rouge: Louisiana State University Press, 1989), p. 39. Historians of slavery have generally neglected consideration of black spiritual traditions as actual
sites of struggle and resistance. See the statements of Eugene Genovese and Donald Mathews, which typify this perspective. Genovese argues that Conjure and
other African American folk religious beliefs "represented a tactical withdrawal
into a black world that . . . offered no direct threat to the [slave] regime"; Mathews says, "black folk religion . . . could not assail slavery, since it explained away
many of the problems of life as the work of evil spirits or a prankish devil" (Genovese, *Roll, Jordan, Roll: The World the Slaves Made* [New York: Vintage Books,
1976], p. 222; Mathews, *Religion in the Old South* [Chicago: University of
Chicago Press, 1977], p. 213). Far from being accommodative, supernatural traditions could support or encourage the enslaved to fight, rebel, escape, or commit destructive acts of sabotage. Within some African American communities,
conjuring specialists were sought for guidance concerning impending matters of
urgency or crisis. In the narratives of the fugitive bondmen William Wells Brown,
William Grimes, and Anthony Burns, the authors relate how each consulted with
diviners prior to making their attempts to attain their freedom. In each case, the
faith that they put in the counsel of the specialists encouraged the men as they
acted decisively in their escape from slavery. See William Wells Brown, *Narrative of William Wells Brown, a Fugitive Slave* (Boston: The Anti-Slavery Office,
1847), pp. 91–93; Charles E. Stevens, *Anthony Burns* (Boston: John P. Jewett,
1856), pp. 168–69. See also James Lindsay Smith, *The Autobiography of James
L. Smith, including also Reminiscences of Slave Life, Recollections of the War,
Education of Freedmen, Causes of the Exodus, etc.* (Norwich: Society of the
Founders of Norwich, Connecticut, 1881), p. 171 for another account of a Conjurer's assistance to a fugitive slave.

12. Rawick, *American Slave,* Texas Narratives vol. 5, p. 161; added emphasis.

13. Drew Gilpin Faust, *James Henry Hammond and the Old South: A Design for Mastery* (Baton Rouge: Louisiana State University Press, 1985), pp. 82,
93. See also Levine, *Black Culture and Black Consciousness,* p. 75; Blassingame,
Slave Community, p. 45; Eugene Genovese notes that while the Conjurer "helped
build an inner and autonomous black world for his brothers and sisters," he simultaneously "reinforced the image of the master as a great power" because ul-

timately he himself was beholden to whites *(Roll, Jordan, Roll,* pp. 222–23). This point is called into question by the authors of slave narratives, such as Douglass and Wells Brown, who both claimed to have turned on oppressive slavemasters after the bidding of black Conjurers.

14. Brown, *My Southern Home*, p. 61; Edward Pollard, *Black Diamonds Gathered in the Darkey Homes of the South* (New York: Pudney and Russell, 1859), p. 119; W. H. Councill, Synopsis of Three Addresses (Normal, Alabama, 1900), reprinted in *After Africa: Extracts from British Travel Accounts and Journals of the Seventeenth, Eighteenth, and Nineteenth Centuries Concerning the Slaves, Their Manners and Customs in the British West Indies*, ed. Roger Abrahams and John Szwed (New Haven: Yale University Press, 1983), p. 37; Rawick, *American Slave*, Texas Narratives vol. 8, no. 2, p. 61. Robert Farris Thompson notes a similar use of occult beliefs for black children in the contemporary South in *Another Face of the Diamond: Pathways Through the Black Atlantic South*, ed. Judith McWillie (New York: INTAR, Hispanic Arts Center, 1989), p. 77. On the uses of supernatural lore among slaves, see Thomas Webber, *Deep Like the Rivers: Education in the Slave Quarter Community, 1831–1865* (New York: W. W. Norton, 1978), 220–23. See also Raymond, "Religious Life of the Negro Slave," p. 822; See also Cross, "Witchcraft in North Carolina," pp. 222–23; B. A. Botkin, *Lay My Burden Down: A Folk History of Slavery* (Chicago: University of Chicago Press, 1945), p. 29.

15. Olmsted, *Journey to the Seaboard States*, p. 389; Brown, *My Southern Home*, pp. 21–22, 68; letter to the editor, *American Missionary*, June 1867, p. 126.

16. Brown, *My Southern Home*, p. 76; Henry Bibb, *Narrative of the Life and Adventures of Henry Bibb, an American Slave, Written by Himself* (New York, 1850), p. 30; Botkin, *Lay My Burden Down*, pp. 31–33. See also Newbell Niles Puckett, *Folk Beliefs of the Southern Negro* (Chapel Hill: University of North Carolina Press, 1926), pp. 264–66; Hurston, "Hoodoo in America," 378.

17. Cited in B. A. Botkin, ed., *A Treasury of Southern Folklore: Stories, Ballads, Traditions, and Folkways of the People of the South* (New York: Crown, 1950), p. 632.

18. Frederick Douglass, *My Bondage and My Freedom*, reprinted in *Autobiographies* (New York: New American Library, 1969), p. 280. See also Gilbert E. Cooley, "Root Doctors and Psychics in the Region," *Indiana Folklore* 10 (1977): 191–200. For examples of various terms describing Conjure practitioners, see the following: F. Roy Johnson, *The Fabled Doctor Jim Jordan: A Story of Conjure* (Murfreesboro, N.C.: Johnson Publishing, 1963), p. 2; Puckett, *Folk Beliefs of the Southern Negro*, p. 204; James Haskins, *Hoodoo and Voodoo: Their Tradition and Craft as Revealed by Actual Practitioners* (Bronx: Original Publications, 1978); Norman Whitten, "Contemporary Patterns of Malign Occultism Among Negroes in North Carolina," *Journal of American Folklore* 75 (1962), cited in *Mother Wit from the Laughing Barrel: Readings in the Interpretation of Afro-American Folklore*, ed. Alan Dundes (Jackson: University Press of Mississippi, 1972), p. 409; Mary A. Owen, *Voodoo Tales, as Told Among the Negroes of the Southwest* (New York: G. P. Putnam, 1893), pp. 218–19; Harry Middleton Hyatt, *Hoodoo — Conjuration — Witchcraft — Rootwork: Beliefs Ac-*

cepted by Many Negroes and White Persons, These Being Orally Recorded among Blacks and Whites, 5 vols. (Hannibal, Mo.: Western Publishing, 1970–78; distributed by American University Bookstore,Washington, D.C.); Leonora Herron, "Conjuring and Conjure Doctors," *Southern Workman* 24, no. 7 (1895): 117–18. NOTE TO READERS: for some material from the *Southern Workman* I cite the original journal articles or another source (as for this item in note 20, I cite Dundes's *Mother Wit*). To make the material more accessible, at the first cite of each item I add its corresponding page span in Donald J. Waters, ed., *Strange Ways and Sweet Dreams: Afro-American Folklore from the Hampton Institute* (Boston: G. K. Hall, 1983)—e.g., here [in Waters, *Strange Ways,* pp. 227–29].

19. Ruth Bass, "Mojo," *Scribner's Magazine* 87 (1930), reprinted in *Mother Wit from the Laughing Barrel: Readings in the Interpretation of Afro-American Folklore,* ed. Alan Dundes (Jackson: University Press of Mississippi, 1972), p. 381; Mamie Garvin Fields, with Karen Fields, *Lemon Swamp and Other Places: A Carolina Memoir* (New York: Free Press, 1983), p. 120. See also Gorn, "Black Magic," pp. 303–4; Puckett, *Folk Beliefs of the Southern Negro,* p. 202; Herron, "Conjuring," 117–18; *Southern Workman* 17, no. 12 (1898): 251; Roland Steiner, "Observations on the Practice of Conjuring in Georgia," *Journal of American Folklore* 14 (1901): 177.

20. J. E. McTeer, *High Sheriff of the Lowcountry,* ed. Kent Nickerson (Beaufort, S.C.: Beaufort Book, 1970), p. 21; John Michael Vlach, *The Afro-American Tradition in Decorative Arts* (Cleveland: Cleveland Museum of Art, 1978), p. 42, 227–43; Brown, *My Southern Home,* p. 71; Georgia Writers' Project, *Drums and Shadows: Survival Studies Among the Georgia Coastal Negroes* (Athens: University of Georgia Press, 1940), pp. 24, 65; Leonora Herron and Alice Bacon, "Conjuring and Conjure Doctors" (1895), in *Mother Wit from the Laughing Barrel: Readings in the Interpretation of Afro-American Folklore,* ed. Alan Dundes (Jackson: University Press of Mississippi, 1972), p. 362 [in Waters, *Strange Ways,* pp. 227–29 and 235–42]; "Conjure Doctors in the South," *Southern Workman* 7, no. 4 (1878): 31 [in Waters, *Strange Ways,* pp. 131–39]. Transvestitism is briefly mentioned in an account of a school or Conjurers or "Voodoo" practitioners in Missouri in the late nineteenth century. See Mary A. Owen, "Among the Voodoos" (paper presented at the Second International Folk-lore Congress, 1891), p. 231. Another study written early in the twentieth century noted that African American hoodoo men nearly "always have long hair." See Puckett, *Folk Beliefs of the Southern Negro,* p. 203; Herron, "Conjuring," p. 118. On gender inversion among Conjure practitioners see also the comments of Robert Tallant, *Voodoo in New Orleans* (New York: Macmillan, 1946), p. 41.

21. Charles C. Jones, Jr., *Negro Myths from the Georgia Coast, Told in the Vernacular* (Boston: Houghton Mifflin, 1888), p.169; Charles Chesnutt, "Superstitions and Folklore of the South," *Modern Culture* 13 (1901). On black women and magic traditions in the United States, see Yvonne Chireau, "The Uses of the Supernatural: Toward a History of Black Women's Magical Practices," in *A Mighty Baptism: Race, Gender, and the Creation of American Protestantism,* ed. Susan Juster and Lisa MacFarlane (Ithaca: Cornell University Press, 1996); see also *DeBow's Review* 31, July–December 1861, p. 98.

22. Petition of Leroy Beauford, General Assembly, 1800, petition no. 174,

South Carolina State Archives, Columbia, cited in Philip D. Morgan, "Black Society in the Lowcountry, 1760–1810," in *Slavery and Freedom in the Age of the American Revolution,* ed. Ira Berlin and Ronald Hoffman (Urbana: University of Illinois Press, 1986), p. 138; Hurston, "Hoodoo in America"; Owen, "Among the Voodoos," pp. 230–32. The relationship of black American magic practices in the United States with other supernatural traditions in African diaspora religions has not been explored, and numerous overlaps suggest a broader influence of New World religions. See, for example, Rawick, *American Slave,* Texas Narratives vol. 7, p. 2784, for an account of a Conjurer whose ritual acts and paraphernalia are evocative of Kongo-derived *Palo Mayombe,* also known as black magic in Afro-Cuban religion today. See also Helen Tunnicliff Catterall, ed., *Judicial Cases Concerning American Slavery and the Negro* (New York: Negro Universities Press, 1968), Mississippi cases, vol. 3, p. 368; Puckett, *Folk Beliefs of the Southern Negro,* p. 190; and see "Notes and Queries," *Journal of American Folklore* 2 (1889): 233, for reference to a "Voodoo" cult operating in nineteenth-century Philadelphia.

23. Hurston, *Sanctified Church,* p. 16. For a similar account of a Conjurer's "call," see Johnson, *Fabled Doctor Jim Jordan,* p. 56.

24. Bass, "Mojo," p. 381; see also Puckett, *Folk Beliefs of the Southern Negro;* Herron, "Conjuring," p. 118.

25. Anonymous slave, quoted in Sallie M. Park, "Voodooism in Tennessee," *Atlantic Monthly,* September 1889, p. 376; Sarah Handy, "Negro Superstitions," *Lippincott's Monthly Magazine,* 1891, p. 736; Donald J. Waters, ed., *Strange Ways and Sweet Dreams: Afro-American Folklore from the Hampton Institute* (Boston: G. K. Hall, 1983), p. 134; Philip Alexander Bruce, *The Plantation Negro as a Freeman: Observations on his Character, Condition, and Prospects in Virginia* (New York: G. P. Putnam, 1889), p. 116–25; McTeer, *High Sheriff,* p. 22; Fields, *Lemon Swamp,* pp. 116–17; see Eric Foner, *Nothing but Freedom: Emancipation and Its Legacy* (Baton Rouge: Louisiana State University Press, 1983), p. 50, for postwar "Black Codes" with some bearing on Conjure practitioners. On Conjurers and monetary profit, see also Louis Pendleton, "Notes on Negro Folklore and Witchcraft in the South," *Journal of American Folklore* 3 (1890): 204–5; and Tallant, *Voodoo in New Orleans,* pp. 33–35; Peter Mitchel Wilson, *Southern Exposure* (Chapel Hill: University of North Carolina Press, 1927), pp. 108–10; "Conjure Doctors in the South," p. 30.

26. Albert Raboteau, "The Afro-American Traditions," in *Caring and Curing: Health and Medicine in the Western Religious Traditions,* ed. Ronald Numbers and Darrel Amundsden (New York: Macmillan, 1986), p. 551.

27. Owen, "Among the Voodoos," p. 232; W. D. Siegfried, *A Winter in the South and Work Among the Freedmen* (Newark, N.J.: Jennings Brothers Printers, 1870); Ruth Bass, "The Little Man," in *Mother Wit from the Laughing Barrel: Readings in the Interpretation of Afro-American Folklore,* ed. Alan Dundes (Jackson: University Press of Mississippi, 1972), p. 394. For the fusion of African American folk beliefs and Catholicism in an early-twentieth-century black community along the Mississippi River, see Ruth Bass, "Ole Miss'," in *Folk-Say: A Regional Miscellany,* ed. B. A. Botkin (Norman: University of Oklahoma Press, 1931), vol. 3, pp. 48–69.

28. Hurston, *Sanctified Church,* pp. 17–18; Whitten, "Malign Occultism," p. 410; Hortense Powdermaker, *After Freedom: A Cultural Study in the Deep South* (New York: Viking Press, 1939), pp. 294–95. On charms containing psalms and biblical verses see Botkin, *Lay My Burden Down,* p. 339. German- and French-language magical booklets were first published in the United States during the early nineteenth century and consulted as reference texts by healers within German Jewish and Pennsylvania Dutch communities. Eventually, English-language editions of these manuals made their way into the hands of Anglo- and African American practitioners of folk magic. Belief in the inherent supernatural power of certain books, letters, and written materials may have intensified when literacy acquired a near-sacred significance for African Americans in the post-Emancipation era. Three early-twentieth-century sources mentioning "letters" or "books" point to the potential spiritual significance of writings. The concept of the mystical power of the word that is written, so prominent in Islamic lore, was fused with the African notion of spirit-embedding charms, which were adopted by black Americans.

29. See Ruth Bass, "Fern Seed—For Peace," in *Folk-Say: A Regional Miscellany,* ed. B. A. Botkin (Norman: University of Oklahoma Press, 1931), pp. 145–56; Puckett, *Folk Beliefs of the Southern Negro,* pp. 557–59. For the use of plants in folk healing in the black Christian tradition see Karen Baldwin, "Mrs. Emma Dupree: 'That Little Medicine Thing,'" *North Carolina Folklore Journal* 32 (1984): 50–53; W. S. Harrison, *Sam Williams: A Tale of the Old South* (Nashville, Tenn.: Publishing House of the Methodist Episcopal Church, 1892), p. 64 ff; Charles Perdue, Thomas E. Barden, and Robert K. Phillips, eds., *Weevils in the Wheat: Interviews with Virginia Ex-Slaves* (Charlottesville: University Press of Virginia, 1976), p. 246.

30. Jacob Stroyer, *My Life in the South* (Salem: Salem Observer Book and Job Print), 1879, pp. 57–58; Handy, "Negro Superstitions," p. 738. Describing a similar ritual, a former slave from Tennessee, Byrl Anderson, told how his white master would "tell many a fortune . . . by hanging the Bible on a key and saying certain words." Anderson recalled, "When the Bible would come to me, it would just spin. That meant that I was [a] lucky and righteous man" (Perdue et al., *Weevils in the Wheat,* p. 11). See also Rawick, *American Slave,* Texas Narratives vol. 4, no. 2, p. 5.

31. Perdue et al., *Weevils in the Wheat,* p. 278; Roland Steiner, "Braziel Robinson Possessed of Two Spirits," *Journal of American Folklore* 13 (1900), reprinted in *Mother Wit from the Laughing Barrel: Readings in the Interpretation of Afro-American Folklore,* ed. Alan Dundes (Jackson: University Press of Mississippi, 1972), p. 378; see also the narrative of Ank Bishop, an ex-slave in Alabama, in Virginia Pounds Brown, *Toting the Lead Row: Ruby Pickens Tartt, Alabama Folklorist* (University: University of Alabama Press, 1981), p. 127.

32. Owen, "Among the Voodoos," pp. 239, 243; Johnson, *Fabled Doctor Jim Jordan,* p. 22. See Mamie Garvin Fields's description of the the Gullah Conjurer Jimmy Brisbane, a successful root doctor who hosted weekly prayer meetings where clients and church members were brought together in his home on John's Island, South Carolina (Fields, *Lemon Swamp,* p. 121). Doctor Buzzard, known also as "Doctor Eagle" in some parts of the South, was a figure of mythic pro-

portions, about whom little of historical fact is known. For a tentative account of the history of this figure, see Roger Pinckney, *Blue Roots: African-American Folk Magic of the Gullah People* (New York: Llewellyn Publications, 1998).

33. Rawick, *American Slave*, Texas Narratives vol. 2, s.s. 2, pp. 16–17; George Schuyler, *Black and Conservative: The Autobiography of George S. Schuyler* (New Rochelle, N.Y.: Arlington House, 1966); Powdermaker, *After Freedom*, p. 286.

34. "About the Conjuring Doctors," *Southern Workman* 7, no. 5 (1878): 38–39 [in Waters, *Strange Ways*, pp. 142–45]; Bacon and Herron, "Conjuring," p. 117; Carl Carmer, *Stars Fell on Alabama* (New York: Farrar and Rinehart, 1934), p. 218; Puckett, *Folk Beliefs of the Southern Negro*, p. 565; Whitten, "Malign Occultism,", pp. 411 ff.

35. Botkin, *Lay My Burden Down*, p. 37. See also Levine, *Black Culture and Black Consciousness*, p. 57.

36. Handy, "Negro Superstitions," pp. 735–36; Johnson, *Fabled Doctor Jim Jordan*, p. 22; Rawick, *American Slave*, Texas Narratives vol. 7, pt. 6, p. 2782; Botkin, *Lay My Burden Down*, p. 34.

37. Clipping "Life in Arkansas," *Boston Herald*, May 29, 1897, p. 20, in Newbell Puckett Papers, Cleveland Public Library; Octave Thanet, "Folklore in Arkansas," *Journal of American Folklore* 5 (1892): 122; Puckett, *Folk Beliefs of the Southern Negro*, p. 205.

38. See Louise Westling, ed., *He Included Me: The Autobiography of Sarah Rice* (Athens: University of Georgia Press, 1989), p. 44.

39. Murphy, "Survival of African Music," pp. 334–35.

40. Zora Neale Hurston, *Mules and Men* (New York: J. B. Lippincott, 1935), p. 228.

41. Thaddeus Norris, "Negro Superstitions," *Lippincott's Monthly Magazine*, July 1870, reprinted in *The Negro and His Folklore in Nineteenth-Century Periodicals*, ed. Bruce Jackson (Austin: University of Texas Press, 1967), p. 139; oral narrative, Rev. P. L. Harvey, folder 2, pp. 1–4, University of Virginia Special Collections, Lynchburg; clipping from the *New York Times*, Sunday, December 20, 1874, Newbell Puckett Papers, Cleveland Public Library; Rawick, *American Slave*, Georgia Narratives vol. 13, pt. 4, p. 248.

42. This is not to say that congregations never formally censured church-going Conjure practitioners. Several nineteenth-century church trials reveal cases in which charges were brought against church-going Conjurers for harmful magic or witchcraft, including two that resulted in expulsion of the members. Transcripts can be found in the records of following church minutes: First Baptist Church of Washington, D.C., June 11, 1830, Betty Orr expelled for conjuring practices; Welsh Neck Baptist Church of South Carolina, October 1832, Cupid expelled for conjuring practices.

43. On the "magical" orientation of African American religion see Mechal Sobel, *Trabelin' On: The Slave Journey to an Afro-Baptist Faith* (Westport, Ct.: Greenwood Press, 1979), pp. 99–135; Raboteau, *Slave Religion*, p. 250; Levine, *Black Culture and Black Consciousness*, p. 37. For an apt theory of conjuring as "work" that utilizes Claude Lévi-Strauss's concept of *bricolage*, see David H. Brown, "Conjure/Doctors: An Exploration of a Black Discourse in America, Antebellum to 1940," *Folklore Forum* 23, nos. 1–2 (1990): 20.

44. Clifton Johnson, ed., God Struck Me Dead: Religious Conversion Experiences and Autobiographies of Ex-Slaves (Philadelphia: Pilgrim Press, 1969), p. 127; Rawick, American Slave, South Carolina Narratives vol. 3, pt. 4, p. 252; Georgia Writers' Project, Drums and Shadows, p. 25; Rawick, American Slave, Mississippi Narratives vol. 7, p. 142 and Georgia Narratives vol. 12, p. 18.

CHAPTER 2. "AFRICA WAS A LAND A' MAGIC POWER SINCE DE BEGINNIN' A HISTORY"

1. Paul Edwards, ed., Equiano's Travels: His Autobiography; The Interesting Narrative of the Life of Olaudah Equiano or Gustavus Vassa the African (London: Heinemann, 1980), p. 121. Born in 1745 in what is present-day eastern Nigeria, Equiano was one of the first Africans to provide an eyewitness account of the slave trade in a published autobiography. Equiano was educated in England and America by benevolent whites, who renamed him Gustavus Vassa, after a sixteenth-century Swedish monarch. Traveling extensively in Europe, the Caribbean, and America, he wrote of his adventures at sea in a narrative that was published in several editions during his lifetime and later translated into Dutch, French, and German. For background on Equiano see Angelo Costanzo, Surprising Narrative: Olaudah Equiano and the Beginnings of Black Autobiography (Westport, Conn.: Greenwood Press, 1987). For the context of the religious thought and views of the world of which Equiano was a part, see Paul Edwards and Rosalind Shaw, "The Invisible Chi in Equiano's Interesting Narrative," Journal of Religion in Africa 19, no. 2 (1989): 146–56.

2. Africans were taken as slaves from the western and central-western regions of the continent, areas broadly designated by Europeans as Upper Guinea (the present-day Senegambia, Guinea-Bissau, and Sierra Leone), Lower Guinea (Ghana, Togo, Benin, Nigeria, Cameroon, and the Ivory Coast) and Angola (including Gabon, Congo, Zaire, and northern Angola). Although specific African populations would predominate within particular slave societies in the New World, ethnic distinctions were blurred over time as indigenous African American cultures developed. See Melville Herskovits, The Myth of the Negro Past (Boston: Beacon Press, 1958); Robert Farris Thompson, Flash of the Spirit: African and Afro-American Art and Philosophy (New York: Vintage Books, 1983); Georgia Writers' Project, Drums and Shadows: Survival Studies Among the Georgia Coastal Negroes (Athens: University of Georgia Press, 1940), pp. 195–249. Maude Southwell Wahlman, Signs and Symbols: African Images in African-American Quilts (New York: Studio Books, 1993); Suzanne Preston Blier, African Vodun: Art, Psychology, and Power (Chicago: University of Chicago Press, 1995). Geoffrey Parrinder, West African Religion: A Study of the Beliefs and Practices of Akan, Ewe, Yoruba, Ibo, and Kindred Peoples (London: Epworth Press, 1961); Benjamin Ray, African Religions: Symbol, Ritual, and Community (Englewood Cliffs, N.J.: Prentice Hall, 1979).

3. Anne Hilton, The Kingdom of Kongo (Oxford: Oxford University Press, 1985), p. 9. Wyatt MacGaffey, Religion and Society in Central Africa: The BaKongo of Lower Zaire (Chicago: University of Chicago Press, 1986). Peter Morton-Williams, "An Outline of the Cosmology and Cult Organization of the

Oyo Yoruba," in *Peoples and Cultures of Africa: An Anthropological Reader,* ed. Elliot Skinner (Garden City, N.Y.: Natural History Press, 1973), pp. 654–63. Daryll Forde, ed., *African Worlds: Studies in the Cosmological Ideas and Social Values of African Peoples* (London: Oxford University Press, 1954); John Mbiti, *African Religions and Philosophy* (London: Heinemann, 1988), pp. 75–91; Evan Zuesse, *Ritual Cosmos: The Sanctification of Life in African Religions* (Athens: Ohio University Press, 1979), pp. 238–43.

4. This discussion draws from the following studies of African traditional religions: Forde, *African Worlds;* Ray, *African Religions;* and Zuesse, *Ritual Cosmos;* John Mbiti, *African Religions and Philosophy* (Garden City, N.Y.: Doubleday, 1970), p. 203. In African thought, terms such as *Da, ashe,* and *Nommo* refer to what is essentially the same dynamic spirit force that imparts power to and infuses all living things. See especially Leonard Barrett, *Soul-Force: African Heritage in Afro-American Religion* (Garden City, N.Y.: Anchor Press, 1974). See also Dominque Zahan, *Religion, Spirituality, and Thought of Traditional Africa* (Chicago: University of Chicago Press, 1983), pp. 34–35, 45–48, 51–52.

5. E. Bolaji Idowu, *African Traditional Religion: A Definition* (Maryknoll, N.Y.: Orbis Books, 1973), p. 196. Willy de Craemer, Jan Vansina, and Renee Fox, "Religious Movements in Central Africa: A Theoretical Study," *Comparative Studies in Society and History* 18, no. 4 (October 1976): 460.

6. De Craemer et al., "Religious Movements in Central Africa," p. 461; Idowu, *African Traditional Religion,* p. 196.

7. De Craemer et al., "Religious Movements in Central Africa," p. 461; This study essentially restates Emile Durkheim's distinction between magic and religion as an activity that is based in social organization. For Durkheim, magical activity normally involves individuals, who serve as clients of the magician. Magic has no church or community and does not emphasize collective activity; religion recognizes a moral assembly of believers who are bound together by their unified belief in the authority of the collective.

8. Andreas Joshua Ulsheimer, "Voyage of 1603–4," in *German Sources for West African History,* ed. Adam Jones (Wiesbaden: Franz Steiner Verlag, 1983), p. 26.

9. Bosman, who called the fetish a "false god," used the Akan word *bossom,* as did Wilhelm Müller, a Lutheran prelate who served the Danish African Company on the Gold Coast nearly fifty years earlier. Müller distinguished between *o-bossum,* "a general idol" that took its power from the high god, and *summan,* an object that served as a dwelling place for lesser spirits and entities. He concluded that Africans generally used *o-bossum* "to cover everything" they considered sacred and in particular instances referred to household sculptures, statuettes, and other created objects (Willem Bosman, *A New and Accurate Description of the Coast of Guinea, Divided into the Gold, the Slave, and the Ivory Coasts* [1703; reprint, New York: Barnes and Noble, 1967], p. 148; Müller, "Description of the Fetu Country," in *German Sources for West African History,* ed. Adam Jones [Weisbaden: Franz Steiner Verlag, 1983], pp. 158–59, 162). R. S. Rattray, a British anthropologist, was the first scholar in the twentieth century to identify the "fetish" with a "limited class of magical objects" called *summan* in Akan tradition, which he described as the "potential dwelling place of a spirit

or spirits . . . associated with the control of the powers of evil . . . for personal ends . . . as much for defensive as for offensive purposes" (Rattray, *Religion and Art in Ashanti* [London: Oxford University Press, 1927], pp. 11, 24, and his *Ashanti* [Oxford: Clarendon Press, 1923]). Pieter de Marees, another seventeenth-century European writer, called African fetishes "relics," possibly referring to funerary statuettes among Akan peoples (de Marees, *Description and Historical Account of the Gold Kingdom of Guinea*, trans. and ed. Albert van Dantzig and Adam Jones [Oxford: Oxford University Press for the British Academy, 1987], p. 69).

10. Joseph M. Murphy, *Working the Spirit: Ceremonies of the African Diaspora* (Boston: Beacon Press, 1994), p. 180; added emphasis.

11. Within the various colonies of the New World different circumstances served to facilitate the survival of African religions under slavery. In Catholic societies, for example, while baptizing slaves and permitting their association in religious confraternities and soldalities, slaveholders unwittingly provided shelter for the secret practice and retention of traditional African religions. The result in many cases was a synthesis of Catholicism and traditional African religions. For studies, see Roger Bastide, *African Civilizations in the New World* (New York: Harper and Row, 1971); Murphy, *Working the Spirit;* Thompson, *Flash of the Spirit;* George Eaton Simpson, *Black Religions in the New World* (New York: Columbia University Press, 1978). A synopsis of some of these studies with an analysis of the continuity and discontinuity of meaning in African New World religions can be found in Albert Raboteau, *Slave Religion: The "Invisible Institution" in the Antebellum South* (New York: Oxford University Press, 1978). On African slave ethnic distribution in the Americas see Philip Curtin, *The Atlantic Slave Trade: A Census* (Madison: University of Wisconsin Press, 1969); Michael Mullin, *Africa in America: Slave Acculturation and Resistance in the American South and the British Caribbean, 1736–1831* (Urbana: University of Illinois Press, 1992), pp. 281–88. On Africans in the Anglo-American colonies, see Daniel C. Littlefield, *Rice and Slaves: Ethnicity and the Slave Trade in Colonial South Carolina* (Baton Rouge: Louisiana State University Press, 1981); and Darold Wax, "Preferences for Slaves in Colonial America," *Journal of Negro History* 58 (1973): 371–401.

12. Marcus Jernigan, "Slavery and Conversion in the American Colonies," *American Historical Review* 21 (1916): 504–11; Raboteau, *Slave Religion;* Luther Jackson, "Religious Development of the Negro in Virginia from 1760 to 1860," *Journal of Negro History* 16 (1931): 168–239.

13. "Rev. Philip Reading to Rev. Samuel Smith," October 10, 1748, and (from John Waring) "A Letter to an American Planter from His Friend in London," October 10, 1770, both in *Religious Philanthropy and Colonial Slavery: The American Correspondence of the Associates of Dr. Bray, 1717–1777*, ed. John C. Van Horne (Urbana: University of Illinois Press, 1985), pp. 100, 293–94; see also Alexander Hewatt, *An Historical Account of the Rise and Progress of the Colonies of South Carolina and Georgia* (London: Alexander Donaldson, 1779) vol. 2, p. 100; Frank Klingberg, *An Appraisal of the Negro in Colonial South Carolina: A Study in Americanization* (Washington, D.C.: Associated Publishers, 1941), p. 51; David Humphreys, *An Account of the Endeavors Used by the*

Society for the Propagation of the Gospel in Foreign Parts (London, 1730), pp. 7–8; Raboteau, *Slave Religion,* p. 66.

14. William D. Piersen, *Black Yankees: The Development of an Afro-American Subculture in Eighteenth-Century New England* (Amherst: University of Massachusetts Press, 1988), pp. 74–86. See also Jon Butler, who argues that "African occultism surfaced for the first time on a sustained scale . . . after 1760," primarily because of the importation of Africans and African beliefs "into a newly receptive setting" (Butler, "The Dark Ages of American Occultism, 1760–1848," in *The Occult in America: New Historical Perspectives,* ed. Howard Kerr [Urbana: University of Illinois Press, 1983], p. 66); see also Kenneth Brown, "Structural Continuity in an African-American Slave and Tenant Community," *Historical Archeology* 24 (1990): 7–19; Eric Klingelhofer, "Aspects of Early Afro-American Material Culture: Artifacts from the Slave Quarters at Garrison Plantation, Maryland," *Historical Archeology* 21 (1987): 115–17. For references, see Thomas Alvord, *The Devil in Britain and America* (Ann Arbor: Gryphon Books, 1971); Tom Peete Cross, "Witchcraft in North Carolina," *Studies in Philology* 16, no. 3 (1919): 219; M. Drake Patten, "African-American Spiritual Beliefs: An Archeological Testimony from the Slave Quarter" (proceedings of the Dublin Seminar for New England Folklife, *Wonders of the Invisible World: 1600–1900,* ed. Peter Benes, June, 1992), pp. 44–52; Leland Ferguson, *Uncommon Ground: Archeology and Early African America, 1650–1800* (Washington, D.C.: Smithsonian Institution Press, 1992).

15. With respect to Africans and Anglican settlers in colonial Virginia, Mechal Sobel argues forcefully that resemblances between the two groups' perceptions of time, space, and the natural world made for a two-way "social-cultural interplay" of values and attitudes. "In the traditional cultures of both peoples the natural world was seen as a place of mystery and hidden powers that had to be taken into account. Africans coming to America did not have a deviant rational tradition, but their view of the natural world was very close to the traditional view of most English people. Taboos were highly important; ritual acts were seen as having efficacy; holy places, holy times, and holy people could affect spirit or power. In this area of perceptions and values the possibility of confluence and melding was strong" (Sobel, *The World They Made Together: Black and White Values in Eighteenth-Century Virginia* [Princeton: Princeton University Press, 1987], pp. 5, 78).

16. Ira Berlin, "Time Space and the Evolution of Afro-American Society on British Mainland North America," *American Historical Review* 85 (1980): 44–78. See also Sidney Mintz and Richard Price, *The Birth of African American Culture: An Anthropological Perspective* (Boston: Beacon Press, 1992). It is also probable that American Indian contact with Africans facilitated cultural exchanges as well. In this respect the probability of black-white-red syncretism was as feasible in North America as it was in other parts of the Western Hemisphere, although demographic and social factors made for significant differences in the extent of American Indian cultural retentions. See, for example, Richard Price, *Maroon Societies* (Baltimore: Johns Hopkins University Press, 1979), pp. 11–16; Daniel Usner, "Indian-Black Relations in Colonial and Antebellum Louisiana," in *Slave Cultures and the Cultures of Slavery,* ed. Stephan Palmie (Knoxville: University of

Tennessee Press, 1995); Sobel, *World They Made Together,* p. 99; Peter Wood, *Black Majority: Negroes in Colonial South Carolina from 1670 through the Stono Rebellion* (New York: W. W. Norton, 1974), p. 289; and John Boles, *Black Southerners; 1619–1869* (Lexington: University Press of Kentucky, 1984), pp. 145–52. There is a growing body of literature which stresses African and African American contributions to the American religious experience. See Sobel, *World They Made Together;* and John Boles, ed., *Masters and Slaves in the House of the Lord: Race and Religion in the American South, 1740–1870* (Lexington: University Press of Kentucky, 1988), pp. 10–11; Alfloyd Butler, *The Africanization of American Christianity* (New York: Carlton, 1980); Charles Joyner, "Cultural Interaction in the Old South," in *Black and White Cultural Interaction in the Antebellum South,* ed. Ted Ownby (Jackson: University Press of Mississippi, 1993), pp. 3–22.

17. Jon Butler, *Awash in a Sea of Faith: Christianizing the American People* (Cambridge, Mass.: Harvard University Press, 1990); John Brooke, *The Refiner's Fire: The Making of Mormon Cosmology, 1644–1844* (New York: Cambridge University Press, 1994). For a theoretical statement on African-based traditions in America, see Herskovits, *Myth of the Negro Past,* pp. 242–43; and Raboteau, *Slave Religion,* p. 59.

18. Herbert Leventhal, *In the Shadow of the Enlightenment: Occultism and Renaissance Science in Eighteenth-Century America* (New York: New York University Press, 1976); Jon Butler, "Magic, Astrology, and the Early American Religious Heritage, 1600–1760," *American Historical Review* 84 (1979): 317–46.

19. Arna Bontemps and Langston Hughes, *The Book of Negro Folklore* (New York: Arno Press, 1969), pp. 58–59; Margaret Jackson, "Folklore in Slave Narratives Before the Civil War," *New York Folklore Quarterly* 11, no. 1 (1985): 11–12; See also Katherine L. Dvorak, "Chapter," in *Masters and Slaves in the House of the Lord: Race and Religion in the American South, 1740–1870,* ed. John Boles (Lexington: University Press of Kentucky, 1988), p. 176; on African spiritual traditions, see Parrinder, *West African Religion.*

20. Maria Leach, *Whistle in the Graveyard: Folktales to Chill Your Bones* (New York: Viking Press, 1974); Mary Lyons, *Raw Head, Bloody Bones: African-American Tales of the Supernatural* (New York: Macmillan, 1991); Newbell Niles Puckett, *Folk Beliefs of the Southern Negro* (Chapel Hill: University of North Carolina Press, 1926); Sobel, *World They Made Together,* pp. 45, 97–99; Richard Dorson, *American Negro Folktales* (Greenwich, Conn.: Fawcett Publications, 1967), pp. 15–16. On folklore as rich source material in American religious history, see Donald Byrne, *No Foot of Land: Folklore of American Methodist Itinerants* (Metuchen, N.J.: Scarecrow Press, 1975); F. Roy Johnson, *SUPERnaturals Among Carolina Folk and Their Neighbors* (Murfreesboro, N.C.: Johnson Publishing, 1974), pp. 9–14; Leventhal, *Shadow of the Enlightenment,* pp. 101 ff. On African American folk beliefs and folklore see also William Montgomery, *Under Their Own Vine and Fig Tree: The African-American Church in the South, 1865–1900* (Baton Rouge: Louisiana State University Press, 1993), pp. 289 ff; Elliot Gorn, "Black Spirits: The Ghostlore of Afro-American Slaves," *American Quarterly* 36, no. 4 (1984): 551. Raboteau, *Slave Religion,* pp. 61–66; Mechal Sobel, *Trabelin' On: The Slave Journey to an Afro-Baptist Faith* (Princeton: Princeton University Press, 1988); John Blassingame, *The Slave Community:*

Plantation Life in the Antebellum South (New York: Oxford University Press, 1972), p. 29; Dena Epstein, *Sinful Tunes and Spirituals: Black Folk Music to the Civil War* (Urbana: University of Illinois Press, 1977), pp. 38–46; on Euro-American Protestant lore and the supernatural see David W. Hall, *Worlds of Wonder, Days of Judgment: Popular Religious Belief in Early New England* (New York: Knopf, 1989); and Richard Dorson, *America in Legend: Folklore from the Colonial Period to the Present* (New York: Pantheon, 1973); Newbell Niles Puckett, "Religious Folk-Beliefs of Whites and Negroes," *Journal of Negro History* 16 (1931); Guion Johnson, "Characteristics of Antebellum North Carolina Folklore," *North Carolina Historical Review* 6 (1929): 155.

21. Morgan Godwyn, *The Negro's and Indian's Advocate, Suing for Their Admission into the Church, or A Persuasive to the Instructing and Baptizing of the Negro's and Indians in Our Plantations* (London, 1680).

22. Jean Barbot, "Letter 8," in *Barbot on Guinea: The Writings of Jean Barbot on West Africa, 1678–1712*, ed. P. E. H. Hair (London: Hakluyt Society, 1992), pp. 86, 93–94; John Atkins, *A Voyage to Guinea, Brazil and the West Indies, with Remarks on the Gold, Ivory and Slave-Trade* (London: printed for Caesar Ward and Richard Chandler, 1735), p. 56; John Mathews, *A Voyage to the River Sierra Leone on the Coast of Africa* (London: B. White and Son, 1788), p. 132; J. Spencer Trimingham, *A History of Islam in West Africa* (London: Oxford University Press, 1962).

23. Hilton, *Kingdom of Kongo*, pp. 15–17; Christian missionaries in early Kongo, adopting endogenous categories in their efforts to convert Africans, identified the Bible, the Eucharist, crosses, and even churches as *nkisi*. See Hilton, *Kingdom of Kongo*, p. 94; and John Thornton, *The Kingdom of Kongo: Civil War and Transition, 1641–1718* (Madison: University of Wisconsin Press, 1983), p. 62. On the visual tradition of Kongo charms as magical objects see Wyatt MacGaffey, *Art and Healing of the Bakongo, Commented by Themselves: Minkisi from the Laman Collection* (Bloomington: Indiana University Press, 1991).

24. European traders in seventeenth- and eighteenth-century West Africa routinely described these "puppets" and "idols," sometimes as physical objects of wood or clay that possessed individual personalities. Although the African practice of anthropomorphizing created objects was adopted by blacks in America, similar customs were popular among European Americans as well. See Thompson, *Flash of the Spirit*, p. 118; Wyatt MacGaffey, "Complexity, Astonishment and Power: The Visual Vocabulary of Minkisi," *Journal of Southern African Studies* 14, no. 2 (January 1988); his *Art and Healing of the Bakongo*; Blier, *African Vodun*, 249 ff; and Barbot, "Letter 27," in *Barbot on Guinea*, p. 228.

25. Rawick, *American Slave*, Texas Narratives vol. 5, pt. 3, pp. 143–44; Norman Whitten, "Aspects and Origins of Negro Occultism in Piedmont Village" (master's thesis, University of North Carolina, Chapel Hill, 1961); Hortense Powdermaker, *After Freedom: A Cultural Study in the Deep South* (New York: Viking Press, 1939); Alice Bacon, "Conjuring and Conjure Doctors, pt. 2," *Southern Workman* 24, no. 12 (1895): 209–10 [in *Waters, Strange Ways*: pp. 238–42]; see also Thompson, *Flash of the Spirit*, pp. 142–45; Ellen Orr, "The Bottle Tree," *Mississippi Folklore Review* 4 (Winter 1969); Rawick, *American Slave*, Texas Narratives vol. 5, pt, 3, pp. 143–44.

26. For Conjure formulae, see especially Harry Middleton Hyatt, *Hoodoo — Conjuration — Witchcraft — Rootwork: Beliefs Accepted by Many Negroes and White Persons, These Being Orally Recorded Among Blacks and Whites,* 5 vols. (Hannibal, Mo.: Western Publishing, 1970–78; distributed by American University Bookstore, Washington, D.C.); and Puckett, *Folk Beliefs of the Southern Negro.*

27. Robert Tallant, *Voodoo in New Orleans* (New York: Macmillan, 1946), pp. 224–25; MacGaffey, *Religion and Society in Central Africa,* p. 70; Thompson, *Flash of the Spirit;* on Funza and other Kongolese *nkisi,* see Wyatt McGaffey and John Janzen, *An Anthology of Kongo Religion: Primary Texts from Lower Zaire* (Lawrence: University of Kansas Press, 1974), p. 34. High John the Conquerer root has been identified both with St.-John's-wort and the Adam and Eve plant of the genus *hypericum.* See Elsie Clews Parsons, "Folklore of the Sea Islands, South Carolina" *Memoirs of the American Folklore Society* 16 (1923): 212; see also Bontemps and Hughes, *Book of Negro Folklore,* p. 22; Faith Mitchell, *Hoodoo Medicine: Sea Islands Herbal Remedies* (Berkeley: Reed, Cannon and Johnson, 1978); Sharon Sharp, "Folk Medicine" in *Encyclopedia of Southern Culture,* ed. Charles Reagan Wilson and William Ferris (Chapel Hill: University of North Carolina Press, 1989), p. 508; "Remedies to Cure Conjuration," *Southern Workman* 28, no. 3 (1899): 112; David Conway, *The Magic of Herbs* (London: Cape Publishing, 1973).

28. Increase Mather, *An Essay for the Recording of Illustrious Providences* (place: printed by Samuel Green, 1684), pp. 260–61; Richard Godbeer, *The Devil's Dominion: Magic and Religion in Early New England* (Cambridge: Cambridge University Press, 1992), pp. 38–39; Chadwick Hansen, *Witchcraft at Salem* (New York: G. Braziller, 1969).

29. See, for example, Atkins, *Voyage to Guinea,* p. 101; Adam Jones, ed., *German Sources for West African History* (Wiesbaden: Franz Steiner Verlag, 1983), p. 118; and de Marees, *Gold Kingdom of Guinea,* p. 70; For black Conjurers "feeding" their charms see Mary A. Owen, "Among the Voodoos" (paper presented at the Second International Folk-lore Congress, 1891), p. 230; and Jeanette Robinson Murphy, "The Survival of African Music" (1899), in *The Negro and His Folklore in Nineteenth-Century Periodicals,* ed. Bruce Jackson (Austin: University of Texas Press, 1967), p. 335; B. A. Botkin, *Lay My Burden Down: A Folk History of Slavery* (Chicago: University of Chicago Press, 1945), p. 30; Raboteau, *Slave Religion,* p. 82.

30. As John Thornton has noted, such communications between humans and entities from the invisible world often functioned as the basis of religious knowledge in precolonial Africa (Thornton, *Africa and Africans in the Making of the Atlantic World, 1400–1680* [Cambridge: Cambridge University Press, 1992], p. 236); see Müller, "Description of the Fetu Country," p. 172; Atkins, *Voyage to Guinea,* p. 102; and Jones, *German Sources for West African History,* p. 256.

31. *Maryland Journal and Baltimore Advertiser,* October 5, 1784, p. 320; Chloe Russel[l], *The Compleat Fortuneteller and Dream Book* (Boston: Tom Hazard, n.d.); Piersen, *Black Yankees,* p. 84; see also Yvonne Chireau, "The Uses of the Supernatural: Toward a History of Black Women's Magical Practices," in *A Mighty Baptism: Race, Gender, and the Creation of American Protestantism,* ed.

Susan Juster and Lisa MacFarlane (Ithaca: Cornell University Press, 1996); and Peter Benes, "Fortunetellers, Wise Men and Magical Healers in New England, 1644–1850" (proceedings of the Dublin Seminar for New England Folklife, *Wonders of the Invisible World: 1600–1900*, ed. Peter Benes, June, 1992), p. 135; Benes states (pp. 127–28) that up to the mid nineteenth century, the cunning "trades" in America were dominated by African and American Indian practitioners.

32. On black cunning persons in New England, see Benes, "Fortunetellers, Wise Men"; and William D. Piersen, "Black Arts and Black Magic: Yankee Accommodations to African Religion"(proceedings of the Dublin Seminar for New England Folklife, *Wonders of the Invisible World: 1600–1900,* ed. Peter Benes, June, 1992); *Gazette of the State of Georgia,* October 19, 1788, p. 2; *South Carolina Gazette,* April 8, 1756, p. 1 (original emphasis); Leventhal, *Shadow of the Enlightenment,* pp. 137–67; Sobel, *World They Made Together,* p. 98; Butler, *Awash in a Sea of Faith,* p. 86. African and African American healers with herbal and homeopathic skills were frequently recognized in colonial America for their medical contributions. See Peter Wood, "People's Medicine in the Early South," *Southern Exposure 6* (Summer 1978): 52; and his *Black Majority,* p. 289; on medicine in colonial New England see also Gordon Jones, ed., *The Angel of Bethesda* (Barre, Mass: American Antiquarian Society, 1972). There is reference to another eighteenth-century specialist of note in Fayetteville, North Carolina, a "Guinea-born" fugitive by the name of Sampson, a fortuneteller and Conjurer" who was about "fifty years old," speaking "bad English," indicating that he was probably a "New Negro," or African-born *(Hall's Wilmington Gazette* [North Carolina], June 8, 1797, p. 4).

33. Thomas Winterbottom, *An Account of the Native Africans in the Neighborhood of Sierra Leone* (London: C. Whittingham, 1803), vol. 1, p. 252. On European cunning persons, see Alan MacFarlane, *Witchcraft in Tudor and Stuart England: A Regional and Comparative Study* (New York: Harper and Row, 1970), p. 122; and Godbeer, *Devil's Dominion;* Brooke, *Refiner's Fire.*

34. Lillie E. Barr, "Three Months on a Southern Plantation," *New York Independent,* June 30, 1881, p. 2. John Hale, *A Modest Enquiry Into the Nature of Witchcraft and How Persons Guilty of That Crime May Be Convicted* (Boston: Kneeland and Adams, 1702), pp. 131, 146–47.

35. Butler, *Awash in a Sea of Faith,* pp. 83–97.Two studies of magic and religion among whites in medieval England and colonial New England, by Keith Thomas (*Religion and the Decline of Magic* [New York: Oxford University Press, 1997]) and Richard Godbeer (*Devil's Dominion),* have clarified a dynamic range of relationships between these two categories of supernatural belief and practice.

36. Curtin, *Atlantic Slave Trade;* James Rawley, *The Transatlantic Slave Trade: A History* (New York: W. W. Norton, 1981).

37. Mintz and Price, *Birth of African-American Culture;* Berlin, "Time Space and Evolution."

38. Alan Kulikoff, *Tobacco and Slaves: The Development of Southern Cultures in the Chesapeake, 1680–1800* (Chapel Hill: University of North Carolina Press, 1986), see esp. ch. 8; Philip D. Morgan, "Slave Life in Piedmont Virginia, 1720–1800," in *Colonial Chesapeake Society,* ed. Lois Green Carr, Philip D. Mor-

gan, and Jean Russo (Chapel Hill: University of North Carolina Press, 1988); Marvin L. Michael Kay and Lorin Lee Cary, *Slavery in North Carolina, 1748–1775* (Chapel Hill: University of North Carolina Press, 1995), pp. 24–25.

39. Edward Warren, *A Doctor's Experiences on Three Continents* (Baltimore: Cushings and Bailey Press, 1885), p. 200.

40. Georgia Writers' Project, *Drums and Shadows*, p. 25. On African-based ritualism in black American Conjure see Owen, "Among the Voodoos," p. 238; Eugene Genovese, *Roll, Jordan, Roll: The World the Slaves Made* (New York: Vintage Books, 1976), p. 223; George Brandon, "Sacrificial Practices," in *African-isms in American Culture*, ed. Joseph Holloway (Bloomington: Indiana University Press, 1990); Tallant, *Voodoo in New Orleans*, p. 33. On black supernaturalism and linguistic parallels between Africa and Afro-America see Winifred Vass, *The Bantu-speaking Heritage of the United States* (Los Angeles: Center for Afro-American Studies, University of California, 1979); Thompson, *Flash of the Spirit*, pp. 105, 107, 283; J. L. Dillard, *Lexicon of Black English* (New York: Seabury Press, 1977), p. 111. In the South, notes Philip D. Morgan, African words were associated with magic as late as the twentieth century (*Slave Counterpoint: Black Culture in the Eighteenth-Century Chesapeake and Lowcountry* [Chapel Hill: University of North Carolina Press, 1998], p. 622).

41. Henry Cogswell Knight [pseud.; Arthur Singleton], *Letters from the South and West* (Boston: Richardson and Lord, 1842), p. 75; added emphasis. Norman Whitten, "Contemporary Patterns of Malign Occultism Among Negroes in North Carolina" (1962), reprinted in *Mother Wit from the Laughing Barrel: Readings in the Interpretation of Afro-American Folklore*, ed. Alan Dundes (Jackson: University Press of Mississippi, 1972), p. 405; Ruth Bass, "Mojo" (1930), in *Mother Wit from the Laughing Barrel: Readings in the Interpretation of Afro-American Folklore,* ed. Alan Dundes (Jackson: University Press of Mississippi, 1972), p. 386; on cunning doctors in the postbellum South, see a detailed description in the *Southern Workman* (1878): 28; Alan D. Watson, "North Carolina Slave Courts, 1715–1785," *North Carolina Historical Review* 60, no. 1 (1983); on blacks and whites described as "Conjurers" in early America see Samuel Drake, *Annals of Witchcraft in New England and Elsewhere in the United States* (New York: Benjamin Bloom, 1967), p. 215; Cross, "Witchcraft in North Carolina"; on Conjurers as *obeah* men, see *African Repository* 1 (1826): 1. Blacks and Indians were sometimes described with a similar language. American Indian shamans, familiar figures in the early South, were called "Conjurers" in the works of some colonial expositors. See John Lawson, *History of Carolina* (Raleigh, N.C.: Strother and Marcom, 1860), pp. 30, 119. On the common cultural roots of blacks and Indians, see Alden Vaughan, "From White Men to Redskin: Changing Anglo-American Perspectives of the American Indian," *American Historical Review* 87 (1982): 927.

42. Harriet Collins quoted in Martia Graham Goodson, "Medical-Botanical Contributions of African Slave Women to American Medicine," *Western Journal of Black Studies* 11, no. 4 (1987): 200; Roland Steiner, "Observations on the Practice of Conjuring in Georgia," *Journal of American Folklore* 14 (1901): 177; Hubert Aimes, "African Institutions in America," *Journal of American Folklore* 18 (1902): 15–32; Daniel Robinson Hundley, *Social Relations in Our Southern*

States (Baton Rouge: Louisiana State University Press, 1860), p. 33; Charles Chesnutt, "Superstitions and Folklore of the South" (1901), reprinted in *Mother Wit from the Laughing Barrel: Readings in the Interpretation of Afro-American Folklore,* ed. Alan Dundes (Jackson: University Press of Mississippi, 1972), p. 371; F. Roy Johnson, *The Fabled Doctor Jim Jordan: A Story of Conjure* (Murfreesboro, N.C.: Johnson Publishing, 1963), p. 3. For discussions of the black American-American Indian cultural nexus, see Wood, "People's Medicine in the Old South," p. 51; J. Leitch Wright, Jr., *The Only Land They Knew: The Tragic Story of the American Indian in the Old South* (New York: Free Press, 1981), pp. 265, 248–78.

CHAPTER 3. "FOLKS CAN DO YUH LOTS OF HARM"

1. Folklore Folder no. 100156, Georgia Narratives, Richmond County, Georgia, Manuscripts Division, Library of Congress.

2. Vincent Harding, "Religion and Resistance Among Antebellum Negroes, 1800–1860," in *The Making of Black America: Essays in Negro Life and History,* ed. August Meier and Elliot Rudwick (New York: Athenaeum, 1969), vol. 1, p. 181.

3. This harsh response was typical of authorities in British mainland North America, where even rumors of slave rebellion were ruthlessly stifled by civil authorities. See Kenneth Scott, "The Slave Insurrection in New York in 1712," *New York Historical Society Quarterly* 45, no. 1 (1961): p. 46; Joseph Carroll, *Slave Insurrections in the United States, 1800–1865* (1938; reprint, New York: Negro Universities Press, 1968), pp. 14–15. The New York plot contrasts with an ill-fated conspiracy in colonial New York—dubbed the "Great Negro Plot" in contemporary narratives—that implicated slaves, free blacks, and whites in a plan to burn and pillage the city. Inconclusive as far as evidence of supernatural beliefs and practices among the participants, cryptic statements in the case record intimate that a Catholic priest had bound the conspirators to loyalty by means of secret oaths, which may have appealed to unassimilated Africans. Other allegations stated that a black "doctor" had administered poison to two of the prisoners. These statements, though unsubstantiated, advance the intriguing possibility that the participants in this rumored insurrection may have adopted supernatural rituals, as one historian has suggested (Jeanne Chase, "The 1741 Conspiracy to Burn New York: Black Plot or Black Magic?," *Social Science Information* 22, no. 6 [1983]: 979). On the background of the New York conspiracy see Daniel Horsmanden, *The New-York Conspiracy or a History of the Negro Plot with the Journal of the Proceedings against the Conspirators at New-York in the Years 1741–1742, 1810* (1810; reprint, New York: Negro Universities Press, 1968), pp. 252–53, 264, 289, 368; Ferenc Szasz, "The New York Slave Revolt of 1741: A Re-Examination," *New York History* 48 (1967): 224; Thomas Davis, *A Rumor of Revolt: "The Great Negro Plot" in Colonial New York* (Amherst: University of Massachusetts Press, 1985), p. 54.

4. Letter of the Reverend John Sharpe to the Society for the Propagation of the Gospel in Foreign Parts, in Roswell Randall Hoes, "The Negro Plot of 1712," *New-York Genealogical and Biographical Record* 21 (1890): 162–63; Scott,

"Slave Insurrection in New York," p. 46. Particularly among Coromantee, an ethnic group inclusive of speakers of the Akan and Ga-Adangme dialects, oaths unified warriors in preparation for combat. The oath secured a covenant between the forces of the spirit world and the parties sealing it with blood, a sign of kinship and a customary ingredient in African rituals of spiritual invocation.

5. Wyatt MacGaffey, *Art and Healing of the BaKongo, Commented by Themselves: Minkisi from the Laman Collection* (Bloomington: Indiana University Press, 1991), p. 121; Willem Bosman, *A New and Accurate Description of the Coast of Guinea, divided into the Gold, the Slave, and the Ivory Coasts* (1703; reprint, New York: Barnes and Noble, 1967), p. 149. Another early description of African oath taking can be found in Adam Jones, ed., *German Sources for West African History* (Wiesbaden: Franz Steiner Verlag, 1983), pp. 175–76. On Akan oath traditions, see especially R. S. Rattray, *Religion and Art in Ashante* (London: Oxford University Press, 1927), pp. 205–15; K. A. Busia, "The Ashante of the Gold Coast," in *African Worlds: Studies in the Cosmological Ideas and Social Values of African peoples,* ed. Daryll Forde (London: Oxford University Press, 1954); Madeline Manoukian, *Akan and Ga-Adangme Peoples* (London: International African Institute, 1964).

6. See David Barry Gaspar, *Bondmen and Rebels: A Study of Master Slave Relations in Antigua, with Implications for Colonial British America* (Baltimore: Johns Hopkins University Press, 1985), pp. 242–45; Michael Craton, *Testing the Chains: Resistance to Slavery in the British West Indies* (Ithaca: Cornell University Press, 1982), p. 122. Orlando Patterson, *The Sociology of Slavery: An Analysis of the Origins, Development and Structure of Negro Slave Society in Jamaica* (Rutherford, N.J.: Fairleigh Dickinson University Press, 1969), p. 272; for a description of the blood oath in the New World context, see Bryan Edwards, *A History, Civil and Commercial, of the British Colonies of the West Indies,* 2d ed. (London: J. Stockdale, 1794), vol. 2, p. 85. See also Monica Schuler, "Akan Slave Rebellions in the British Caribbean," *Savacou* 1, no. 1 (June 1970): 16; Michael Mullin, *Africa in America: Slave Acculturation and Resistance in the American South and the British Caribbean, 1736–1831* (Urbana: University of Illinois Press, 1992), p. 67; Craton, *Testing the Chains,* pp. 99–139.

7. Jacob Stroyer, *My Life in the South* (Salem: Newcomb and Gauss, 1898), pp. 58–59. For an account of another African American magical oathing ritual, see Thaddeus Turpin, "Religion Among the Negro Slaves of South Carolina," *Christian Advocate* 8 (January 1834): 419, 436, 437. For examples of Christianized oathtaking in the West Indies, see Schuler, "Akan Slave Rebellions," p. 23; Shirley Gordan, *God Almighty Make Me Free: Christianity in Pre-Emancipation Jamaica* (Bloomington: Indiana University Press, 1996), p. 98. For an example of an oath-curse by an African American Christian, see Charles Raymond, "The Religious Life of the Negro Slave," *Harper's New Monthly Magazine,* August 1863, p. 824.

8. Charles C. Jones, *Religious Instruction of the Negroes in the United States* (1842; reprint, Savannah: Negro Universities Press, 1969), p. 128. The same concerns had been raised in the aftermath of another colonial insurrection in the New York plot, which involved catechumens from a missionary school of the Society for the Propagation of the Gospel in Foreign Parts. In this case Elias Neau,

the Anglican cleric who operated the school, found himself accused of fostering the slaves' desire for freedom. Ultimately, Neau and the members of his class were vindicated, but a negative association between black religion and black rebellion had been evoked and would persist for generations to come (see John C. Van Horne, ed., *Religious Philanthropy and Colonial Slavery: The American Correspondence of the Associates of Dr. Bray, 1717–1777* [Urbana: University of Illinois Press, 1985], pp. 32–35; Faith Vibert, "The Society for the Propagation of the Gospel," *Journal of Negro History* 18 [1933]: 176). See also Sylvia Frey, *Water from the Rock: Black Resistance in a Revolutionary Age* (Princeton: Princeton University Press, 1991); Eugene Genovese, *Roll Jordan, Roll: The World the Slaves Made* (New York: Vintage Books, 1976), pp. 592–94.

9. In the West Indies, bondpersons made ready for rebellion by fortifying themselves by supernatural means. In the great 1760 uprising of slaves in St. Mary's parish, Jamaica, also known as Tacky's Revolt, plotters were supported by an "old Coromantin obeah-man," who, according to an eighteenth-century historian, "administered a powder, which, being rubbed on their bodies, was to make them invulnerable" (Edward Long, *History of Jamaica* [1774; reprint, London: Frank Cass, 1970]). Analogous rites were established in slave communities from Barbados to the Guianas, where bondpersons were brought together under the leadership of *obeah* men, practitioners whose authority extended equally over affairs of the spirit and matters of life and death (Craton, *Testing the Chains,* pp. 122, 258, and Mullin, *Africa in America,* pp. 179 ff.). The role of supernaturalism, and especially African-based ritual in slave rebellions in America, has not been fully explored. For example, one of the largest slave revolts in the United States, occurring in Louisiana in 1811 and involving some 300 to 500 rebels, has turned up little evidence of such practices in a cultural setting where we might most expect them. On African ritual in American rebellions see Mullin, *Africa in America,* esp. chs. 3 and 8; John Thornton, "African Dimensions of the Stono Rebellion," *American Historical Review* 96 (1991): 1101–13; William Suttles, "African Religious Survivals as Factors in American Slave Revolts," *Journal of Negro History* 56 (1971): 98. See also Gerald Mullin, *Flight and Rebellion: Slave Resistance in Eighteenth-Century Virginia* (London: Oxford University Press, 1972), pp. 159 ff; and Frey, *Water from the Rock,* p. 321.

10. Philip D. Morgan, *Slave Counterpoint: Black Culture in the Eighteenth-Century Chesapeake and Lowcountry* (Chapel Hill: University of North Carolina Press, 1998), pp. 648–51.

11. Mullin, *Flight and Rebellion,* p. 160. All of chapter 3's text references to the *Confessions* and quoted passages from it come from Henry I. Tragle, ed., *The Southampton Slave Revolt of 1831: A Compilation of Source Material* (Amherst: University of Massachusetts Press, 1971).

12. Peter Wood, "Nat Turner: The Unknown Slave as Visionary Leader," in *Black Leaders of the Nineteenth Century,* ed. Leon Litwack and August Meier (Urbana: University of Illinois Press, 1988), p. 40. For a discussion that places Turner in the context of an Afro-Baptist traditional worldview, see Mechal Sobel, *Trabelin' On: The Slave Journey to An Afro-Baptist Faith* (Princeton: Princeton University Press, 1988), pp. 161–68. Reprinted primary documents on the Nat Turner uprising can be located in several compilations. The best single

source is Tragle's work, *Southampton Revolt*, which has a bibliographic overview of sources on Turner's character (pp. 469–89). And see Kenneth Greenberg, ed., *The Confessions of Nat Turner and Related Documents* (Boston: Bedford Books, 1996), which recapitulates the debate over historical portrayals of Turner (pp. 26–31); Eric Foner, ed., *Nat Turner* (Englewood Cliffs, N.J.: Prentice Hall, 1971); and the critique in John Henrik Clarke, ed, *William Styron's Nat Turner: Ten Black Writers Respond* (Boston: Beacon Press, 1968).

13. Editorial, *Constitutional Whig*, Richmond, Virginia, 26 September 1831, reprinted in Tragle, *Southampton Revolt*, p. 92.

14. Although he rejected the title of Conjurer, Turner displayed many of the attributes that were associated with Conjurers and supernatural practitioners in this time, including prescient visions, dreams, invulnerability, anomalous bodily markings, and magical powers over nature and the elements (Tragle, *Southampton Revolt*, pp. 100, 222, 307, 309, 420–21).

15. In 1815, in a move that enraged officials in the white-dominated Methodist Society, blacks resigned from three of Charleston's largest biracial churches in response to the abolishment of their quarterly conference, which had functioned as a semiautonomous organization for blacks since the early 1800s. In 1817 several new churches were established under the auspices of the African Association, an organization by which blacks consolidated a new institutional base and facilitated connections with the African Methodist Episcopal churches of the North. For historical background of these events as they pertained to the controversy see Margaret Washington Creel, *"A Peculiar People": Slave Religion and Community-Culture Among the Gullahs* (New York: New York University Press, 1988); and Vincent Harding, *There Is a River: The Black Struggle for Freedom in America* (New York: Vintage Books, 1981), pp. 66–68. For a reconstruction of the events preceding the conspiracy see John Lofton, *Insurrection in South Carolina* (Yellow Springs, Ohio: Antioch Press, 1964).

16. Robert S. Starobin, *Denmark Vesey: The Slave Conspiracy of 1822* (Englewood Cliffs, N.J.: Prentice Hall, 1970), p. 14; John Oliver Killens, ed., *The Trial Record of Denmark Vesey* (Boston: Beacon Press, 1970), pp. xii, 14 (hereafter cited as *Trial Record*). The most accessible compilations of primary sources relating to the Vesey conspiracy can be found in these volumes. See also Sterling Stuckey, *Slave Culture: Nationalist Theory and the Foundations of Black America* (New York: Oxford University Press, 1987), pp. 46–51; Mullin, *Africa in America*, p. 50; Creel, *Peculiar People*, p. 154.

17. L. H. Kennedy and T. Parker, *An Official Report of the Trials of Sundry Negroes Charged with an Attempt to Raise an Insurrection in the State of South-Carolina* (Charleston, 1822), reprinted in Starobin, *Denmark Vesey*, pp. 21–22, 64; Frey, *Water from the Rock*, pp. 322–23; Harding, "Religion and Resistance," pp. 185–86. The religious dynamic of the conspiracy has been acknowledged by scholars (Creel, *Peculiar People*, pp. 148–66; Stuckey, *Slave Culture*, pp. 43–53; and Sobel, *Trabelin' On*, pp. 166–67).

18. Lofton, *Insurrection*, pp. 148–54, 183–85; on the impact of the Vesey conspiracy on black churches in the South, see Donald Mathews, *Religion in the Old South* (Chicago: University of Chicago Press, 1977), p. 204.

19. Creel, *Peculiar People*, p. 153. On characteristics of Gullah religion, see

also Patricia Jones-Jackson, *When Roots Die: Endangered Traditions in the Sea Islands* (Athens: University of Georgia Press, 1987), pp. 22–31; Charles Joyner, *Down by the Riverside: A South Carolina Slave Community* (Urbana: University of Illinois Press, 1984), pp. 141–71. On harming practices in the Vesey plot, see W. Freehling, "Denmark Vesey's Peculiar Reality," in *New Perspectives on Race and Slavery in America,* ed. Robert Abzug and Stephen Maizlish (Lexington: University Press of Kentucky, 1986); Kennedy and Parker, "Trials of Sundry Negroes," reprinted in Starobin, *Denmark Vesey,* pp. 32; Stuckey, *Slave Culture,* p. 50. "Examination of Billy [Bulkley],"in Killens, *Trial Record,* pp. 130, 131; Kennedy and Parker, "Trials of Sundry Negroes," 42; Sobel, *Trabelin' On,* p. 167.

20. A blacksmith by the name of Tom Rusell is depicted in the trial record as Gullah Jack's "partner," whom Jack had taught the art of conjuring (Killens, *Trial Record,* p. 79). Another supernatural specialist amid the conspirators was Philip, a blind "seer or fortuneteller" who was "born with a caul" in the manner of black Conjurers, who may have also been one of the spiritual elders in the Gullah religion, portrayed by Creel as the "healers, interpreters of dreams, signs and visions" in the Gullah community (*Peculiar People,* pp. 385, 315); see Killens, *Trial Record,* pp. 165, 31; Starobin, *Denmark Vesey,* pp. 101–2; and Sobel, *Trabelin' On,* p. 166.

21. See George Eaton Simpson, *Religious Cults of the Caribbean: Trinidad, Jamaica, Haiti* (Rio Piedras: Institute of Caribbean Studies, University of Puerto Rico, 1970); Joseph Murphy, *Working the Spirit: Ceremonies of the African Diaspora* (Boston: Beacon Press, 1994), pp. 114–44; Monica Schuler, *Alas, Alas Kongo: A Social History of Indentured African Immigration in Jamaica, 1841–1865* (Baltimore: Johns Hopkins University Press, 1980); Leonard Barrett, "African Religion in the Americas: The Islands in Between," in *African Religions: A Symposium,* ed. Newell S. Booth (New York: NOK, 1977), pp. 195–98. On shared ritual structures in diaspora traditions, see especially Walter Pitts, *Old Ship of Zion: The Afro-Baptist Ritual in the African Diaspora* (New York: Oxford University Press, 1993); Stephen Glazier, *Marchin' the Pilgrims Home: A Study of the Spiritual Baptists of Trinidad* (Salem, Wis.: Sheffield Publishing, 1983). On African Christianity see Harold W. Turner, *Religious Innovation in Africa: Collected Essays on New Religious Movements* (Boston: G. K. Hall, 1979); David Barrett, *Schism and Renewal in Africa: An Analysis of Six Thousand Contemporary Religious Movements* (Nairobi: Oxford University Press, 1969); and Bennetta Jules-Rosette, ed., *The New Religions of Africa: Priests and Priestesses in Contemporary Cults and Churches* (Norwood, N.J.: Ablex Publishing, 1979).

22. Barrett, "African Religion in the Americas." On slavery as sorcery, see especially Monica Schuler, "Afro-American Slave Culture," in *Roots and Branches: Current Directions in Slave Studies* (New York: Pergamon Press, 1979), pp. 121–37.

23. Samuel A. Cartwright, "Negro Consumption," *New Orleans Medical and Surgical Journal* (May 1851), cited in *Advice Among Masters: The Ideal of Slave Management in the Old South,* ed. James Breeden (Westport, Ct.: Greenwood Press, 1980), p. 170; added emphasis. Also called "African Consumption" the ailment described by Cartwright has been identified as military tuberculosis, a

highly fatal and contagious disease among enslaved African Americans in the 1800s (Todd L. Savitt, *Medicine and Slavery: The Diseases and Health Care of Blacks in Antebellum Virginia* [Urbana: University of Illinois Press, 1978]). Although poisoning was most often practiced by individuals against individuals, the use of poisoning as a weapon of revolt is mentioned not only in the Vesey conspiracy, but in at least two other accounts of slave rebellion. See mention of the "secret poisonings and bloody insurrections" by Christian slaves in colonial South Carolina, in Peter Wood, *Black Majority: Negroes in Colonial South Carolina from 1670 through the Stono Rebellion* (New York: W. W. Norton, 1974), p. 299; and in Carroll, *Slave Insurrections*, p. 70.

24. Philip D. Morgan, "Slave Life in Piedmont Virginia, 1720–1800," in *Colonial Chesapeake Society*, ed. Lois Green Carr, Philip D. Morgan, and Jean Russo (Chapel Hill: University of North Carolina Press, 1988), p. 454; see also Philip J. Schwartz, *Twice Condemned: Slaves and the Criminal Laws of Virginia, 1705–1865* (Baton Rouge: Louisiana State University Press, 1988), pp. 92–113; petition of Spotslyvania County residents, December 20, 1795, Executive Papers, Virginia State Library, cited in Morgan, "Slave Life in Piedmont Virginia," p. 455.

25. Schwartz, *Twice Condemned*, p. 101. "Petition in Regard to a Slave, 1773," Virginia State Archives, miscellaneous documents, Colonial and State, reprinted in *Virginia Magazine of History and Biography* 18 (December 1910): 394–95. Poisons were also found to be used by slaves to induce sickness, thus enabling them to avoid required tasks and labor. See Jean W. Robinson, "Black Healers During the Colonial Period and Early Nineteenth-Century America" (Ph.D. diss., Southern Illinois University, Carbondale, 1979), pp. 64–65; "Trial of Jacob," October 18, 1779, Johnston County miscellaneous records, State Archives, cited in Alan D. Watson, "North Carolina Slave Courts, 1715–1785," *North Carolina Historical Review* 60, no. 1 (1983): 28.

26. Of course, not all incidents of poison were attributed to African American supernatural practitioners and magicians. And yet their activities were so closely linked that this perception was carried to the types of sentences that courts meted out for poisoning crimes. Typical punishments for the offense of poisoning included hanging, castration, and execution by burning, an action usually reserved for those guilty of witchcraft. See an eighteenth-century account in John Ashton, *The Devil in Britain and America* (London: Ward and Downey, 1896), pp. 311–13; and Carroll, *Slave Insurrections*, p. 70. Wood, *Black Majority*, p. 290; Allen D. Candler and Lucian Knight, eds., *Colonial Records of the State of Georgia* (Atlanta: Franklin Printing and Publishing, 1904), vol. 18, pp. 641–44, cited in William D. Piersen, *Black Legacy: America's Hidden Heritage* (Amherst, University of Massachusetts Press, 1993), p. 114; Watson, "North Carolina Slave Courts," pp. 30–31; and Alan D. Watson, "Impulse Toward Independence: Resistance and Rebellion among North Carolina Slaves, 1750–1775," *Journal of Negro History* 62 (1978): 320; Marvin L. Michael Kay and Lorin Lee Cary, *Slavery in North Carolina, 1748–1775* (Chapel Hill: University of North Carolina Press, 1995), p. 109; Donna Spindel, *Crime and Society in North Carolina, 1663–1776* (Baton Rouge: Louisiana State University Press, 1989), pp. 65, 73, 78, 130; Schwartz, *Twice Condemned*, esp. ch. 4; Morgan, "Slave Life in Piedmont Virginia," p. 441; Alan Kulikoff, *Tobacco and Slaves: The Development of South-*

ern Cultures in the Chesapeake, 1680–1800 (Chapel Hill: University of North Carolina Press, 1986), p. 329; Wood, *Black Majority,* pp. 289–92. See also Ulrich B. Philips, *Life and Labor in the Old South* (Boston: Little Brown, 1929), pp. 165, 283; Herbert Aptheker, *Negro Slave Revolts in the United States* (New York: International Publishers, 1939), pp. 143, 241; Mechal Sobel, *The World They Made Together: Black and White Values in Eighteenth-Century Virginia* (Princeton: Princeton University Press, 1987), p. 99; Winthrop Jordan, *White Over Black: American Attitudes Toward the Negro, 1550–1812* (New York: Oxford University Press, 1968), p. 393.

27. See Schwartz, *Twice Condemned,* pp. 92–113; petition of Spotslyvania County residents, December 20, 1795, cited in Morgan, "Slave Life in Piedmont Virginia," pp. 454–55; see also *Slave Counterpoint,* p. 614.

28. Clarence Alvord, "Transcripts from the Cahokia Record," *Collections of the Illinois State Historical Library,* Virginia Series, 1778–90 (Springfield, 1907), vol. 2, pp. 13–21; Pieter Kalm, *Peter Kalm's Travels in North America* (New York: Wilson-Erickson, 1937), vol. 1, p. 210; cf. Helen Tunnicliff Catterall, ed., *Judicial Cases Concerning American Slavery and the Negro* (New York: Octagon Books, 1926), Louisiana cases, vol. 3, p. 404; records of the Superior Council of Louisiana, October 21 and 25, 1729.

29. Petition of Leroy Beauford, General Assembly, 1800, petition no. 174, South Carolina State Archives, Columbia. I am grateful to Sharla Fett for sharing these materials with me.

30. Secretary of State Court Records, Box 312, *The King v. Sarah Wiggins,* 1772, North Carolina Department of Archives and History, Raleigh. In another case from Virginia, a white mother who delivers a mulatto baby used as her defense in divorce proceedings the claim that a Negro, Robin, "had overcome her by saying that he wou'd conger" in order to procure a husband for her (Benjamin Butt Divorce Petition, Norfolk County, December 7, 1803, Legislative Papers, Petitions, Virginia State Library. I am grateful to Martha Hodes for providing these citations). See also Watson, "North Carolina Slave Courts," p. 30; Bertram Wyatt-Brown, *Southern Honor: Ethics and Behavior in the Old South* (New York: Oxford University Press, 1982), pp. 313–16.

31. See Frank Klingberg, *An Appraisal of the Negro in Colonial South Carolina: A Study in Americanization* (Washington, D.C.: Associated Publishers, 1941), p. 103. Laura Porteus, "The Gri-Gri Case," *Louisiana Historical Quarterly* 17 (January 1934): 56–61. On the African use of alligator as an ingredient in poisoning, see Thomas Winterbottom, *An Account of the Native Africans in the Neighborhood of Sierra Leone* (London: C. Whittingham, 1803), vol. 1, p. 266; for another New World application of alligator poison see Mullin, *Africa in America,* p. 353 n. 12; Joseph Waring, *The History of Medicine in South Carolina* (Spartanburg, S.C.: Reprint Company, 1971), cited in Wood, *Black Majority,* pp. 290–91. See also Wood, "People's Medicine in the Early South," p. 52. Garden, a renowned botanist and physician in Charleston, was the grandson and namesake of the Anglican commissary of the early 1700s.

32. Thomas Bluett, *Some Memoirs of the Life of Job, the Son of Solomon the High Priest of Boonda in Africa* (London: Richard Ford, 1734); and "Olaudah Equiano of the Niger Ibo," both reprinted in Philip Curtin, *Africa Remem-*

bered: Narratives by West Africans from the Era of the Slave Trade (Madison: University of Wisconsin Press, 1967), p. 80; Winterbottom, Account of the Native Africans, p. 266; Robert Voeks, "African Medicine and Magic in the Americas," Geographical Review 83 (January 1993): 66–76.

33. Susan McClure, "Parallel Usage of Medicinal Plants," Economic Botany 36 (1982): 291; Governor's Office, Committee of Claims Reports, 1760–64, and Pasquotank County Court Minutes, 1737–65, North Carolina State Archives, Raleigh, cited in Kay and Cary, Slavery in North Carolina, p. 187; Morgan, Slave Counterpoint, p. 613; Voeks, "African Medicine and Magic," pp. 66–76. On the adoption of American Indian plant and animal lore for poisoning by blacks, see J. Leitch Wright, Jr., The Only Land They Knew: The Tragic Story of the American Indian in the Old South (New York: Free Press, 1981), pp. 265–66; on other African American uses of plants as poisons, see William Ed Grime, Botany of the Black Americans (St. Clair Shores, Mich.: Scholarly Press, 1976).

34. 32 Md. Arch. 178, December 1766, cited in Catterall, Judicial Cases Concerning Slavery, Maryland cases 1926–37, vol. 4, p. 46; Archives of Virginia, Executive Papers, June 1–July 27, 1802, cited in Carroll, Slave Insurrections, p. 63. On the use of snakes' heads, "groundpuppies" and other substances in Conjure preparations see Fanny Bergen, "Plant and Animal Lore," Memoirs of the American Folklore Society 8 (1899): esp. 14–15, 62; Stewart Culin, "Concerning Negro Sorcery in the United States," Journal of American Folklore 3 (1890): 286; Newbell Niles Puckett, Folk Beliefs of the Southern Negro (Chapel Hill: University of North Carolina Press, 1926).

35. Daniel Robinson Hundley, Social Relations in Our Southern States (Baton Rouge: Louisiana State University Press, 1860), p. 332; on medicines in African culture, see Rattray, Religion and Art in Ashanti, p. 18; John Mbiti, African Religions and Philosophy (London: Heinemann, 1988), p. 197. Material objects for black American harming traditions resonate with the spiritually powerful creations of West and Central African peoples, including the minkisi of Kongo, the bochio of the Fon peoples of Benin, and the sumang of the Akan in Ghana. See Robert Farris Thompson, Flash of the Spirit: African and Afro-American Art and Philosophy (New York: Vintage Books, 1983), pp. 117–21; Suzanne Preston Blier, African Vodun: Art, Psychology, and Power (Chicago: University of Chicago Press, 1995), pp. 48–54.

36. It is likely that many black poison specialists in America were themselves obeah practitioners from the West Indies, although it is difficult to determine the birthplace or national origins of most practitioners. Some black American practitioners were known as obeah or obi specialists or were so named. See for example in Virginia, reference to the trial of "Obee" a slave convicted of poisoning ("Trial of Obee, June 29, 1778," Spotsylvania Order Book, cited in Morgan, Slave Counterpoint, p. 441). See also Watson, "North Carolina Slave Courts," p. 31, for the trial of an "Ober" Negro for poisoning.

37. See Melville Herskovits, The Myth of the Negro Past (Boston: Beacon Press, 1958), p. 242. This "moral ambivalence," insists Theophus Smith, means that conjure cannot be reduced, in such one-dimensional terms, to evil magic, demonic machinations, or "malign occultism"—the traditional distinction between white and black magic (Theophus H. Smith, Conjuring Culture: Biblical

Formations of Black America [New York: Oxford University Press, 1994], p. 145, see also pp. 43, 52–53). James Haskins calls the good-evil dichotomy "an outright heresy" in black American conjuring traditions, or at the least, "far more European than African or even Afro-American" (Haskins, *Hoodoo and Voodoo: Their Tradition and Craft as Revealed by Actual Practitioners* [Bronx: Original Publications, 1978]).

38. Douglas Fraser, *African Art as Philosophy* (New York: Interbook Publishing, 1974), p. 3; Albert Raboteau, *Slave Religion: The "Invisible Institution" in the Antebellum South* (New York: Oxford University Press, 1978), p. 287. A discussion that considers the "dual potential" of black magic practice is in Smith, *Conjuring Culture*, pp. 43, 52–53. For a similar perspective of the West African sacred cosmos in slavery, see Sobel, *Trabelin' On*, p. 13.

39. Irving E. Lowery, *Life on the Old Plantation in Ante-Bellum Days, or A Story Based on Facts* (Columbia, S.C.: State Co. Publishers, 1911), p. 81–84.

40. Morgan, *Slave Counterpoint*, p. 618; James Lindsay Smith, *The Autobiography of James L. Smith, including also Reminiscences of Slave Life, Recollections of the War, the Education of Freedmen, Causes of the Exodus, etc.* (Norwich: Society of the Founders of Norwich, Connecticut, 1881), pp. 5–6; Walker diary, June 5, 1832, February 19, 1833, John Walker Papers, Southern Historical Collection, cited in William Dosite Postell, *The Health of Slaves on Southern Plantations* (Baton Rouge: Louisiana State University Press, 1951), pp. 108–9. See also Piersen, *Black Legacy*, p. 100.

41. Catterall, *Judicial Cases Concerning Slavery,* South Carolina cases, vol. 2, pp. 413–14. Another case only incidentally involving a black Conjurer and a white client was that of James Reel, a slaveowner who was brought to trial in 1822 in Craven County, North Carolina, over a dispute involving his will. The court record noted that Reel had gone to consult a "Negro conjurer" on several occasions, and that he had told him that he was being "tricked" by "persons who wanted his property." See Francis L. Hawks, *North Carolina Reports: Cases Argued and Adjudged in the Supreme Court of North Carolina, 1822–1823* (Raleigh: Turner and Hughes, 1843–45), vol. 9, p. 67.

42. Hundley, *Social Relations,* p. 337; Sarah Handy, "Negro Superstitions," *Lippincott's Monthly Magazine,* 1891, p. 737; Puckett, *Folk Beliefs of the Southern Negro,* p. 224.

43. Puckett, *Folk Beliefs of the Southern Negro,* p. 247. For further definition and elaboration of these terms, see Harry Middleton Hyatt, *Hoodoo — Conjuration — Witchcraft — Rootwork: Beliefs Accepted by Many Negroes and White Persons, These Being Orally Recorded Among Blacks and Whites,* 5 vols. (Hannibal, Mo.: Western Publishing, 1970–78; distributed by American University Bookstore, Washington, D.C.).

44. Raboteau, *Slave Religion,* p. 276.

45. Mary Jackson, n.d., Folklore Folder, Georgia Folklore, Works Progress Administration (WPA) records, Manuscripts Division, Library of Congress; Rossa Belle Cooley, *The Homes of the Freed* (New York: New Republic, 1926), pp. 40–41; M. S. Lea, "Two-Head Doctors," *American Mercury,* October 1927, p. 238; Daniel Webster Davis, "Conjuration," *Southern Workman* 27, no. 12 (1898): 252. See also Rawick, *American Slave,* Georgia Narratives vol. 13, pt. 3,

p. 345, for a Conjure curse by a black woman to make another "nappy and kinky headed."

46. Mamie Garvin Fields, with Karen Fields, *Lemon Swamp and Other Places: A Carolina Memoir* (New York: Free Press, 1983), p. 117; Jeanette Robinson Murphy, "The Survival of African Music in America" (1899), in *The Negro and His Folklore in Nineteenth-Century Periodicals*, ed. Bruce Jackson (Austin: University of Texas Press, 1967), p. 335.

47. Kent Nickerson, ed., *High Sheriff of the Lowcountry* (Beaufort, S.C.: Beaufort Book, 1970), p. 25; Roland Steiner, "Observations on the Practice of Conjuring in Georgia," *Journal of American Folklore* 14 (1901): 174–75.

48. Alice Bacon, "Conjuring and Conjure Doctors, pt. 2," *Southern Workman* 24, no. 12 (1895): 210. Julien Hall, "Negro Conjuring and Tricking," *Journal of American Folklore* 10 (1897): 241–43; Zora Neale Hurston, *Mules and Men* (Philadelphia: J. B. Lippincott, 1935), pp. 197–99.

49. Georgia Writers' Project, *Drums and Shadows: Survival Studies Among the Georgia Coastal Negroes* (Athens: University of Georgia Press, 1940), p. 3.

50. Culin, "Concerning Negro Sorcery," p. 282; Richard Dorson, *Negro Tales from Pine Bluff, Arkansas, and Calvin, Michigan* (Bloomington: Indiana University Press, 1958), p. 207; Steiner, "Practice of Conjuring in Georgia," p. 174.

51. Georgia Writers' Project, *Drums and Shadows*, pp. 1, 4.

52. Myrta Lockett Avary, *Dixie After the War: An Exposition of Social Conditions Existing in the South During the Twelve Years Succeeding the Fall of Richmond* (Garden City, N.Y.: Doubleday and Page, 1906), p. 234; Philip Alexander Bruce, *The Plantation Negro as a Freeman: Observations on His Character, Condition, and Prospects in Virginia* (New York: G. P. Putnam, 1889), pp. 119–22; Charles C. Jones, Jr. *Negro Myths from the Georgia Coast, Told in the Vernacular* (Boston: Houghton Mifflin, 1888), p. 171.

53. B. A. Botkin, *Lay My Burden Down: A Folk History of Slavery* (Chicago: University of Chicago Press, 1945), pp. 33–34; John Patterson Green, *Recollections of the Inhabitants, Localities, Superstitions, and KuKlux Outrages of the Carolinas* (Cleveland: Library of American Civilization, 1880), p. 45; Steiner, "Practice of Conjuring in Georgia," p. 174.

54. Rawick, *American Slave,* Indiana Narratives vol. 6, pt. 2, pp. 193–94; Richmond County Folklore Folder, n.d., records of the Federal Writers' Project, WPA interviews, Manuscripts Division, Library of Congress; Rawick, *American Slave,* Georgia Narratives vol. 4, s.s. 1.

55. Ashton, *Devil in Britain,* pp. 311–15; Tom Peete Cross, "Witchcraft in North Carolina," *Studies in Philology* 16, no. 3 (1919): 220–24; Richard B. Davis, "The Devil in Virginia in the Seventeenth Century," *Virginia Magazine of History and Biography* 65 (April 1957); James Kences, "Some Unexplored Relationships of Essex Country Witchcraft to the Indian Wars of 1675 and 1689," *Essex Institute Historical Collections* 20 (1984); Herbert Leventhal, *In the Shadow of the Enlightenment: Occultism and Renaissance Science in Eighteenth-Century America* (New York: New York University Press, 1976), p. 120. On race and witchcraft see Timothy McMillan, "Black Magic: Witchcraft, Race and Resistance in Colonial New England," *Journal of Black Studies* 1 (September 1994). In the early South, responses to witchcraft occurred in contained outbursts. See,

for example, E. S. Riley, "Witchcraft in Early Maryland," *Southern Magazine,* April 1873, p. 435; Francis Neale Parker, "Witchcraft in Maryland," *Maryland Historical Magazine* 31 (December 1936): 271–72. In Virginia, where the first American prosecutions of witchcraft took place, numerous scourgings, banishings, and investigations effectively established that colony's intolerance for malign spiritual practices prior to the end of the seventeenth century. See Darrett Rutman, "The Evolution of Religious Life in Early Virginia," *Lex et Scientia* 14 (1978): 193–96; Edward W. James, "Grace Sherwood, The Virginia Witch," *William and Mary Quarterly,* s. 1, 3 (1894–95); Sobel, *World They Made Together,* p. 79. Awareness of the powers of witches also persisted among members of the population of colonial North and South Carolina. In 1702, for example, the Society for the Propagation of the Gospel missionary Francis LeJau described his shock at the outcome of a grand jury case that had dismissed a witchcraft indictment. The accused, he charged, was "evidently guilty," having "kill'd several Persons by the Devils" with "notorious" means. It is noteworthy that LeJau was silent concerning witchcraft among the African slaves he worked among and encountered daily (Frank Klingberg, ed., *The Carolina Chronicle of Dr. Francis LeJau, 1706–1717* [Berkeley: University of California Press, 1956], p. 25; see also Samuel Drake, *Annals of Witchcraft in New England and Elsewhere in the United States* [New York: Benjamin Bloom, 1967], p. 215).

56. In the New England witchcraft cases, several blacks were included among the accusers and the accused. See William D. Piersen, *Black Yankees: The Development of an Afro-American Subculture in Eighteenth-Century New England* (Amherst: University of Massachusetts Press, 1988), p. 80; see also Cross, "Witchcraft in North Carolina," p. 219.

57. According to one source, the hag is the "disembodied spirit of an old woman who practices witchcraft," rather than a shape-shifting female human. See Federal Writers Program, *South Carolina Folktales* (Folcroft, Pa.: Folcroft Library Editions, 1976), pp. 89, 92; see also Joyner, *Down by the Riverside;* Basil Duke, *Reminiscences of General Basil W. Duke* (New York: Deale Publishing, 1906), p. 32; Sobel, *Trabelin' On,* p. 69; Raboteau, *Slave Religion,* p. 287. For a tentative discussion of African American moral constructs in occultism, see Norman Whitten, "Aspects and Origins of Negro Occultism in Piedmont Village" (master's thesis, University of North Carolina, Chapel Hill, 1960), pp. 56–61.

58. Edward Evans-Pritchard, *Witchcraft, Oracles and Magic among the Azande* (Oxford: Clarendon Press, 1937), pp. 64, 72.

59. Clyde Kluckhohn, *Navaho Witchcraft* (Millwood, N.Y.: Kraus Reprint, 1975), p. 224.

60. Basil Davidson, *The African Genius: An Introduction to African Cultural and Social History* (Boston: Little, Brown, 1969), pp. 129–30. See also Evan Zuesse, *Ritual Cosmos: The Sanctification of Life in African Religions* (Athens: Ohio University Press, 1979), p. 228.

61. Georgia Writer's Project, *Drums and Shadows,* p. 17; Puckett, *Folk Beliefs of the Southern Negro,* p. 151; Hundley, *Social Relations,* p. 330; Cross, "Witchcraft in North Carolina"; Mary A. Owen, "Among the Voodoos" (paper presented at the Second International Folk-lore Congress, 1891), p. 241; cf. her *Voodoo Tales, as Told Among the Negroes of the Southwest* (New York: G. P.

Putnam, 1893), pp. 10–11. For other witch-riding traditions, see Wayland Hand, ed., *Popular Beliefs and Superstitions from North Carolina*, vol. 7 of Frank C. Brown Collection of North Carolina Folklore (Durham, N.C. Duke University Press, 1964), pp. 115–19. The problem of the gender of witches in black American traditions is not easily resolved. The folklorist Fanny Bergen argues that most older black women were often believed to be witches, but Elsie Clews Parsons makes note of a "witch-man" who was a powerful specialist in one southern black community (Bergen, *Current Superstitions Collected from the Oral Traditions of English-Speaking Folk* [Boston: Houghton Mifflin, 1896], p. 128; and Parsons, "Folklore of the Sea Islands, South Carolina," *Memoirs of the American Folklore Society* 16 [1923]: 61). Newbell Niles Puckett describes some witches as evil succubi who steal married women, suggesting a masculine identity, as does Tom Peete Cross, who notes that "a male witch sometimes causes his neighbor to leave his bed, and then, entering the house, enjoys his wife" (Puckett, *Folk Beliefs of the Southern Negro*, p. 151; Cross, "Folklore from the Southern States," *Journal of American Folklore* 22 [1909]: 251). Another sources notes that "Witches are the wives of hoodoo men" (Richard Dorson, "Negro Witch Stories on Tape," *Midwest Folklore* 2, no. 4 [1952]: 233). While some accounts make occasional references to a gendered male witch, by far, most witches in black folk narratives are female.

62. Georgia Writers' Project, *Drums and Shadows*, p. 58; Dorson, "Negro Witch Stories on Tape," p. 233. For descriptions of witches in nineteenth-century folklore, see Fanny Bergen, "Two Negro Witch-Stories," *Journal of American Folklore* 12 (1899): 145–46; Mary Minor, "How to Keep Off Witches," *Journal of American Folklore* 11 (1898): 71; three articles by Elsie Clews Parsons, all in the *Journal of American Folklore*, on tales from Guilford County, N.C. (30 [1917]: 168–200), Aiken, S.C. (34 [1921]: 2–39), and Elizabeth County, Va. (35 [1922]: 250–327); as well as Alice Bacon, "Hags and Their Ways," *Southern Workman* 23, no. 2 (1894): 26–27. According to one authority, "many of the ideas traditionally associated with witches in Europe seem in this country to have become associated with conjurers" (Hand, *Popular Beliefs and Superstitions*, p. 120).

63. Alice Bacon, "Out of Her Skin," *Journal of American Folklore* 35 (1922). On similar witch beliefs in other parts of the country see also Henry Davis, "Negro Folklore in South Carolina," *Journal of American Folklore* 27 (1910): 247; Jesse Harris, "Some Southern Illinois Witch Lore, *Southern Folklore Quarterly* 10 (1946): 183–90; Parsons, "Tales from Guilford County," 209–10; Parsons, "Folklore of the Sea Islands," p. 63; Hyatt, *Hoodoo — Conjuration*, vol. 1, p. 141. Puckett remarks that the skin motif is unique to African lore in the New World and shows up with a number of variations throughout the American South and in parts of the Caribbean (*Folk Beliefs of the Southern Negro*, p. 154); see also Herskovits, *Myth of the Negro Past*, pp. 258–59. On "nightmares," see *Southern Workman* 23 (1894): 161; and Puckett, *Folk Beliefs of the Southern Negro*, p. 158. Puckett traces the connection of witches and horses to England but does make note (p. 159) of the relation between spiritual possession and "horses" appearing in New Orleans as well.

64. In the riding belief we glimpse an interpretive link between insomnia or

body aches and the witch's nightly activities. Other symptoms blamed on witch visitations include sores in the mouth (from a bridle?) and excessive restlessness, suggesting that victim is being ridden during slumber. Another source of this tradition recalls the African-based practice of spirit possession, in which the possessed individual is called the "horse" in New World religions. See Hand, *Popular Beliefs and Superstitions*, p. 118; and "Conjure Doctors in the South," *Southern Workman* 7, no. 4 (1878), reprinted in *Strange Ways and Sweet Dreams: Afro-American Folklore from the Hampton Institute*, ed. Donald J. Waters (Boston: G. K. Hall, 1983), pp. 138–39.

65. *Southern Workman* 23, no. 2 (1894): 26–27; Puckett, *Folk Beliefs of the Southern Negro*, p. 156; Dorson, *Negro Tales from Pine Bluff*, p. 198; Cross, "Folklore from the Southern States," p. 252; Zora Neale Hurston, "Hoodoo in America," *Journal of American Folklore* 44 (1931): 394. For an excellent compilation of antiwitchcraft beliefs, see Hand, *Popular Beliefs and Superstitions*, pp. 121–32.

66. Davis, "Negro Folklore in South Carolina," pp. 241–54; "Beliefs of Southern Negroes Concerning Hags," *Journal of American Folklore* 7 (1894): 66. On similar practices in black American spiritual traditions, see Thompson, *Flash of the Spirit*, p. 145; and Sobel, *World They Made Together*, p. 97; Puckett, *Folk Beliefs of the Southern Negro*, p. 188; F. Roy Johnson, *The Fabled Doctor Jim Jordan: A Story of Conjure* (Murfreesboro, N.C.: Johnson Publishing, 1963), p. 14; Herbert Gutman, *The Black Family in Slavery and Freedom, 1750–1925* (New York: Vintage Books, 1976), pp. 282–83. On African and African American religious connotations of broomstick jumping, see Piersen, *Black Legacy*, pp. 176–77; and Raboteau, *Slave Religion*, pp. 228–29.

67. Stroyer, *My Life in the South*, pp. 53–54.

68. Grimes's curious treatment of the witch might be read as a coded reflection on his own repressed sexual desires, or a critique of the slaveowner's domination of a slave's erotic life. Perhaps these anecdotes should be seen as fantasies, rendered complex and disturbing by the physical subordination suffered by the black male slave. For the full account see *The Life of William Grimes, The Runaway Slave, Written by Himself* (New York, 1825), pp. 24–25.

CHAPTER 4. "MEDICAL DOCTORS CAN'T DO YOU NO GOOD"

1. Addie Battle's testimony, in James Blackwell, "A Comparative Study of Five Negro Store-front Churches in Cleveland" (master's thesis, Western Reserve University, Cleveland, 1949), pp. 312–15.

2. Ibid. On women preachers in the black Spiritualist tradition, see Yvonne Chireau, "Prophetess of the Spirits," in *Women Preachers and Prophets Through Two Millennia of Christianity*, ed. Beverly Kienzle and Pamela Walker (Berkeley: University of California Press, 1998).

3. On conceptions of healing and affliction in African American religious life, see Theophus H. Smith, *Conjuring Culture: Biblical Formations of Black America* (New York Oxford University Press, 1994); and Karen McCarthy Brown, *Mama Lola: A Vodou Priestess in Brooklyn* (Berkeley: University of California Press, 1991).

4. Bruce Jackson, "The Other Kind of Doctor: Conjure and Magic in Black American Folk Medicine," in *American Folk Medicine: A Symposium*, ed. Wayland Hand (Berkeley: University of California Press, 1976), p. 268; Rawick, *American Slave*, Texas Narratives vol. 5, p. 143.

5. Rawick, *American Slave*, Alabama Narratives vol. 6, pt. 1, p. 69; see also Georgia Narratives vol. 12, pt. 1, pp. 76, 139; Janie Hunter, quoted in Jackson, "Other Kind of Doctor," p. 268.

6. John Haller, *Outcasts from Evolution: Scientific Attitudes of Racial Inferiority, 1859–1900* (Urbana: University of Illinois Press, 1971), pp. 57–59; see also George Frederickson, *The Black Image in the White Mind: The Debate on Afro-American Character and Destiny, 1817–1914* (New York: Harper and Row, 1972), esp. chs. 2 and 3.

7. Cited in Stewart Culin, "Concerning Negro Sorcery in the South," *Journal of American Folklore* 3 (1890): 285. Gaines M. Foster, "The Limitations of Federal Health Care for Freedmen," *Journal of Southern History* 48 (1982): 347–72; Marshall Legan, "Disease and the Freedmen in Mississippi during Reconstruction," *Journal of the History of Medicine and Allied Sciences* (July 1973): 257–67.

8. Attitudes of present-day black Americans also reflect strong suspicions toward professional healthcare, including hospital facilities, viewed by some Sea Islands elderly as "places of death." See J. Herman Blake, "Doctor Can't Do Me No Good: Social Concomitants of Health Care Attitudes and Practices among Elderly Blacks in Isolated Rural Populations," in *Black Folk Medicine: The Therapeutic Significance of Faith and Trust*, ed. Wilbur Watson (New Brunswick, N.J.: Transaction Books, 1988), p. 36. For folklore beliefs of African Americans, see Tom Schick, "Healing and Race in the South Carolina Low Country," in *Africans in Bondage: Studies in Slavery and the Slave Trade*, ed. Paul Lovejoy (Madison: University of Wisconsin Press, 1986), p. 109; Todd L. Savitt, *Medicine and Slavery: The Diseases and Health Care of Blacks in Antebellum Virginia* (Urbana: University of Illinois Press, 1978); Gladys Marie Fry, *Night Riders in Black Folk History* (Athens: University of Georgia Press, 1991), ch. 6; Lyle Saxon, Edward Dreyer, and Robert Tallant, comp., *Gumbo Ya-Ya: A Collection of Louisiana Folktales* (Greenwich, Conn.: Fawcett Publications, 1967), pp. 75–76; Alison Davis and John Dollard, *Children of Bondage: The Personality Development of Negro Youth in the Urban South* (New York: Harper and Row, 1964), p. 45.

9. Georgia Writers' Project, *Drums and Shadows: Survival Studies Among the Georgia Coastal Negroes* (Athens: University of Georgia Press, 1940), pp. 61, 165; Michael Anthony Cooke, "The Health of Blacks During Reconstruction, 1862–1870" (Ph.D. diss., University of Maryland, College Park, 1983), p. 112; Schick, "Healing and Race," p. 109.

10. See cases of whites' adoption of black American/African curing regimens, including treatments for yaws, syphilis, snakebite, and the development of inoculation techniques for smallpox, in William D. Piersen, *Black Legacy: America's Hidden Heritage* (Amherst: University of Massachusetts Press, 1993), pp. 99–117; Jean W. Robinson, "Black Healers During the Colonial Period and Early Nineteenth-Century America" (Ph.D. diss., Southern Illinois University, Carbondale, 1979); Peter Wood, *Black Majority: Negroes in Colonial South Car-*

olina from 1670 through the Stono Rebellion (New York: W. W. Norton, 1974), pp. 289–92; and his article, "People's Medicine in the Early South," *Southern Exposure* 6 (Summer 1978). Schick, "Healing and Race," p. 111; Savitt, *Medicine and Slavery*, pp. 174, 179; Walter Fisher, "Physicians and Slavery in the Antebellum Medical Journal," in *The Making of Black America: Essays in Negro Life and History*, ed. August Meier and Elliot Rudwick (New York: Athenaeum, 1969), vol. 1, p. 164; Martia Graham Goodson, "Medical-Botanical Contributions of African Slave Women to American Medicine," *Western Journal of Black Studies* 11, no. 4 (1987): 198–203; Sarah Handy, "Negro Superstitions," *Lippincott's Monthly Magazine*, 1891, p. 737; Charles Perdue, Thomas E. Barden, and Robert K. Phillips, *Weevils in the Wheat: Interviews with Virginia Ex-Slaves* (Charlottesville: University Press of Virginia, 1976), p. 120.

11. Daniel Webster Davis, "Conjuration," *Southern Workman* 27, no. 12 (1898): 251; Laura Towne diary, August 13, 1863, p. 130, Manuscripts, Southern Historical Collection; George Rawick, *From Sundown to Sunup: The Making of the Black Community* (Westport, Conn.: Greenwood Press, 1972), p. 48. See also Willie Lee Rose, *Rehearsal for Reconstruction: The Port Royal Experiment* (New York: Oxford University Press, 1964), p. 98; Francis R. Packard, *Medicine in the United States* (New York: P. B. Hoeber, 1931), vol. 1, pp. 1227–28. On domestic medicine, see Ronald Numbers, "Do-It-Yourself the Sectarian Way," in *Medicine Without Doctors: Home Health Care in American History*, ed. Guenter B. Risse, Judith Walzer Leavitt, and Ronald Numbers (New York: Science History Publishers, 1977); Todd L. Savitt, *Fevers, Agues, and Cures: Medical Life in Old Virginia* (Richmond: Virginia Historical Society, 1990); D. E. Cadwallader and F. J. Wilson, "Folklore Medicine among Georgia's Piedmont Negroes after the Civil War," *Collections of the Georgia Historical Society* 45 (1965), cited in Goodson, "Medical-Botanical Contributions of African Slave Women," p. 200; F. Roy Johnson, *The Fabled Doctor Jim Jordan: A Story of Conjure* (Murfreesboro, N.C.: Johnson Publishing, 1963), p. 3; Roland Steiner, "Observations on the Practice of Conjuring in Georgia," *Journal of American Folklore* 14 (1901): 177; see also Wood, *Black Majority*, pp. 120–21; Rawick, *From Sundown to Sunup*, p. 48.

12. Rawick, *American Slave*, Texas Narratives, pt. 1, p. 243 and pt. 6, p. 2785; Zora Neale Hurston, *Mules and Men* (New York: J. B. Lippincott, 1935), p. 288; Clifton Johnson, ed., *God Struck Me Dead: Religious Conversion Experiences and Autobiographies of Ex-Slaves* (Philadelphia: Pilgrim Press, 1969), p. 141.

13. Zora Neale Hurston, "Hoodoo in America," *Journal of American Folklore* 44 (1931): 317; Arvilla Payne-Jackson, *Folk Wisdom and Mother Wit: John Lee, An African American Herbal Healer* (Westport, Conn.: Greenwood Press, 1993), p. 15. Newbell Puckett noted a "mixture of herbs and hoodoo constituting African-American medicine" among southern practitioners (Puckett, *Folk Beliefs of the Southern Negro* [Chapel Hill: University of North Carolina Press, 1926], p. 358).

14. Rawick, *American Slave*, Texas Narratives, pt. 3, p. 13; see also Ophelia Settle Egypt and Charles Johnson, eds., *Unwritten History of Slavery: Autobiographical Accounts of Negro Ex-Slaves* (Nashville, Tenn.: Social Science Institute, Fisk University, 1945), pp. 212, 316.

15. Roland Steiner, "Braziel Robinson Possessed of Two Spirits" (1900), reprinted in *Mother Wit from the Laughing Barrel: Readings in the Interpretation of Afro-American Folklore*, ed. Alan Dundes (Jackson: University Press of Mississippi, 1972), p. 379; Georgia Folklore, pp. 249–50, records of the Federal Writers' Project, WPA records, 1936–37, Manuscripts Division, Library of Congress.

16. Karen Baldwin, "Mrs. Emma DuPree: 'That Little Medicine Thing,'" *North Carolina Folklore Journal* 32 (1984): 50–53.

17. M. S. Lea, "Two-Head Doctors," *American Mercury*, October 1927, p. 236; Johnson, *God Struck Me Dead*, p. 46. See also Hurston, "Hoodoo in America," p. 320.

18. Cited in Puckett, *Folk Beliefs of the Southern Negro*, p. 567.

19. Johnson, *God Struck Me Dead*, p. 150.

20. W. S. Harrison, *Sam Williams: A Tale of the Old South* (Nashville, Tenn.: Publishing House of the Methodist Episcopal Church, 1892), p. 61; Rossa Belle Cooley, *The Homes of the Freed* (New York: New Republic, 1926), pp. 39–41, 55; Negro Superstitions folder, p. 71, Florida Folklore, WPA records, 1938, Manuscripts Division, Library of Congress. See also Savitt, *Medicine and Slavery*, p. 239; Botkin, *Lay My Burden Down*, p. 37; Cooke, "Health of Blacks During Reconstruction," p. 199.

21. Perdue et al., *Weevils in the Wheat*, p. 310; Johnson, *Fabled Doctor Jim Jordan*, p. 46; Rawick, *American Slave*, South Carolina Narratives vol. 2, p. 106. A black woman in Washington, D.C., detailed a case for a journalist in which a "hoodoo man" approached her, saying that "with the help of the Bible" that he could cure her of an existing malady. "He read from the good book and prayed aloud for the salvation of her soul," explained the writer, "before he preceded to mutter" the incantations that would bring about her healing (Lea, "Two-Head Doctors," p. 237).

22. Puckett, *Folk Beliefs of the Southern Negro*, p. 205; "Witchcraft and Divination in Macon County," *Bulletin of the Tennessee Folklore Society* 9 (1943): 11; Rawick, *American Slave*, North Carolina Narratives vol. 15, pp. 157, 375; Georgia Writers' Project, *Drums and Shadows*, pp. 117, 121, 133, 184; "Conjure Doctors in the South," *Southern Workman* 7, no. 4 (1878): 30–31. On the use of cards for divination, see James Lindsay Smith, *The Autobiography of James L. Smith, including also Reminiscences of Slave Life, Recollections of the War, Education of Freedmen, Causes of the Exodus, etc.* (Norwich: Society of the Founders of Norwich, 1881), p. 56; on the use of cups, crystals, and gourds by Conjurers and specialists, see Gilbert Osofsky, *Puttin on Old Massa: The Slave Narratives of Henry Bibb, William Wells Brown, and Solomon Northup* (New York: Harper and Row, 1969), p. 215. On the frizzly chicken, see *Southern Workman* 24 (1895): 78; see also Michael Bell, "Pattern, Structure and Logic in Afro-American Hoodoo Performance" (Ph.D. diss., Indiana University, Bloomington, 1980), p. 67, who states that the "frizzled" chicken is actually the name for a Friesland hen.

23. "Virginia Hayes Shepherd," WPA Folklore file, Virginia Narratives, University of Virginia, Box no. 2, Folder 2; see also *Southern Workman* 28, no. 8 (1899), reprinted in *Strange Ways and Sweet Dreams: Afro-American Folklore*

from the Hampton Institute, ed. Donald J. Waters (Boston: G. K. Hall, 1983), pp. 314–15; Norman Whitten, "Aspects and Origins of Negro Occultism in Piedmont Village" (master's thesis, University of North Carolina, Chapel Hill, 1960), p. 37.

24. Georgia Writers' Project, *Drums and Shadows,* p. 177; Folklore Folder, p. 276, Georgia Folklore, Manuscripts Division, Library of Congress.

25. Rawick, *American Slave,* Texas Narratives; B. A. Botkin, *Lay My Burden Down: A Folk History of Slavery* (Chicago: University of Chicago Press, 1945), p. 37; Georgia Folklore, p. 252, Manuscripts Division, Library of Congress; Georgia Writers' Project, *Drums and Shadows,* p. 23.

26. *Southern Workman* 28, no. 8 (1899): 315; Alice Bacon, "Conjuring and Conjure Doctors, pt. 2," *Southern Workman* 24, no. 12 (1895): 210; *Southern Workman* 7, no. 5 (1878): 30; Georgia Folklore, p. 251, Manuscripts Division, Library of Congress.

27. Charles Chesnutt, "Superstitions and Folklore of the South" (1901), reprinted in *Mother Wit from the Laughing Barrel: Readings in the Interpretation of Afro-American Folklore,* ed. Alan Dundes (Jackson: University Press of Mississippi, 1972), p. 372.

28. Payne-Jackson, *Folk Wisdom,* p. 13; Carl Carmer, *Stars Fell on Alabama* (New York: Blue Ribbon Press, 1934), p. 214; Kenneth Kiple, *Another Dimension to the Black Diaspora: Diet, Disease and Racism* (Cambridge, Cambridge University Press, 1981). For an excellent recent analysis of similar examples of healing specialties and folk medicine among African American slaves see Charla Fett, *Working Cures* (Chapel Hill: University of North Carolina Press, 2001).

29. Rawick, *American Slave,* Georgia Narratives vol. 13, p. 277; Bacon, "Conjuring," 210; Georgia Writers Project, *Drums and Shadows,* p. 13; Hurston, *Mules and Men,* p. 196.

30. Narratives of animal intrusion are found in numerous studies of African American religion and folklore, including Georgia Writers' Project, *Drums and Shadows,* p. 54; excerpt of a letter, *Southern Workman* 7, no. 4 (1878): 28 [in Waters, *Strange Ways,* pp. 130–31]; Puckett, *Folk Beliefs of the Southern Negro,* pp. 434–35; and Harry Middleton Hyatt, *Hoodoo — Conjuration — Witchcraft — Rootwork: Beliefs Accepted by Many Negroes and White Persons, These Being Orally Recorded among Blacks and Whites* (Hannibal, Mo.: Western Publishing, 1970–78; distributed by American University Bookstore, Washington, D.C.), pp. 3077–3109.

31. Portia Smiley, "Folklore from Virginia," *Journal of American Folklore* 32 (1919): 379; letter excerpt, *Southern Workman* 7, no. 4 (1878): 28; Chesnutt, "Superstitions and Folklore," p. 373.

32. Could the conjured body have represented the social body—defiled by an invader within its boundaries? Is the conjured body a limited wilderness, a bounded territory for the invasive creatures, whose polluting unnatural (supernatural) presence contrasts with their normal environment—outside, in the natural habitat? As Mary Douglas has shown, the human body functions as a terrain of "natural symbols." In this cosmology, lower creatures are the primary metaphors for impurity and disorder. The "unclean animal," she notes, "is that which creeps, crawls or swarms upon the earth. This form of movement is ex-

plicitly contrary to holiness. . . . Whether we call it teeming, trailing, creeping, crawling or swarming, it is an indeterminate form of movement. . . . There is no order in them" (Douglas, *Purity and Danger: An Analysis of the Concepts of Pollution and Taboo* [London: Routledge and Kegan Paul, 1966], p. 56). See also Kiple, *Another Dimension to the Black Diaspora*, p. 131; Wayland Hand, "Physical Harm, Sickness, and Death by Conjury," *Acta Ethnographica Academiae Scientiarum Hungaricae* 19 (1970): 173; Norman Whitten, "Contemporary Patterns of Malign Occultism Among Negroes in North Carolina," *Journal of American Folklore* 75 (1962): 313.

33. Georgia Writers' Project, *Drums and Shadows,* p. 27; Handy, "Negro Superstitions," p. 736. See also Saxon et al., *Gumbo Ya-Ya,* p. 248. In some African-derived folklore traditions, the serpent was viewed as a symbol of spiritual power (Hurston, *Mules and Men,* pp. 203–15). In an interesting parallel, a seventeenth-century catechism by Kongolese Christians describes the spoken confession of sins as corresponding with the manifestation of deadly scorpions emerging from the mouth with the penitent's words; cited in John Thornton, "Sin and Evil in Kongo Christianity" (manuscript, 1997). I am grateful to the author for sharing this reference with me.

34. Rawick, *American Slave,* Texas Narratives vol. 4, pt. 2, p. 64.

35. Christians viewed the sanctification process as the culmination of one's inner spiritual development, while others believed that sanctification was an instantaneous occurrence, a "second blessing" that was imparted following the event of conversion. Some understood sanctification to be a state that was unattainable before a believer passed on. On the various interpretations of holiness-pentecostal theology see Donald Dayton, *The Theological Roots of Pentecostalism* (Metuchen, N.J.: Scarecrow Press, 1987), esp. chs. 2–4; and Vinson Synan, ed., *Aspects of Pentecostal-Charismatic Origins* (Plainfield, N.J.: Logos International, 1975). On the doctrinal roots of perfection see John Leland Peters, *Christian Perfection and American Methodism* (Grand Rapids, Mich.: Zondervan, 1956); and on its social sources see Timothy Smith, *Revivalism and Social Reform in Mid-Nineteenth Century America* (Baltimore: Johns Hopkins University Press, 1980), esp. pp. 103–47.

36. Vinson Synan, *The Holiness-Pentecostal Movement in the United States* (Grand Rapids, Mich.: Eerdmans Press, 1971), p. 80. According to Synan (p. 58), several major intellectual developments in this period, including Darwinism, higher criticism, natural science, the social gospel and the rationale underlying the ecumenist restructuring of the Federal Council of Churches were seen as "false doctrines." See also Robert Mapes Anderson, *Vision of the Disinherited: The Making of American Pentecostalism* (New York: Oxford University Press, 1979), pp. 31–32.

37. Although the earliest proponents of Pentecostalism had roots in holiness churches in the south, it was in the Los Angeles revival that many historians assert that the foundations of a national Pentecostal movement were laid in 1906, under William Seymour. On the historical origins of Pentecostalism, see James Tinney, "Competing Theories of Historical Origins for Black Pentecostalism" (manuscript, 1979, James Tinney Collection, Howard University). For the biographical background of the founders of Pentecostalism, see Synan, *Pentecostal*

Movement, pp. 99–103; Sarah E. Parham, *The Life of Charles F. Parham, Founder of the Apostolic Faith Movement* (New York: Garland Publishing,1930); James Goff, *Fields White Unto Harvest: Charles F. Parham and the Missionary Origins of Pentecostalism* (Fayetteville: University of Arkansas Press, 1989); James Tinney, "William J. Seymour: Father of Modern Day Pentecostalism," *Journal of the Interdenominational Theological Center* 4 (Fall 1976); Douglas Nelson, "For Such a Time as This: The Story of Bishop William J. Seymour and the Azusa Street Revival"(Ph.D. diss., Birmingham University, 1981).

38. John Nichol, *Pentecostalism* (Plainfield, N.J.: Logos International, 1971), p. 15; Nils Bloch-Hoell, *The Pentecostal Movement: Its Origin, Development, and Distinctive Character* (London: Allen and Unwin, 1964), pp. 147–51; David Edwin Harrell, Jr., *All Things Are Possible: The Healing and Charismatic Revivals in Modern America* (Bloomington: Indiana University Press, 1975); Dayton, *Theological Roots of Pentecostalism;* editorial, *The Apostolic Faith* 1, no. 1 (September 1906): 2.

39. C. H. Mason, "Storms—Storms—Storms," in *Yearbook of the Church of God in Christ* (Memphis, Tenn.: Church of God in Christ Publishing House, 1926), p. 9. James Tinney, "A Theoretical and Historical Comparison of Black Political and Religious Movements" (Ph.D. diss., Howard University, Washington, D.C., 1978), p. 234; David Tucker, *Black Pastors and Leaders, Memphis, 1819–1972* (Memphis, Tenn.: Memphis State University Press, 1975), p. 92. In a recent biography, Ithiel Clemmons argues that Mason was "committed to preserving the African spirit cosmology" and other "distinctive African cultural expressions." The ethicist Cheryl Sanders notes that Pentecostal healing practices designated "as African and magical—such as prayer, anointing the sick with oil, laying on of hands, and the commission of special cloths or handkerchiefs—are also found in the New Testament" (Clemmons, *Bishop C. H. Mason and the Roots of the Church of God in Christ* [Bakerfield, Calif.: Pneuma Life Publishing, 1996], pp. 33–34, 78; and Sanders, *Saints in Exile: The Holiness-Pentecostal Experience in African-American Religion and Culture* [New York: Oxford University Press, 1996], p. 8).

40. J. O. Patterson, German Ross, and Julia Mason Atkins, *History and Formative Years of the Church of God in Christ with Excerpts from the Life and Works of Its Founder, Bishop C. H. Mason* (Memphis, Tenn.: Church of God in Christ Publishing House, 1969), pp. 22–23 (hereafter cited as *History and Formative Years*); L. A. Berry, testimonial, *The Whole Truth,* February 1934, p. 9; testimonial, *The Whole Truth,* October 1931, p. 2.

41. Testimonials in *The Whole Truth,* October 1931, p. 2; January 1933, p. 14; and October 1911, p. 4. Grant Wacker has noted that similar techniques became associated with the predominantly white Pentecostal healing ministries that enjoyed popularity in the middle of the twentieth century: "early Pentecostals were never reluctant to claim incredible healings, including resurrections from the dead, but the mid-century evangelists routinely claimed as healings that seemed not so much miraculous as simply preposterous. Decayed teeth were filled, halos photographed, screaming demons tape-recorded, and bloody cancers coughed up and put on display. [A minister] told of one woman whose stomach had been surgically removed" (Wacker, "The Pentecostal Tradition," in *Caring*

and Curing: Health and Medicine in the Western Religious Traditions, ed. Ronald Numbers and Darrel Amundsden [New York: Macmillan, 1986], pp. 523–24); cf. Anderson, *Vision of the Disinherited,* pp. 95–98; and Harrell, *All Things Are Possible,* pp. 87–91. Similar claims were commonplace for Conjurers and black supernatural doctors, who often demonstrated sensational visual proofs of their healings.

42. St. Clair Drake and Horace Cayton, *Black Metropolis: A Study of Negro Life in a Northern Community* (New York: Harcourt, Brace, 1945), p. 645.

43. Lelia Mason Byas, *Bishop C. H. Mason, Church of God in Christ Founder* (Memphis, Tenn.: Church of God in Christ Publishing House, 1995), p. 23; Patterson et al., *History and Formative Years,* pp. 14, 19; C. G. Brown, *C. H. Mason, A Man Greatly Used of God* (Memphis, Tenn.: Church of God in Christ Publishing House, 1926), pp. 12, 52–53. A famous late-nineteenth-century white evangelist, Maria Woodworth-Etter, widely known for her healing gifts, was once dubbed a "voodoo priestess" because of the "unusual physical manifestations" that accompanied her works. Wayne Warner, *The Woman Evangelist: the Life and Times of Charismatic Evangelist Maria Woodworth-Etter* (Metuchen, N.J.: Scarecrow Press, 1986), p. 79; Wacker, "Pentecostal Tradition," pp. 519–20; Synan, *Pentecostal Movement,* pp. 188, 73. See also Patterson et al., *History and Formative Years,* pp. x, xii, 14, 19; James Tinney, "Competing Strains of Hidden and Manifest Theologies in Black Pentecostalism" (manuscript, 1980, James Tinney Collection, Howard University), p. 8; Bloch-Hoell, *Pentecostal Movement,* pp. 36–37, 54. Although it is not known if Pentecostals identified Mason with conjuring, at least one historian has noted a corresponding relationship (Tucker, *Black Pastors and Leaders,* p. 92): "Hundreds from the masses were attracted to … the magical powers of the Elder. At a time when the lower classes still feared their spirits and 'hants,' there was considerable appeal in the all-night services where one could hear unknown languages, witness healings and the exorcising of devils, and examining the collection of misshapen potatoes and crooked roots which the Elder called examples of the 'mystical wonder of God.' When Mason was criticized for bringing magic into the church, he provided his justification by pointing to the Scriptures, which, he said, made it clear that Jesus himself believed in healings, spirits, and demons."

44. Annie Foster, testimonial, *The Grace Magazine* 7, no. 18 (December 1941): 6. Other testimonial accounts of the miraculous healing powers of Bishop Grace can be found in Georgia Writers' Project, *Drums and Shadows,* p. 45; Rawick, *American Slave,* Georgia Narratives vol. 4, s.s. 1, pt. 2, pp. 3–4; and Albert Whiting, "The United House of Prayer for All People: A Case Study of a Charismatic Sect" (Ph.D. diss., American University, Washington, D.C., 1952); pp. 101–75. Grace founded what became his national church, the United House of Prayer for All People, in Wareham, Massachusetts, in 1919. Like Father Divine, his more renowned contemporary, Grace emphasized supernatural approaches to this-worldly afflictions such as poverty, hunger, and disease. See Arthur Huff Fauset, *Black Gods of the Metropolis: Negro Religious Cults in the Urban North* (Philadelphia: University of Pennsylvania Press, 1944); Lenwood Davis, *Daddy Grace: An Annotated Bibliography* (New York: Greenwood Press, 1992).

45. Hortense Powdermaker, *After Freedom: A Cultural Study in the Deep South* (New York: Viking Press, 1939), pp. 290–93.

46. Georgia Writers' Project, *Drums and Shadows*, pp. 84–85.

47. Within this diverse and rapidly growing population, the Spiritual churches demonstrated remarkable growth. In the black "Bronzeville" district on Chicago's south side, for example, one church in twenty in 1928—a total of seventeen churches—had a Spiritual congregation; in 1938, that figure had increased to one in ten—a total of fifty-one. This count did not include the vast number of unaffiliated Spiritualists who operated house altars and served as advisors, whose number was said to be more than a hundred in the district on the eve of the Second World War. On the early presence of Spiritual congregations in Chicago, see Drake and Cayton, *Black Metropolis*, p. 642; Alan Spear, *Black Chicago: the Making of a Negro Ghetto, 1890–1920* (Chicago: University of Chicago Press, 1967), pp. 175–77. For other metropolitan areas, see Edith [Lockley] White, *The Spiritualist Sect in Nashville* (New York: Vintage Books, 1970), p. 27; Claude McKay, *Harlem: Negro Metropolis* (New York: E. P. Dutton, 1940), pp. 73–85. On the historical origins of he movement, see Hans Baer, *The Black Spiritual Movement: A Religious Response to Racism* (Knoxville: University of Tennessee Press, 1984), p. 18.

48. Drake and Cayton, *Black Metropolis*, p. 642. Most Spiritual churches maintain an affiliation with a parent association. One of the largest of these is the Metropolitan Spiritual Churches of Christ Association, located in Kansas City, which has over one hundred affiliate congregations in cities such as Chicago, Detroit, Baltimore, and St. Louis. See Baer, *Black Spiritual Movement*, pp. 25–26; and James Daniel Tyms, "A Study of Four Religious Cults Operating Among Negroes" (master's thesis, Howard University, Washington, D.C., 1938).

49. In the same decade of the founding of Leaf Anderson's Eternal Life Spiritual Church in Chicago, Spiritual congregations appeared in cities throughout the United States. It is not clear whether these early churches were affiliated with Leaf Anderson's original association. The presence of Spiritual churches in various metropolitan areas was reported by contemporary observers in the early part of the twentieth century. See Ira D. Reid, "Let Us Prey!" *Opportunity* 4 (1926): 168–70; Miles Mark Fisher, "Organized Religion and the Cults," *Crisis*, January 1937, p. 8; White, *Spiritualist Sect in Nashville*, p. 27. The history and manifestations of black Spiritual traditions in New Orleans, although beyond the scope of this chapter, are the subject of two recent studies. See Claude Jacobs and Andrew Kaslow, *The Spiritual Churches of New Orleans: Origins, Beliefs and Rituals of an African-American Religion* (Knoxville: University of Tennessee Press, 1991); see also Michael Smith, *Spirit World: Pattern in the Expressive Folk Culture of Afro-American New Orleans* (New Orleans: New Orleans Folklife Society, 1984); Hurston, "Hoodoo in America"; and Robert Tallant, *Voodoo in New Orleans* (New York: Macmillan, 1946); Baer, *Black Spiritual Movement*, p. 110. See also Hans Baer, "Black Spiritual Churches: A Neglected Socio-Religious Institution," *Phylon* 42 (Fall 1981): 210.

50. Hurston, "Hoodoo in America," p. 318; Tallant, *Voodoo in New Orleans*, p. 169; Joseph Washington, *Black Sects and Cults* (Garden City, N.Y.: Doubleday, 1972), p. 113.

51. African American Spiritual churches are unique for their adoption of traditions from Roman Catholicism. Spiritual altars, adorned with crucifixes, candles, and other iconographic embellishments, provide a visual link with Catholicism, while the robes, vestments and clothing of Spiritual ministers mirror that of Roman Catholic priests and clerics. It is difficult to determine whether these innovations were the product of Roman Catholic confluences in *vodou,* or whether such traditions were inherited directly from the folk practices of ethnic Catholics in New Orleans. The features of Catholicism that appear in the black Spiritual tradition contribute to the movement's sense of itself as a faith with an archaic institutional heritage, and, according to Hans Baer, they provide an atmosphere of respectability for members of the movement who seek religious symbols of social status. Other Spiritual practices derived from popular Catholic traditions include prayers to the Blessed Mother and the Trinity, the use of holy oil, and the celebration of saints' feast days, especially the feast of Saint Joseph, a holiday that remains popular in New Orleans among black Spiritualists and Italian American women today. Nevertheless, although some black Spiritualists refer to themselves as "sanctified Catholics," the religious content and significance of their traditions hold different meanings for the two groups. See David Estes, "Across Ethnic Boundaries: Saint Joseph's Day in a New Orleans Afro-American Spiritual Church," *Mississippi Folklore Register* 21 (1987): 11–12; Louisiana Writers' Project, in Saxon et al., *Gumbo Ya-Ya,* p. 105; Baer, *Black Spiritual Movement,* p. 153. On similar Italian American occult worldviews, see Rudolph Vecoli, "Cult and Occult in Italian-American Culture," in *Immigrants and Religion in Urban America,* ed. Randall Miller and Thomas Marzik (Philadelphia: Temple University Press, 1977), p. 29. See also Lyle Saxon, *Fabulous New Orleans* (New York: Century, 1928), pp. 306–7; Baer, *Black Spiritual Movement,* p. 218.

52. In the present-day Spiritual tradition, the emphasis on efficacious ritual remains strong. In Nashville, Tennessee, one researcher observed a ceremony that involved the use of the sacramental bread, distributed by a Spiritual minister as crackers wrapped in small packets of tissue paper, to members of the congregation. "She instructed them to crush the cracker fragments on Monday morning and place them outside their homes," he reported, "and assured them that they would be sure to receive a blessing from the Lord" (Baer, *Black Spiritual Movement,* p. 122).

53. Baer, *Black Spiritual Movement,* p. 134. See also Tallant, *Voodoo in New Orleans,* pp. 169, 170; Federal Writers' Project, *New Orleans City Guide* (New York: Houghton Mifflin, 1938), pp. 210–11. Some of what appear to be Catholic ritual influences in the New Orleans Spiritualist churches may in fact be derived from the Afro-Haitian religion of *vodou,* widely practiced among blacks in New Orleans in the late eighteenth and early nineteenth century. Potential influences in the Spiritualist churches can be discerned from similarities in organization, the strong commitment to female leadership and spirit mediumship, which is a feature of spirit possession rituals in *vodou.*

54. Edith Lockley, "The Spiritualist Sect in Nashville: A Study in Personality Reorganization" (bachelor's thesis, Virginia Union University, Richmond, 1933), pp. 136, 182, 123, 97, 152, 160, 180–82. Lockley White's revised thesis

was published without much of the primary data and interview materials as *The Spiritualist Sect in Nashville* (1970).

55. Drake and Cayton, *Black Metropolis*, p. 643.

56. Hurston, "Hoodoo in America," p. 317. By midcentury many congregations became officially known as Spiritual churches rather than Spiritualists, ostensibly to differentiate themselves from the American spiritualist movement, which some in the black community perceived as "ungodly" (Baer, *Black Spiritual Movement*, pp. 51, 115).

57. Definitions of health and illness among black Americans are examined in Wilbur Watson, ed., *Black Folk Medicine: The Therapeutic Significance of Faith and Trust* (New Brunswick, N.J.: Transaction Books, 1988); Loudell Snow, *Walking Over Medicine* (Boulder, Colo.: Westview Press, 1993); Carole Hill and Holly Mathews, "Traditional Health Beliefs and Practices Among Southern Rural Blacks: A Complement to Biomedicine," in *Perspectives on the American South: An Annual Review of Society, Politics, and Culture*, ed. Merle Black (New York: Gordon and Breach, 1981); and Carole Hill, "Folk Medicine," in *Encyclopedia of Southern Culture*, ed. Charles Reagan Wilson and William Ferris (Chapel Hill: University of North Carolina Press, 1989), p. 472.

CHAPTER 5. "WE ALL BELIEVED IN HOODOO"

1. Text and notes from Scott Joplin, "Treemonisha: Opera in Three Acts," reprinted in *The Complete Works of Scott Joplin*, ed. Vera Brodsky Lawrence (New York: New York Public Library, Readex Books, 1981), vol. 2, pp. 5–6, 199–201.

2. Lawrence Levine, *Black Culture and Black Consciousness: Afro-American Folk Thought from Slavery to Freedom* (New York: Oxford University Press, 1977), pp. 138–45, 152; Eric Foner, *Reconstruction: America's Unfinished Revolution, 1863–1877* (New York: Harper and Row, 1988), p. 397; Leon Litwack, *Been in the Storm So Long: The Aftermath of Slavery* (New York: Random House, 1980), pp. 224–25. Here I identify African American "folk" culture with a dynamic combination of forces, including the values and styles by which African Americans formulated shared understandings of community and religious self-identity. Although associated with the masses of rural, Christianized southern blacks in the mid nineteenth century, black folk or vernacular religion was not constituted solely by institutionalized expressions but rather, organic and enduring and intimately tied to black culture, was sustained and passed on from the slaves to their descendants.

3. Robert Russa Moton, *Finding a Way Out: An Autobiography* (Garden City, N.Y.: Doubleday and Page, 1920), p. 65. Members of a nonindigenous group primarily from northern states and consisting of missionaries, clergy, and teachers measured cultural differences among members of the native population and threw into relief the caste differences between an assimilated population of African American elites from urbanized areas and a larger majority hailing from a rural and agrarian class, the so-called black masses who included the sons and daughters of the enslaved, those most recently "up" from slavery. The debate over class and culture in African American life is discussed in E. Franklin Frazier, *Black*

Bourgeoisie (New York: Collier Books, 1962), pp. 56–76, 98–111; and Evelyn Brooks Higginbotham, *Righteous Discontent: The Women's Movement in the Black Baptist Church, 1880–1920* (Cambridge, Mass.: Harvard University Press, 1993), pp. 13–14.

4. Foner, *Reconstruction*, p. 25; Joe Richardson, *Christian Reconstruction: The American Missionary Association and Southern Blacks, 1861–1890* (Athens: University of Georgia Press, 1986), pp. 17–33; James McPherson, *The Abolitionist Legacy: From Reconstruction to the NAACP* (Princeton: Princeton University Press, 1975), pp. 143–88; Jacqueline Jones, *Soldiers of Light and Love: Northern Teachers and Georgia Blacks, 1865–1873* (Athens: University of Georgia Press, 1980), pp. 24–25; Ronald E. Butchart, *Northern Schools, Southern Blacks, and Reconstruction: Freedmen's Education, 1862–1875* (Westport, Conn.: Greenwood Press, 1980), pp. 35–37.

5. Levine, *Black Culture and Black Consciousness*, pp. 141–44; Litwack, *Been in the Storm So Long*, pp. 453–55.

6. *American Missionary*, June 1867, p. 126; *Spirit of Missions*, November 1868, p. 852; McPherson, *Abolitionist Legacy*, p. 62; Jones, *Soldiers of Light and Love*, p. 25; Katherine L. Dvorak, *An African-American Exodus: The Segregation of Southern Churches* (Brooklyn, N.Y.: Carlson Publishing, 1991), pp. 49–52; Foner, *Reconstruction*, pp. 88–95; Litwack, *Been in the Storm So Long*, pp. 468–71; Genovese, *Roll, Jordan, Roll*, pp. 97–112.

7. Laura Towne, *Letters and Diary, 1862–1888*, ed. Rupert Sargent Holland (Cambridge: Riverside Press, 1912), p. 20; C. Thurston Chase, "The Educational Situation," Freedman's Bureau records, August 1865–May 1869, quoted in Robert Morris, *Reading, 'Riting, and Reconstruction: The Education of Freedmen in the South, 1861–1870* (Chicago: University of Chicago Press, 1981), p. 89; Charlotte Forten, quoted in Rose, *Rehearsal for Reconstruction*, p. 93; *American Missionary*, June 1868, p. 134; D. S. Cartwright, "Negro Freedom an Impossibility under Nature's Law," *DeBow's Review* 30, May 1861, p. 648; M.R.S., "A Visitor's Account of Our Sea Island Schools," *Pennsylvania Freedman's Bulletin*, October 1866, reprinted in Dena Epstein, *Sinful Tunes and Spirituals: Black Folk Music to the Civil War* (Urbana: University of Illinois Press, 1977), p. 282. Letter to the editor, *Southern Workman* 7, no. 4 (1878): 31 (added emphasis); Willie Lee Rose, *Rehearsal for Reconstruction: The Port Royal Experiment* (New York: Oxford University Press, 1964), p. 74.

8. Letter to the editor, *American Missionary*, June 1868, p. 134; Rose, *Rehearsal for Reconstruction*, p. 74.

9. James Sparkman, "The Negro," Sparkman Family Papers, Southern Historical Collection, quoted in Charles Joyner, *Down by the Riverside: A South Carolina Slave Community* (Urbana: University of Illinois Press, 1984), p. 144; Myrta Lockett Avary, *Dixie After the War: An Exposition of Social Conditions Existing in the South During the Twelve Years Succeeding the Fall of Richmond* (Garden City, N.Y.: Doubleday and Page, 1906), p. 203; Arney Childs, ed., *Rice Planter and Sportsman: The Recollections of J. Motte Alston, 1821–1909* (Columbia: University of South Carolina Press, 1953), p. 48; George Frederickson, *The Black Image in the White Mind: The Debate on Afro-American Character and Destiny, 1817–1914* (New York: Harper and Row, 1972), pp. 259–61.

10. Cheveux Gris, "The Negro in his Religious Aspect," *Southern Magazine,* October 1878, p. 501; Letitia Burwell [pseud.; Page Thacker], *Plantation Reminiscences* (Richmond, Va., 1878), p. 57; Charles Stearns, *The Black Man of the South and the Rebels, or The Characteristics of the Former and the Recent Outrages of the Latter* (New York: American News, 1872), p. 347.

11. W. C. Gannett, "The Freedmen at Port Royal," *North American Review,* July 1865, p. 28; *American Missionary,* July 1866, pp. 199–200; *American Missionary,* September 1865, p. 197; Rose, *Rehearsal for Reconstruction,* pp. 90–91.

12. *American Missionary,* July, 1866, p. 199; *Spirit of Missions,* April, 1868, p. 316; Richardson, *Christian Reconstruction,* p. 155; H. G. Spaulding, "Under the Palmetto" (1863), reprinted in Jackson, *The Negro and his Folklore,* p. 66; correspondence, *Southern Workman* 7, no. 9 (1878): 67 [in Waters, *Strange Ways,* 145–47].

13. W. A. L. Campbell to E. M. Cravath, October 1874, American Missionary Association papers, cited in Richardson, *Christian Reconstruction,* p. 150; Elizabeth Kilham, "Sketches in Color," *Putnam's Monthly,* March 1870, reprinted in *The Negro and His Folklore in Nineteenth-Century Periodicals,* ed. Bruce Jackson (Austin: University of Texas Press, 1977), p. 133; Thomas Cardozo to Samuel Hunt, June 23, 1865, American Missionary Association papers; Frederick Douglass, "The Emancipated Man Wants Knowledge," in *The Nation Still in Danger, or Ten Years After the War* (New York: American Missionary Association, 1875), p. 12.

14. "Conjure Doctors in the South," *Southern Workman* 7, no. 4 (1878): 31; John Patterson Green, *Recollections of the Inhabitants, Localities, Superstitions, and KuKlux Outrages of the Carolinas* (Cleveland: Library of American Civilization, 1880), pp. 47–48; Charles Chesnutt, "Superstitions and Folklore of the South," *Modern Culture* 13 (1901): 231; Octavia V. Rogers Albert, *The House of Bondage, or Charlotte Brooks and Other Slaves* (New York: Hunt and Eaton, 1890), p. 99. See also Higginbotham, *Righteous Discontent,* pp. 43 ff.

15. Octave Thanet, "Folklore in Arkansas," *Journal of American Folklore* 5 (1892): 122; Louis Pendleton, "Notes on Negro Folk-Lore and Witchcraft in the South," *Journal of American Folklore* 3 (1890): 203; Daniel Webster Davis, "Conjuration," *Southern Workman* 27, no. 12 (1898): 252.

16. Rawick, *American Slave,* Texas Narratives vol. 5, pt. 4, p. 184.

17. James Anderson, *The Education of Blacks in the South, 1860–1935* (Chapel Hill: University of North Carolina Press, 1988), pp. 16–17, 34–36. Hampton's most famous graduate, Booker T. Washington, embodied the ideals of accommodation and social conservatism that Hampton taught (Frazier, *Black Bourgeoisie,* pp. 56–76).

18. For background on life at Hampton Institute in its first few decades, see especially Mary Frances Armstrong and Helen Ludlow, *Hampton and Its Students* (New York: G. P. Putnam, 1875); and Mary Frances Armstrong, *Hampton Institute: Its Work for Two Races* (Hampton, Va.: Normal School Press, 1885). For recollections by the founder, see Samuel C. Armstrong, "The Founding of the Hampton Institute," in *Twenty-two years of Hampton Normal and Agricultural Institute* (Hampton, Va.: Normal School Press, 1890); for contemporary

studies of Hampton and its role in southern education, see Anderson, *Education of Blacks,* esp. ch. 2, "The Hampton Model of Normal School Industrial Education, 1868–1915"; and Robert F. Engs, *Freedom's First Generation: Black Hampton, Virginia, 1861–1890* (Philadelphia: University of Pennsylvania Press, 1979).

19. Anderson, *Education of Blacks,* pp. 37–47; Engs, *Freedom's First Generation,* pp. 144–58.

20. "Conjure Doctors," pp. 26, 30. On nineteenth-century theories of racial extinction, see Frederickson, *Black Image in the White Mind,* pp. 228–55.

21. "Conjure Doctors," p. 30.

22. Ibid., p. 26. As the historian James Anderson has shown, Armstrong's directives and Hampton's educational policies translated into a political conservatism that balanced the interests of both southern white paternalists and benevolent northerners and proved to be ultimately detrimental to black political aspirations (*Education of Blacks,* pp. 79–109).

23. Horace Frissell, "Negro and Indian Folklore," n.d., Hampton Press Service, Folklore File, Hampton University Archives; Alice Bacon, "Work and Methods of the Hampton Folklore Society," *Journal of American Folklore* 11 (1893): 18; see Donald J. Waters, ed., *Strange Ways and Sweet Dreams: Afro-American Folklore from the Hampton Institute* (Boston: G. K. Hall, 1983), p. 41; see also Ronald Lamarr Sharps, "Happy Days and Sorrow Songs: Interpretations of Negro Folklore by Black Intellectuals, 1893–1928" (Ph.D. diss., George Washington University, Washington, D.C., 1991), chs. 1 and 2.

24. The goals of the folklore society at Hampton were elucidated in a introductory statement by the teacher who helped to organize the group, Alice Bacon. Before the annual meeting of the American Folklore Society in 1897 Bacon read a platform that proclaimed that the folklore society "arose . . . not in enthusiasm for the collection of folklore" but "from a strong desire on the part of some of those connected with the Hampton work to bridge over, if possible, the great gulf fixed between the minds of the educated and the uneducated, the civilized and the uncivilized." The study of folklore would allow Hampton students "to enter more deeply into the daily life of the common people, and to understand more thoroughly their ideas and motives," she believed ("Work and Methods of the Hampton Folk-Lore Society," p. 17). Interpretation of the past through folklore was a tool for understanding the present conditions and prospects of blacks in the United States, and as such, she stressed, of value to the proponents of racial uplift. Teachers and students in the folklore society were soon fully involved in preserving the memory of indigenous African American traditions, the substance of a usable past.

25. Waters, *Strange Ways and Sweet Dreams,* pp. 20, 36. *Southern Workman* 22, no. 12 (1893): 101; Sharps, "Happy Days and Sorrow Songs," pp. 64–67.

26. Waters, *Strange Ways and Sweet Dreams,* p. 43.

27. See *Southern Workman* 22, no. 12 (1893): 179–80; and 23, no. 1 (1894): 5, 131–33.

28. It was during Boas's tenure as editor of the *Journal of American Folklore* that a series of seminal articles on conjuring was published as part of a "Negro Numbers" sequence of single-topic issues devoted to blacks in the United States,

the Antilles, and Africa. White writers dealing with Conjure and black folklore published at this time in the pages of the journal included Stewart Culin, Julien Hall, Sarah Handy, and Ruby Andrews Moore. Black writers also actively contributed to the discussion of African American folklore, including Monroe Work, Portia Smiley, Clement Richardson, and A. S. Perkins, most of them, significantly, graduates of Hampton Institute. These black collectors would publish their reports in the "Negro Numbers" series under the direction of the anthropologist Elsie Clews Parsons. On Boas, see William Willis, "Franz Boas and the Study of Black Folklore," in *The New Ethnicity: Perspectives from Ethnology* (St. Paul: Western Publishing, 1973), p. 309–15; see also George W. Stocking, ed., *The Shaping of American Anthropology: A Franz Boas Reader* (New York: Basic Books, 1974), pp. 308–30.

29. Bacon, "Work and Methods," p. 17; *Southern Workman* 22, no. 12 (1893): 180; Newbell Niles Puckett, "Race Pride and Folklore," *Opportunity: A Journal of Negro Life* 4 (1926): 82. In the decades between 1890 and 1920 Conjure and black supernatural beliefs became a lively topic of exploration by scholars and other contributors to the *Journal of American Folklore*. While many of the contributors were gentleman scholars and collectors of obscure and "primitive" memorabilia, their extensive documentation of African American folk life in this period provided vital historical evidence of the persistence of Conjure and other supernatural beliefs among southern blacks.

30. On southern authors, including Joel Chandler Harris and the "new" southern paternalism in literature, see Frederickson, *Black Image in the White Mind*, pp. 204–11.

31. Simon Bronner, *American Folklore Studies: An Intellectual History* (Lawrence: University Press of Kansas, 1986), p. 53. A sampling of late-nineteenth- and early-twentieth-century literature with Conjure themes would include Mary A. Owen, *Voodoo Tales* (1893); and her *Ole Rabbit* (1893); Mamie Sims, *Negro Mystic Lore* (1907); Virginia Boyle, *Devil Tales* (1900); James Melville Beard, *KKK Sketches, Humorous and Didactic* (1877); from an earlier period, Edward Pollard, *Black Diamonds Gathered in the Darkey Homes of the South* (1859); and Edmund Kirke, *My Southern Friends* (1863), plus numerous short pieces in the popular magazine press. For relevant discussions on the use of Conjure by black authors, see Helen Jaskoski, "Power Unequal to Man: The Significance of Conjure in Works by Five African-American Authors," *Southern Folklore Quarterly* 38 (1974): 91–108; and Margaret Jackson, "Folklore in Slave Narratives before the Civil War," *New York Folklore Quarterly* 11 (1955): 5–19; Robert Hemenway, "The Functions of Folklore in the Conjure Woman," *Journal of the Folklore Institute* 13, no. 3 (1976): 283; David Britt, "Charles Chesnutt's Conjure Tales," *CLA Journal* 15, no. 3 (1972).

32. Levine, *Black Culture and Black Consciousness*, pp. 155, 162–70; *New York Times*, June 15, 1875, p. 5; Kilham, "Sketches in Color," p. 305; Michael Harris, *The Rise of Gospel Blues* (New York: Oxford University Press, 1992), pp. 110–16.

33. James Weldon Johnson, *The Book of American Negro Spirituals* (New York: Viking Press, 1925), p. 33; Levine, *Black Culture and Black Consciousness*, p. 150; Sterling Stuckey, *Slave Culture: Nationalist Theory and the Foun-*

dations of Black America (New York: Oxford University Press, 1987), pp. 67–73, 104–6; and William Wiggins, *O Freedom! Afro-American Emancipation Celebrations* (Knoxville: University of Tennessee Press, 1987), pp. 35, 88.

34. A relevant discussion can be found in Theophus H. Smith, *Conjuring Culture: Biblical Formations of Black America* (New York Oxford University Press, 1994), p. 115.

35. James Grossman, *Land of Hope: Chicago, Black Southerners, and the Great Migration* (Chicago: University of Chicago Press, 1989), pp. 13–37; Thomas J. Woofter, *Negro Migration: Changes in Rural Organization and Population of the Cotton Belt* (New York: W. D. Gray, 1920), pp. 120–21. Background on the Great Migration in this chapter comes from Joe William Trotter, Jr., ed., *The Great Migration in Historical Perspective* (Bloomington: Indiana University Press, 1991).

36. Richard Wright, *12 Million Black Voices: A Folk History of the Negro in the United States* (New York: Viking Press, 1941), p. 93. On religion and religious meaning in the context of the Great Migration see most recently Milton Sernett, *Bound for the Promised Land: African American Religion and the Great Migration* (Durham, N.C.: Duke University Press, 1997.

37. Hans Baer, *The Black Spiritual Movement: A Religious Response to Racism* (Knoxville: University of Tennessee Press, 1984). On store-front churches and migrant religions, see Sernett, *Bound for the Promised Land*, pp. 194–97.

38. Negro Lore, Florida, pp. 41–44, WPA records, 1938, Manuscripts Division, Library of Congress. On the transformation of black folk magic in an urban environment see Gilbert E. Cooley, "Root Doctors and Psychics in the Region," *Indiana Folklore* 10 (1977): 191–200.

39. For typologies of African American folk healing practitioners see Loudell Snow, "Sorcerers, Saints, and Charlatans: Black Folk Healers in Urban America," *Culture, Medicine, and Psychiatry* 2 (1978): 87–96; Arthur Hall and Peter Bourne, "Indigenous Therapists in a Southern Black Urban Community," *Archives of General Psychiatry* 28 (1973): 137–42.

40. This section focuses on transformations of Conjure practices and traditions as they occurred in public and expressive manifestations of magic. Patterns in southern magic traditions, such as the motifs and structure of hoodoo narratives, and the healing practices and diagnosis of supernatural afflictions, were also recast in the urban settings. These internal dynamics of transformation are more fully discussed in Elon Ali Kulii, "A Look at Hoodoo in Three Urban Areas of Indiana: Folklore and Change" (Ph.D. diss., Indiana University, Bloomington, 1982); and George Brandon, "Regional Variations in Rootwork Symptoms? Some Findings from Folklore, Ethnography and the Clinic," *The Griot,* Spring 1988.

41. *Chicago Defender,* November 5, 1910, p. 7. Curiously, Professor White's ad first appeared in September (*Chicago Defender,* September 24, 1910, p. 4) without the self-designation of "psychic" but within two months had acquired supernatural overtones.

42. See Kulii, "A Look at Hoodoo." I am not arguing that newspaper advertisements for occult specialists were a twentieth-century phenomenon; to be sure, one historian has dated such advertisements to the 1890s, while another has found one notice for a black female spiritualist from 1865. See Henry Car-

rington Bolton, "Fortune-Telling in America Today," *Journal of American Folklore* 9 (1896); and Albert Raboteau, "The Afro-American Traditions," in *Caring and Curing: Health and Medicine in the Western Religious Traditions,* ed. Ronald Numbers and Darrel Amundsden (New York: Macmillan, 1986), p. 554.

43. The rise of the so-called African American "cult" leaders may also be seen as another manifestation of the institutionalizing of Conjure specialists in urban settings. During the early twentieth century several larger-than-life religious figures such as Father Divine and Bishop Grace brought to the city dwellers assurances of security and sacred power. Rabbi Wentworth Matthew, founder of the Commandment Keepers of the Living God of Harlem (the Black Hebrews) refashioned Conjure-style beliefs into a "Cabalistic Science" through which followers were able to "eliminate mental illness, cure fevers, raise the dead, restore sight, heal physical pains, and change minds as well as make friends of enemies." Many practitioners cloaked their practices in the spiritual trappings of Christianity, Islam, Judaism, and eastern religions and were able to tailor their ministries to audiences gripped by poverty and affliction. On African American urban "cultists," see Miles Mark Fisher, "Organized Religion and the Cults," *Crisis,* January 1937, pp. 9–10, 29–30; Frank Rasky, "Harlem's Religious Zealots," *Tomorrow,* 9, November 1949; Raymond Julius Jones, "A Comparative Study of Religious Cult Behavior Among Negroes with Special Reference to Emotional Group Conditioning Factors," *Howard University Studies in the Social Sciences* 2 (1939); Arthur Huff Fauset, *Black Gods of the Metropolis: Negro Religious Cults in the Urban North* (Philadelphia: University of Pennsylvania Press, 1944). For advertisements, see *New York Amsterdam News* from 1923: March 7, pp. 2, 3; March 21, p. 3; and September 5, p. 3; and see its multiple listings for June 22, 1927, p. 12. For a relevant discussion of the adaptability of urban practitioners, see Kulii, "A Look at Hoodoo," pp. 93–112.

44. *Pittsburgh Courier,* September 6, 1924, p. 9. An identical advertisement in national edition of the *Chicago Defender* (September 6, p. 4) attaches the line, "Tell your secrets to the right man." And for typical retail advertisements for conjuring products such as roots, herbs, and other goods see the *Chicago Defender,* April 30, 1921, p. 13.

45. *Chicago Defender,* February 7, 1925; *New York Amsterdam News,* December 13, 1925.

46. On the history of the rise of magical commercialism in the African American community, see Carolyn Long, *Spiritual Merchants* (Knoxville: University of Tennessee Press, 2001).

47. The case of Herman Rucker and Mount Zion African Methodist Episcopal Church in Philadelphia is reviewed in Robert Gregg, *Sparks from the Anvil of Oppression: Philadelphia's African Methodists and Southern Migrants, 1890–1940* (Philadelphia: Temple University Press, 1993), pp. 55–57. On urban healing and supernatural traditions see also Snow, "Sorcerers, Saints," p. 90; St. Clair Drake and Horace Cayton, *Black Metropolis: A Study of Negro LIfe in a Northern City* (New York: Harcourt, Brace, 1945), pp. 476–77.

48. George McCall, "Symbiosis: The Case of Hoodoo and the Numbers Racket," *Social Problems* 10 (1963), reprinted in *Mother Wit from the Laughing Barrel: Readings in the Interpretation of Afro-American Folklore,* ed. Alan Dun-

des (Jackson: University Press of Mississippi, 1972), pp. 419–24; Baer, *Black Spiritual Movement*, pp. 79–81; Drake and Cayton, *Black Metropolis*, pp. 474–78.

49. Although I focus on an early period in the blues, supernatural motifs also proliferated in the decades following World War II, when the blues were produced primarily as urban music. Of course, prior to the blossoming of the blues recording establishment, African American magic had been put to thematic use in music and theater, as seen with the production of Scott Joplin's *Treemonisha*. It is difficult to determine the precise origin of Conjure-themed song, but a popular tune that circulated in the South between 1915 and 1919 (written more than ten years earlier) concluded with the chorus "I've been hoodooed, hoodooed/ hoodooed, hoodooed by a nigger voodoo," thus demonstrating the early thematic influences of magic for black performers. The later growth of themes from black supernaturalism as entertaining subject matter was possibly stimulated by whites' fascination with the products of African American vernacular culture as an antebellum vehicle of entertainment, in folk song and African American singing troupes touring the nation, then later, the world. See Epstein, *Sinful Tunes and Spirituals*; and Eileen Southern, *The Music of Black Americans, A History* (New York: W. W. Norton, 1983), esp. pp. 61–188; and Robert Toll, *Blacking Up: The Minstrel Show in Nineteenth Century America* (New York: Oxford University Press, 1974).

50. Jon Michael Spencer, *Blues and Evil* (Knoxville: University of Tennessee Press, 1993), pp. xxv–xxvi, xxiii; Julio Finn, *The Bluesman: The Musical Heritage of Black Men and Women in the Americas* (London: Quartet Books, 1986), p. 146, 150; Paul Oliver, *Blues Fell This Morning: Meaning in the Blues* (Cambridge: Cambridge University Press, 1990), p. 118.

51. James Cone, *The Spirituals and the Blues: An Interpretation* (New York: Orbis Books, 1991), p. 100. On the blues as a "secular religion" see also Rod Gruver, "The Blues as a Secular Religion," *Blues World*, nos. 29–32 (April–July 1970). Blues are often represented as a secular counterpart to religious music, much as the practices of African American magic are described as the "worldly" counterparts of sacred ritual. Yet this stark, antagonistic juxtaposition of the blues against African American sacred culture tends to obscure the interrelatedness of the blues and black religion. Like African American magic, the blues were forged within a worldview that drew no sharp lines between the sacred and the secular realms. The intersection of the sacred and profane in the blues manifests what Spencer (*Blues and Evil*, p. xxvi) has called the "synchronous duplicity" of black religion, as embodied in the archetype of the African-based trickster figure—the convergence of qualities such as benevolence and malevolence, holiness and carnality, good and evil. The improvisational nature of blues performance, for instance, its use of polyrhythmic syncopation, call-and-response patterns, and the sermonic delivery characteristic in blues vocalizing, all demonstrate the natural kinship between the blues and African American religious music. In blending the roles of priest and performer, the blues artist paralleled the quintessential religious performer, the black preacher (see Charles Keil, *Urban Blues* [Chicago: University of Chicago Press, 1969], p. 164) The blues performer and the black preacher were cultural counterparts or, as Michael Harris has called them, "cultural analogues" (*Rise of Gospel Blues*, p. 154).

52. Lizzie Miles, "Shootin' Star Blues" (1928), lyrics cited in Michael Taft, *Blues Lyric Poetry: An Anthology* (New York: Garland Press, 1983).

53. William Christopher Handy, "Sundown Blues" (1922), lyrics and music in *Blues: An Anthology* (New York: Macmillan, 1972), pp. 150–53. Will Shade and the Memphis Jug band would record a more famous version of the song ("Aunt Caroline Dyer Blues") in 1930. On this tradition see John Quincy Wolf, "Aunt Caroline Dye: The Gypsy in St. Louis Blues, *Southern Folklore Quarterly* 33 (1969): 339–46.

54. See Spencer, *Blues and Evil*, pp. 1–34; Jeffrey Todd Titon, *Early Downhome Blues: A Musical and Cultural Analysis* (Urbana: University of Illinois Press, 1977), p. 182–93; Paul Garon, "Magic and Voodoo in the Blues," *Cultural Correspondence* 10 (Fall 1977): 80–81.

55. Blind Lemon Jefferson, "Low Down Mojo Blues" (1928), #20636–1 Paramount Records, lyrics cited in Taft, *Blues Lyric Poetry.*

56. Leola B. and "Kid" Wesley Wilson, "Keep Your Hands Off My Mojo" (1932), #405146 Okeh Records, in Robert Dixon, John Godrich, and Howard Rye, comp., *Blues and Gospel Records* (New York: Oxford University Press, 1997), p. 858.

57. Clara Smith, "Prescription for the Blues" (1924), #14045-D Columbia Records, in Godwin and Spencer, *Blues and Gospel Records*, p. 66; lyrics cited in Taft, *Blues Lyric Poetry.*

58. On blues as spiritual healing see Smith, *Conjuring Culture*, pp. 122–23, 137–38.

59. As Titon and others have argued, "the church and the blues were structural and functional counterparts" (Titon, *Early Downhome Blues*, p. 19). Blues performances were ritualized, although they were not practiced with liturgical intent, for blues singers adopted a nontheistic idiom; their primary reference point was the self rather than the transcendent divine. For analyses that consider the blues as analogous to collective religious practice see Levine, *Black Culture and Black Consciousness*, 233–37; Keil, *Urban Blues*, pp. 155–60; Spencer, *Blues and Evil*, pp. 37–43. And on the bluesman as shaman, see John Szwed, "Musical Adaptation Among African Americans," *Journal of American Folklore* 82 (1969): 116.

60. Muddy Waters, quoted in Finn, *Bluesman*, p. 60.

CONCLUSION

1. Bruce Dick and Amrijit Singh, *Conversations with Ishmael Reed* (Jackson: University Press of Mississippi, 1995), p. 21; Theophus H. Smith, *Conjuring Culture: Biblical Formations of Black America* (New York Oxford University Press, 1994), p. 18.

2. During World War Two, it was rumored that black servicemen sought Conjurers for assistance in attaining honorable discharges. Other African American males used occult-induced sicknesses as a means of avoiding the draft (J. E. McTeer, *Fifteen Years as a Lowcountry Witchdoctor* [Beaufort, S.C.: Beaufort Book, 1976], p. 26; Mike Michealson, "Can a 'Root Doctor' Actually Put a Hex On or Is It All a Great Put-On?" *Today's Health*, March 1972, p. 58).

3. *Wall Street Journal,* February 24, 1989, pp. A1, A6. While the article does not indicate whether the participants in the plot were white or black, their strategies, indeed, their techniques, the use of image magic, their criminal association with "voodoo" and the fact that these incidents occurred in the Deep South, all suggest an African American cultural influence. Nonetheless, supernatural traditions of African and European origin were historically shared by blacks and whites in the South, as they were in other regions of the country. See Mechal Sobel, *The World They Made Together: Black and White Values in Eighteenth-Century Virginia* (Princeton: Princeton University Press, 1987).

4. Newbell Niles Puckett, *Folk Beliefs of the Southern Negro* (Chapel Hill: University of North Carolina Press, 1926), p. 277; Norman Whitten, "Contemporary Patterns of Malign Occultism Among Negroes in North Carolina," *Journal of American Folklore* 75 (1962): 312. In his role as a high-ranking sheriff in Beaufort County, South Carolina, J. E. McTeer observed such activities among prisoners and accused criminals both within and outside of the system. McTeer related the story of his confrontation with Doctor Buzzard, the famous Gullah root doctor, who had used a mysterious white power in order to control the court. His experiences are recorded in his autobiography *(Fifteen Years as a Lowcountry Witch Doctor)* and in another volume of episodes of his role as conjurer and law enforcement officer (*High Sheriff of the Lowcountry,* ed. Kent Nickerson [Beaufort, S.C.: Beaufort Book, 1970]; for cases, see pp. 24–25). On "chewing the root" in the courtroom see also James Haskins, *Voodoo and Hoodoo: Their Tradition and Craft as Revealed by Actual Practitioners* (Bronx: Original Publications, 1978), p. 176.

5. Zora Neale Hurston, *Mules and Men* (New York: J. B. Lippincott, 1935), p. 230–31; Elliot Gorn, "Religion and Medicine Among Slaves," in *Science and Medicine in the Old South,* ed. Ronald L. Numbers and Todd L. Savitt (Baton Rouge: Louisiana State University Press, 1989), p. 301. The folklorist Frank Schmalleger calls this process a "ritual enactment" occurring within the theater space of the courtroom. "In the belief that the outcome of any event can be influenced through ritual enactment, rootworkers will enter an empty courtroom before trial and invoke forces associated with the four cardinal directions, beseeching them to ensure a successful resolution of the real-life drama about to occur. The process involves sprinkling dust over the courtroom, especially the judge's bench and the jury box. The area touched by the dust is believed to come under the conjurer's control" (Schmalleger, "The Root Doctor and the Courtroom," *North Carolina Folklore,* 29 [1981]: 103). The effectiveness of conjuring as an arbiter in legal matters was in most circumstances determined by the outcome. A guilty verdict, or a conviction, however, was not enough to diminish a believer's trust in the abilities of the supernatural specialist. In many cases failure was legitimated by the internal dynamics of the system, which provided a coherent, self-sustaining explanation. If an outcome was not favorable, a typical interpretation was that the client did not have enough faith in the practitioner or did not follow the instructions to the letter.

6. On African witchcraft, see Max Marwick, ed., *Witchcraft and Sorcery: Selected Readings* (Baltimore: Penguin Books, 1970); Mary Douglas, ed., *Witch-*

craft Confessions and Accusations (London: Tavistock Publications, 1970); Lucy Mair, *Witchcraft* (New York: McGraw Hill, 1969); John Middleton, comp., *Magic, Witchcraft, and Curing* (Garden City, N.Y.: Natural History Press, 1967). On African American witchcraft see Charles Joyner, *Down by the Riverside: A South Carolina Slave Community* (Urbana: University of Illinois Press, 1984).

Index

Page numbers in *italic* type refer to illustrations.

Abraham, Henry, 11, 23, 158–59n1
academia, post-Emancipation, 130–36
Accra (Africa), 50
acculturation, 123, 124
Ada (healer), 97
Adam and Eve (root), 26, 142, 172n27
Adams, William, 5, 27, 102
advertising, of urban Conjure, 141–43,
    202n41, 202–3n42, 203n44
advising, spiritual, 114, 115, 118
affliction, 154; blame for, 107; and blues
    music, 145, 146; bodily intrusion,
    104–6, 191–92n32; cosmology of,
    98–101; harming as defense against,
    89; as imbalance, 93; natural vs.
    supernatural, 102–3; in Pentecostal-
    ism, 109; in Spiritualism, 116–18;
    with supernatural cures, 103, 194n44;
    underlying causes of, 8, 60, 78, 92,
    112–13
Africa. *See names of specific regions,*
    cultures, and traditions
African American spirituality: African
    sources of, 7, 52–53; and blues
    music, 144–49, 204nn49,51, 205n59;
    European sources of, 43–44; histori-
    ography of, 5–6; and intraracial
    tensions, 71, 128–29; negative
    connotations of, 152–53; present-
    day, 151–54, 155; primitive vision

of, 123. *See also* Conjure; super-
    naturalism, African American
African consumption, 69, 179–80n23
African Methodist Church, 65, 88
African religious/spiritual traditions:
    cosmologies of, 37, 172n30; early
    Kongolese Catholicism, 5; and
    fetishism, 40; emergence of, post-
    1750, 53, 54, 55, 169n14; *gris-gris*
    and other charms in, 45, 46, 47;
    herbalism, 93; intersection with
    European American traditions, 7, 26,
    33, 36, 43, 44, 45, 169n15, 171n24;
    in North American slave communi-
    ties, 41, 168n11; magic vs. religion
    in, 39; shouting, 125–26; and slave
    uprisings, 67, 177n9; as source of
    African American healing practices,
    93, 129, 163n22; as source of African
    American spiritual practices, 68,
    152, 173n31, 174n40; visual objects
    from, 37; Western compartmental-
    ization of, 38. *See also names of*
    specific cultures and traditions
Afro-Christian spirituality, 53–54, 67, 92;
    healing and, 107–13; Spiritualism vs.
    other denominations of, 115. *See*
    also Christianity; Conjure; Protest-
    antism; *names of religious denomi-*
    nations

209

Indexer: Kristen Cashman
Compositor: BookMatters, Berkeley
Text: 10/13 Sabon
Display: Sabon